STUDY GUIDE

Sherri L. Jackson
Jacksonville University

Richard A. Griggs
University of Florida

Nancy Hempel
Durham College and University Centre

INVITATION TO PSYCHOLOGY

Canadian Edition

Carole Wade
Carol Tavris
Gary Poole

Prentice
Hall

Toronto

ISBN 0-13-031087-5

Acquisitions Editor: Jessica Mosher
Developmental Editor: Lise Creurer
Production Editor: Sherry Torchinsky
Production Coordinator: Wendy Moran

1 2 3 4 5   04 03 02 01 00

Printed and bound in Canada.

Prentice Hall

CONTENTS

TO THE STUDENT

This Study Guide was designed for use with the First Canadian *Invitation to Psychology* by Carole Wade, Carol Tavris, and Gary Poole. It is not intended to serve as a substitute for the textbook, but rather as a supplement to help you understand the material in the textbook and to access what you have learned from the text. We strongly recommend that you also read the To the Student section in the text. It will familiarize you with the pedagogical features of the text and provide you with some valuable suggestions for studying the text. We have designed the pedagogical program employed in the Study Guide to correspond with the structure of the textbook in order to maximally impact your learning. There are two major study strategies that students employ in using study guides in concert with textbooks—(1) studying an entire chapter and then working through the related chapter in the study guide or (2) studying a chapter section by section and working through the related chapter in the study guide by section. We strongly recommend the latter strategy because it devides the learning task into smaller, more manageable chunks. Based on both cognitive research and our own experience in teaching introductory psychology students, this strategy seems to result in better comprehension and learning of the information. To facilitate your use of this strategy, we will briefly detail how you should coordinate studying the text and using your Study Guide for maximal benefit.

First, you should read the Chapter Outline in the text and the Chapter Overview in the Study Guide. These advance organizers will give you a good idea about the content of the chapter and how the chapter is structured. Having this organizational outline and a good idea of what you will be reading about will allow you to better organize and comprehend the chapter information. In addition, you should read the chapter-opening *Psychology in the News* section, which raises some intriguing psychological questions that will be considered at the end of the chapter. You should keep these questions in mind as you study the chapter.

Having surveyed the chapter content and organization, you should now proceed through the chapter section by section. Read each section, using the *What's Ahead* questions as guides to the content in each section. As you work through a section, pay particular attention to key terms, people, and concepts. The marginal glossary will help you in this task. You should also do the *Get Involved* activities. They will help you to better understand the material you are studying. In addition, carefully study the illustrations, tables, and figures. Many students skip over these. Don't do this! Like the other pedagogical devices, they will gently facilitate your learning. Many of the tables present summary/comparative information and thus also make excellent review devices for exams. After you finish the section, you should complete the *Quick Quiz* in the text to start testing your knowledge of the information.

Now you are ready to complete the related units in the comparable chapter in the Study Guide. You should first complete the *Guided Study* unit on this section. We recommend that you use pencil so that you can easily change any incorrect answers. You should re-study the relevant material in the text for any questions you have trouble answering. Once completed correctly, the Guided Study sections will comprise another good review device for exams. Next, you should review the key terms listed in the Study Guide for the section. Make sure you re-study any terms that you have trouble defining before you take the matching test in the Study Guide. This test completes the Study Guide work for the section, and you should proceed to the next section in the textbook. To ensure that you are paying attention and making optimal use of your study time, we recommend that you take breaks between studying the main chapter sections. Distributed study usually leads to better retention than massed study.

When you have finished studying all of the sections in a chapter, you will be ready to review the entire chapter. These are several devices in the textbook and Study Guide to help you do this. First, you should read the chapter-ending Psychology in the News section, which shows you how theories and findings from psychology will help you address the questions generated in the related chapter-opening section. You should then read the *Taking Psychology* with you section in the textbook. It allows you to see how the chapter content can be applied to your own enumerated chapter summary in the textbook and the completed *Guided Study* unit in the Study Guide as well as the *List of Key Terms* in the textbook. Re-study any key terms that are still not familiar to you. The relevant page numbers are provided in the textbook. Now you are ready to test your knowledge of the chapter content.

You should test yourself in two ways. First, you should attempt to answer the *What's Ahead* questions, which are all listed in the *Looking Back* section at the end of the chapter in the textbook. You can compare your answers to sample answers provided in the Study Guide. Review the relevant material in the textbook for any questions you had difficulty answering. The relevant pages are listed after each question in the *Looking Back* section of the textbook. Now, you are ready to take the chapter-specific *Multiple-Choice Progress Test* in the Study Guide. Answers and the text page(s) for each answer are provided to assist you in reviewing the relevant material for questions that you answered incorrectly. We do not annotate answers because we want you to go back to the textbook and re-study the tested material. If you do so and still cannot understand why the indicated answer is the correct one, see your instructor for clarification.

You are now ready to begin. We have tried to make this Study Guide as useful to you as possible. We would like to thank the textbook authors and the publisher for giving us the opportunity to write this Study Guide and our Supplements Editor, Cindy Taylor, for her valuable guidance and prompt replies to our many questions. Most of all, we thank Bernie and Henry for providing us with the continued inspiration to complete all such tasks.

Sherri L. Jackson

Richard A. Griggs

When a decision was made to develop a Canadian Edition of *Invitation to Psychology*, the supplements to the text were also revised to reflect the Canadian content. You will notice many opportunities in this edition's Study Guide and the Companion Website to reflect on how psychological research and concepts relate to the issues you read about in the newspaper, talk about with your friends and wonder about on your own. Take the opportunity to explore the Companion Website (**http://www.pearsoned.ca/wade**) to find out more about any of the exciting ideas you are introduced to in your course. The world of Psychology has endless questions and answers, and there is always something new to discover.

I would like to extend my appreciation to the staff at Pearson Education Canada for their guidance in developing the Canadian supplements. I also offer special thanks to my Developmental Editor, Lise Creurer, for her attention to all the details.

Nancy Hempel

CHAPTER 1

What is Psychology?

CHAPTER OVERVIEW

Chapter 1 begins by defining psychology and discussing what psychology is not. There is also a brief history of psychology and the people and events that led to the birth of psychology. Contributions of several early psychologists are noted, including Wundt and James. Psychology's present is discussed in terms of the five major theoretical perspectives now dominant in psychology. The differences between a clinical psychologist, psychotherapist, psychoanalyst, and psychiatrist are discussed and related to basic versus applied psychology.

Basic guidelines for critical thinking are presented. The guidelines aid in determining whether a psychological claim is merely "psychobabble," in evaluating an argument, and in determining whether a theory is scientific. The importance of understanding and applying the principle of falsifiability is also discussed.

Descriptive methods are covered next, including advantages and disadvantages of such methods as case studies, observational studies, psychological tests, and surveys. Important issues including representative samples, standardization, norms, reliability, and validity are raised. Correlational methods and their uses and limitations are discussed. Coefficient of correlation and positive and negative correlations are defined and explained.

The experimental method is explained in detail using a theoretical study on smoking and driving to illustrate such concepts as independent variable, dependent variable, experimental group, control group, and placebo and experimenter effects. Lastly, a brief discussion of statistical methods is presented. Descriptive statistics such as arithmetic mean and variance are discussed. In addition, inferential statistics are introduced along with the concepts of statistical significance and meta-analysis.

GUIDED STUDY

1. The Science of Psychology

Read the section "The Science of Psychology" and then answer the following questions. If you have trouble answering any of the questions, re-study the relevant material before going on to the review of key terms and the matching test.

1-1.   Psychology is defined as the scientific study of _____ and _____ processes and how they are affected by an organism's _____ _____,

1

_____ _____, and _____ _____. It is important when studying psychology to understand what it is and what it is NOT. The authors note that psychology is not "psychobabble," _____, or _____ _____.

1-2.   Unlike psychologists today, great thinkers from the past did not rely heavily on _____ evidence gathered by observational means. The first psychological laboratory was established in the year _____ by _____ _____. The empirical method that involved carefully trained volunteers observing, analyzing, and describing their own sensations, mental images, and emotional reactions was called _____ _____. William James, an American philosopher, was a leader of _____, which emphasized the function or purpose of behaviour, not its analysis and description.

1-3.   There are currently five major perspectives that are dominant in psychology. The _____ perspective focuses on how physical bodily events affect, behaviour, feelings, and thoughts. The perspective focuses on the environment and how experience influences our actions. Psychologists from this perspective may refer to themselves as _____ when they are especially interested in rewards and punishments. Psychologists who combine behaviourism with research on thoughts and intentions are known as _____-_____ theorists. If you were interested in what goes on in people's heads, you would be following the _____ perspective. On the other hand, if you were interested in studying unconscious dynamics, you would be from the _____ perspective, whose founding father was _____. Lastly, a more recent approach to studying psychology focuses on how society and culture affect behaviour. This is known as the _____ perspective.

Review of Key Terms

The following is a list of the Key Terms from the section "The Science of Psychology." Make sure you are familiar with each term before taking the matching test on these terms.

psychology	William James	learning perspective
empirical	psychodynamic perspective	trained introspection
Wilhelm Wundt	sociocultural perspective	social-learning perspective
behaviourists	psychoanalysis	cognitive perspective
functionalism	biological perspective	Sigmund Freud

Matching Self Test 1

Match the appropriate term from the list of Key Terms with its definition or description.

1. _____   A perspective focusing on how physical bodily events affect behaviour,

feelings, and thoughts.

2. _____ An early psychological approach that emphasized the function or purpose of behaviour and consciousness.

3. _____ The scientific study of behaviour and mental processes and how they are affected by an organism's physical state, mental state, and external environment.

4. _____ Relying on or derived from observation, experimentation, or measurement.

5. _____ The father of psychology who used the method of trained introspection.

6. _____ A perspective focusing on the environment and how experience influences us.

2. What Psychologists Do

Read the section "What Psychologists Do" and then answer the following questions. If you have trouble answering any of the questions, re-study the relevant material before going on to the review of key terms and the matching test.

2-1. Psychologists who seek knowledge for its own sake are said to engage in _____ research. On the other hand, psychologists concerned with the practical uses of knowledge are said to engage in research.

2-2. Psychologists who are clinicians and provide health or mental health services are said to be in _____ _____. Those in psychological practice who use psychotherapies and treat severely disturbed people are typically _____ psychologists. _____ psychologists on the other hand usually help people deal with more minor day-to-day problems. Lastly, _____ psychologists work with students, parents, and teachers to aid student performance. People often confuse the term _____ that refers to anyone who does any type of psychotherapy with the term psychologist. They also often confuse _____, who have medical degrees, with psychologists, who have doctorate degrees.

Review of Key Terms

The following is a list of the Key Terms from the section "What Psychologists Do." Make sure you are familiar with each term before taking the matching test on these terms.

psychological practice	counselling psychologist	psychotherapist
basic psychology	school psychologist	psychiatrist
applied psychology	clinical psychologist	

Matching Self Test 2

Match the appropriate term from the list of Key Terms with its definition or description.

1. _____ The study of psychological issues that have direct practical significance and the application of psychological findings.

2. _____ A psychologist who helps people deal with minor day-to-day problems.

3. _____ A professional in psychological practice who also holds a medical degree (M.D.).

4. _____ The study of psychological issues in order to seek knowledge for its own sake rather than for its practical application.

3. Critical and Scientific Thinking in Psychology

Read the section "Critical and Scientific Thinking in Psychology" and then answer the following questions. If you have trouble answering any of the questions, re-study the relevant material before going on to the review of key terms and the matching test.

3-1. The ability to assess arguments objectively and to resist claims that have no foundation or supporting evidence is known as _____ _____. When using the principles of critical thinking one should start by proposing a _____, which is a statement that attempts to describe or explain a given behaviour. This hypothesis should have some predictive ability and the variables outlined in the hypothesis should also be elaborated upon in very specific, concrete terms known as _____ definitions.

3-2. Critical thinkers are able to analyze their own and others' assumptions and biases. Psychologists put their assumptions to the test by applying the principle of _____. This involves stating a hypothesis in such a way that it can be _____ if contradictory evidence were to be discovered. Critical thinkers also avoid emotional reasoning. They do not make things overly _____ or _____ argue by _____, which can entail arguing from personal experience. When using critical thinking it is also wise to consider other _____ and to tolerate _____. The goal of critical thinking and science is to arrive at an organized system of assumptions and principles that purports to explain certain phenomena and how they are related. This is known as a _____.

Review of Key Terms

The following is a list of the Key Terms from the section "Critical the Scientific Thinking in Psychology." Make sure you are familiar with each term before taking the matching test on these terms.

critical thinking	hypothesis	principle of falsifiability
theory	operational definition	replicate

Matching Self Test 3

Match the appropriate term from the list of Key Terms with its definition or description.

1. _____   The principle that a scientific theory must make predictions that expose the theory to the possibility of disconfirmation.

2. _____   A statement that attempts to predict or to account for a set of phenomena.

3. _____   The ability and willingness to assess claims and to make objective judgments on the basis of well-supported reasons.

4. _____   A precise definition of a term that specifies the operations for observing or measuring the process or phenomenon being defined.

4. Descriptive Studies: Establishing the Facts

Read the section "Descriptive Studies: Establishing the Facts" and then answer the following questions. If you have trouble answering any of the questions, re-study the relevant material before going on to the review of key terms and the matching test.

4-1.   Research methods that allow a researcher to describe and predict behaviour but not to choose one explanation over another are known as _____ methods. One example of such a method involves a detailed description of a particular individual known as a _____ _____. The main drawback of this method is that it is frequently _____ of the people about whom we are trying to draw conclusions.

4-2.   When researchers are trying not to interfere with people and are also attempting to systematically observe them, they are said to be engaging in _____ studies. There are two types of observational studies. One in which the researcher has more control is known as _____ observation. The primary goal of _____ observation is to find out how people or animals act in their normal environments.

4-3.   Assessment instruments used to evaluate such things as personality traits and interests are known as _____ _____. Most of these tests are _____, which means there are uniform procedures for giving and scoring the test. This scoring is usually done by using _____ or established standards of performance. Before using psychological tests, one should be sure that the test is _____, which means that it produces the same results over time and place. In addition, one should also be sure that the test measures what it claims to measure, or that it is

4-4.   In comparison to psychological tests, _____ ask people directly about their experiences, attitudes, or opinions. One of the largest problems with surveys is obtaining a _____ that is _____ of the population. Frequently, survey results suffer from a sampling bias known as _____ This means that those who participated in the survey did so of their own accord and because of this, probably differ in some way from those who decided not to participate in the survey.

Review of Key Terms

The following is a list of the Key Terms from the section "Descriptive Studies: Establishing the Facts." Make sure you are familiar with each term before taking the matching test on these terms.

descriptive methods	laboratory observation	validity
case study	representative sample	surveys
observational studies	norms	psychological tests
naturalistic observation	reliability	volunteer bias

Matching Self Test 4

Match the appropriate term from the list of Key Terms with its definition or description.

1. _____   Procedures used to measure and evaluate personality traits, emotional states, aptitudes, interests, abilities, and values.

2. _____   A group of participants selected from a population for study, that matches the population on important characteristics such as age and gender.

3. _____   A detailed description of a particular individual being studied or treated.

4. _____   A shortcoming of findings derived from a sample of volunteers instead of a representative sample.

5. _____   In test construction, to develop uniform procedures for giving and scoring a test.

6. _____   The ability of a test to measure what it was designed to measure.

7. _____   Measures that yield descriptions of behaviour but not necessarily causal explanations.

5. Correlational Studies: Looking for Relationships

Read the section "Correlational Studies: Looking for Relationships" and then answer the following questions. If you have trouble answering any of the questions, re-study the relevant material before going on to the review of key terms and the matching test.

5-1.   Another type of descriptive research method that enables researchers to examine the degree of relationship between two _____ is known as a _____ study. Some correlations are _____, meaning that high values on one variable correspond to high values on the other and that low values on one variable with low on the other. Height and _____ have this type of relationship. The correlation may

6

also be _____, meaning that there is an inverse relationship, that high values on one variable correspond to low values on the other and vice-versa. An example of a negative correlation is the relationship between the age of a car and the cost of the car. It is important to remember that correlation does not mean _____.

Review of Key Terms

The following is a list of the Key Terms from the section "Correlational Studies: Looking for Relationships." Make sure you are familiar with each term before taking the matching test on these terms.

correlational study	variable	positive correlation
correlation	coefficient of correlation	negative correlation

Matching Self Test 5

Match the appropriate term from the list of Key Terms with its definition or description.

1. _____   An association between increases in one variable and decreases in another.

2. _____   A measure of correlation that ranges in value from -1.00 to +1.00.

3. _____   Characteristics of behaviour or experience that can be measured or described by a numeric scale.

4. _____   A descriptive study that looks for a consistent relationship between two phenomena.

6. The Experiment: Hunting For Causes

Read the section "The Experiment.' Hunting For Causes" and then answer the following questions. If you have trouble answering any of the questions, re-study the relevant material before going on to the review of key terms and the matching test.

6-1.   To actually track down the causes of behaviour, a researcher must use an _____, which allows the researcher to control or manipulate the situation. In an experiment, the manipulated variable is known as the _____ variable, and the measured variable is known as the _____ variable.

6-2.   An experiment minimally requires at least two conditions. In the _____ condition, the participants are given some level of the independent variable. In the _____ condition, the participants are treated exactly as those in the experimental condition except that they are not exposed to the manipulation of the independent variable. It is necessary to _____ assign participants to the experimental and control groups or conditions. Sometimes the control group is given an inactive substance or a fake treatment known as a _____.

6-3. In a _____-blind study, neither the person running the experiment nor the participants know who is in the experimental or control groups. This type of study controls for _____ effects, or expectations of the experimenter that can influence the study. In a _____-blind study, the subjects do not know in which condition, experimental or control, they are serving, but the experimenter does know.

Review of Key Terms

The following is a list of the Key Terms from the section "The Experiment: Hunting for Causes."
Make sure you are familiar with each term before taking the matching test on these terms.

experiment   experimental group   single-blind study

independent variable   control group   experimenter effects

dependent variable   random assignment   double-blind study

control condition   placebo

Matching Self Test 6

Match the appropriate term from the list of Key Terms with its definition or description.

1. _____   An inactive substance or fake treatment used as a control in an experiment or given by a medical practitioner to a patient.

2. _____   An experiment in which neither the participants nor the individuals running the study know which participants are in the control group and which are in the experimental group until after the results are tallied.

3. _____   A variable that an experimenter manipulates in an experiment.

4. _____   Unintended changes in participants' behaviour due to cues inadvertently given by the experiment.

5. _____   A controlled test of a hypothesis in which the researcher manipulates one variable to discover its effect on another.

6. _____   In an experiment, a comparison condition in which participants are not exposed to the independent variable.

7. Evaluating the Findings

Read the section "Evaluating the Findings" and then answer the following questions. If you have trouble answering any of the questions, re-study the relevant material before going on to the review of key terms and the matching test.

7-1. One manner in which psychologists use statistics is to summarize data, possibly in graphs or charts. Such statistics are typically referred to as _____ statistics. Another way to summarize data is to add all of the scores up and divide by the total number of scores. This is referred to as the _____ _____. Another frequently used descriptive statistic that indicates how spread out a distribution of scores may be is the _____. _____ statistics differ from descriptive statistics in that they allow researchers to make inferences concerning the importance of the data. When one has determined that it is very unlikely that the results of an experiment occurred due to chance, the result is said to be _____ _____. Inferential statistics allow researchers to determine statistical significance.

7-2. A _____-_____ is a statistical technique that combines and analyzes data from many studies instead of evaluating the results of each study separately. A special kind of study in which groups of different ages are compared at one time is called a _____ study. When researchers follow the same group of people over a period of time, this is called a _____ study.

Review of Key Terms

The following is a list of the Key Terms from the section "Evaluating the Findings." Make sure you are familiar with each term before taking the matching test on these terms.

descriptive statistics	inferential statistics	longitudinal study
arithmetic mean	statistical significance	meta-analysis
variance	cross-sectional study	

Matching Self Test 7

Match the appropriate term from the list of Key Terms with its definition or description.

1. _____ A measure of the dispersion of scores around the mean.

2. _____ A procedure for combining and analyzing data from many studies; it determines how much of the variance in scores across all studies can be explained by a particular variable.

3. _____ A term used to refer to a result that is extremely unlikely to have occurred by chance.

4. _____ Statistics that organize and summarize research data.

5. _____ A study in which the same subjects are followed and periodically reassessed over a period of time.

SAMPLE ANSWERS TO WHAT'S AHEAD QUESTIONS FROM TEXTBOOK

After you have completed the "Looking Back" section at the end of the chapter by answering the "What's Ahead" questions that preceded each major section of the chapter, compare your answers to the following sample answers. If your answers are not similar to the sample answers, review the pertinent sections of the chapter. The relevant page(s) for each question is(are) provided in the "Looking Back" section in the text.

What's the difference between psychology and plain old common sense?

Psychology is not just a fancy name for common sense. Because it is a science, psychology subjects common sense beliefs to scientific testing. Some are confirmed; some are disconfirmed. Psychological research often produces findings that contradict common sense. Even when common sense is confirmed, the obviousness of the finding may only be an illusion caused by hindsight.

How old is the science of psychology?

During the 19th century, several pioneering researchers began to study psychological issues using scientific methods. And in 1879, the first psychological laboratory was officially established in Leipzig, Germany, by Wilhelm Wundt.

What are the five major perspectives in modern psychology?

The five major perspectives in modem psychology include the biological, learning, cognitive, psychodynamic, and sociocultural perspectives. Each explains behaviour and mental processes in a slightly different manner.

If someone tells you that he or she is a psychologist, why can't you assume the person is a therapist?

You cannot assume that the person is a therapist because not all psychologists are therapists. Many are basic or applied researchers who teach and do research in colleges and universities or conduct research and apply its findings in nonacademic settings.

If you decided to call yourself a "psychotherapist," would doing so be legal?

Yes, a psychotherapist is anyone who does any type of psychotherapy. The term is not legally regulated, and in most provinces you can call yourself a psychotherapist without having any training at all.

How can you distinguish a clinical psychologist from a psychiatrist?

A clinical psychologist typically has a Ph.D. or M.A., whereas a psychiatrist has a medical degree (M.D.) and has done a residency in psychiatry.

What guidelines can you use to tell whether a psychological claim is merely "psychobabble"?

One should use the eight essential critical thinking guidelines in order to make this distinction. These are (1) ask questions, (2) define your terms, (3) examine the evidence, (4) analyze assumptions and biases, (5) avoid emotional reasoning, (6) do not oversimplify, (7) consider other interpretations, and (8) tolerate uncertainty.

Why is a psychological theory unscientific if it explains anything that could conceivably happen?

Because it does not meet the principle of falsifiability. All scientific theories must not only be able to predict what will happen but also what will not happen. A theory that can explain anything never opens itself up to the possibility of falsification.

What is wrong with drawing conclusions about behaviour from a collection of anecdotes?

Anecdotes represent only one or two examples of a category. Critical thinkers require more evidence than this before drawing conclusions.

When are psychological case studies informative and when are they useless?

Case studies are most informative with respect to providing in-depth information on individuals and as a good source of hypotheses. They are even more useful if the person(s) studied is (are) representative of the people about whom the researcher would like to draw conclusions. If the individual(s) is(are) not representative of those about whom we wish to draw conclusions, then the case study is useless for that purpose.

Why do psychologists often do research in laboratories instead of observing people in their everyday lives?

Because the researcher has more control in the laboratory. This means that the researcher can decide how many people or animals are to be observed at a time, can use equipment more easily, and can control the situation in a better fashion than could be done in the natural environment. Thus, this control may enable better description, but laboratory observational studies only allow researchers to describe behaviour and not explain it. Only an experiment allows explanation.

Why should you be skeptical about psychological tests in magazines and newspapers?

Psychological tests in magazines have not been evaluated for either validity or reliability. In order to be valuable a test must be both reliable (consistent) and valid (measure what it claims to measure).

What's the difference between a psychological survey and a poll of listeners by your local radio talk-show host?

A poll from a radio talk-show suffers from volunteer bias. That is, those who respond to the poll do not constitute a representative sample. Only those motivated and interested enough to respond to the poll do so. Thus, this does not constitute a sample representative of the population.

If two things are "negatively" correlated, like grades and TV watching, what's the relationship between them?

A negative correlation means that high values of one variable are associated with low values of the other. In the example of grades and TV watching, students who spend many hours in front of the TV tend to have lower GPAs and those who spend fewer hours in front of the TV tend to have higher GPAs.

If depression and illness are correlated, does that mean depression causes illness?

No, it simply means that there is a relationship between these variables. Remember that a correlation does not show causation. When two variables are correlated, changes in one variable may or may not be causing changes in the other.

Why do psychologists rely so heavily on experiments?

Because the experimental method allows researchers to track down the causes of behaviour and give explanations. None of the other methods allow this.

What, exactly, do control groups control for?

Control groups allow the researcher to evaluate whether the independent variable had an effect by comparing the experimental group, which receives some level of the independent variable, with the control group, which is treated exactly as the experimental group except that they do not receive any level of the independent variable. Without a control group, you cannot be sure that the behaviour you are interested in would not have occurred anyway, even without your manipulation.

In a double-blind experiment, who is "blind" and what aren't they supposed to "see"?

In a double-blind experiment, the experimenter is "blind" as to which condition the participants are participating in and the participants are also "blind" as to which condition they are serving in.

How can psychologists tell whether a finding is impressive or trivial?

Psychologists use inferential statistics to determine whether a finding is impressive or trivial. Inferential statistics tell researchers how likely it is that a result occurred by chance. If a result is impressive, it is said to be statistically significant. This means that the likelihood it occurred by chance is low (5 or fewer times in 100 repetitions of the study).

Why are some findings significant statistically but insignificant in practical terms?
A result may be statistically significant but of minor consequence in everyday life. This means that the result was significant according to inferential statistics but that it has very little application or meaning in terms of real life.

MULTIPLE-CHOICE PROGRESS TEST

Choose the single best answer for each of the following questions. When you have finished this progress test, check your answers with those at the end of the chapter. You should review the indicated pages in the text for the questions you do not answer correctly.

1. According to the text's definition of psychology, behaviour and mental processes are affected by an organism's:
   a. physical state.
   b. mental state.
   c. external environment.
   d. all of the above

2. Which of the following relies heavily on empirical evidence?
   a. astrology
   b. numerology
   c. graphology
   d. none of the above

3. An early research method in which specially trained volunteers carefully observed, analyzed, and described their own sensations, mental images, and emotional reactions was called:
   a. introspection.
   b. functionalism.
   c. psychoanalysis.
   d. phrenology.

4. Phrenology is to _____ as functionalism is to _____.
   a. William James; Joseph Gall
   b. Joseph Gall; William James
   c. Wilhelm Wundt; Sigmund Freud
   d. Sigmund Freud; Wilhelm Wundt

5. The learning perspective is to the psychodynamic perspective as _____ are to _____.
   a. bodily events; social and cultural forces
   b. social and cultural forces; bodily events
   c. environmental conditions; unconscious dynamics
   d. unconscious dynamics; environmental conditions

6. Which of the following therapists is most likely to look for biochemical causes of mental disorders?
   a. a counselling psychologist
   b. a psychiatrist
   c. a clinical psychologist
   d. a social worker

7. If you test a hypothesis by stating it in such a way that it can be refuted by counterevidence, you are:
   a. conducting a single-blind study.
   b. conducting a double-blind study.
   c. using operational definitions.
   d. employing the principle of falsifiability.

8. On a radio talk-show, the host argues that smoking is not dangerous to your health because his grandfather smoked two packs a day for most of his adult life and lived to be 93 years old. The host is guilty of:
   a. reasoning emotionally.
   b. arguing by anecdote.
   c. examining the evidence.
   d. considering alternative interpretations.

9. Which descriptive research method provides in-depth information about an individual being studied or treated?
   a. case study
   b. naturalistic observation
   c. test
   d. survey

10. A test producing the same results from one time to another is to a test measuring what it is supposed to as _____ is to _____.
   a. validity; reliability
   b. reliability; validity
   c. reliability; standardization
   d. standardization; reliability

11. Volunteer bias is a problem that is most likely to occur with which one of the following descriptive research methods?
   a. case study
   b. survey
   c. test
   d. naturalistic observation

12. Which of the following coefficients of correlation indicates the strongest relationship?
    a. +.50
    b. +.10
    c. -.25
    d. -.75

13. If a researcher observes a strong negative correlation between income and mental illness, you can conclude that:
    a. being poor causes mental illness.
    b. having wealth makes you resistant to mental illness.
    c. those with lower incomes tend to suffer from higher rates of mental illness and those with higher incomes tend to suffer from lower rates of mental illness.
    d. lower income levels lead to lower levels of mental illness.

14. Which of the following relationships is a negative correlation?
    a. height and weight
    b. IQ scores and school grades
    c. educational level and annual income
    d. none of the above

15. Only _____ permits a researcher to identify cause and effect.
    a. a correlational study
    b. an experiment
    c. a survey
    d. naturalistic observation

16. In an experiment, the _____ variable is manipulated and the _____ variable is measured.
    a. control; independent
    b. independent; control
    c. independent; dependent
    d. dependent; independent

17. To control for experimenter effects, a researcher conducts a _____ study.
    a. single-blind study
    b. double-blind study
    c. case
    d. correlational

18. The mean and variance are _____ statistics.
    a. inferential
    b. descriptive

        c. correlational

        d. case study

19. Significance tests tell the researcher how likely it is that the results of the study are due to
    _____, and the results are said to be significant if this likelihood is very
    _____.

        a. chance; low

        b. the independent variable; low

        c. chance; high

        d. the independent variable; high

20. Cross-sectional studies of mental abilities across the life span usually find that mental ability
    _____ with age, and longitudinal studies usually find that mental ability
    _____ with age.

        a. declines; declines

        b. declines; does not decline

        c. does not decline; declines

        d. does not decline; does not decline

ANSWERS

GUIDED STUDY

1. The Science of Psychology

1.1	behaviour	external environment
	mental	pseudoscience
	physical state	common sense
	mental state	

1.2.	empirical	trained introspection
	1879	functionalism
	Wilhelm Wundt	

1.3.	biological	cognitive
	learning	psychodynamic
	behaviourists	Sigmund Freud
	social-learning	sociocultural

Matching Self-Test 1

1. biological perspective
2. functionalism
3. psychology

4. empirical
5. Wilhelm Wundt
6. learning perspective

___

2. What Psychologists Do

2.1	basic		applied

2.2.	psychological practice		school
	clinical		psychotherapist
	Counselling		psychiatrists

Matching Self-Test 2

1. applied psychology
2. counselling psychologist

3. psychiatrist
4. basic psychology

___

3. Critical and Scientific Thinking in Psychology

3.1.	critical thinking	hypothesis	operational

3.2.	falsifiability	anecdote	theory
	refuted	explanations	
	simplified	uncertainty	

Matching Self-Test 3

1. principle of falsifiability
2. hypothesis

3. critical thinking
4. operational definition

___

4. Descriptive Studies: Establishing the Facts

4.1.	descriptive	4.2.	observational
	case study		laboratory
	unrepresentative		naturalistic

4.3.	psychological tests	4.4.	surveys
	standardized		sample
	norms		representative
	reliable valid		volunteer bias

Matching Self-Test 4

1. psychological tests	4. volunteer bias	7. descriptive methods
2. representative sample	5. standardization	
3. case study	6. validity	

---

5. Correlational Studies: Looking for Relationships

5.1	variables	positive	negative
	correlational	weight	causation

Matching Self-Test 5

1. negative correlation	3. variable
2. coefficient of correlation	4. correlational study

---

6. The Experiment: Hunting for Causes

6.1	experiment	6.2.	experimental	6.3.	double
	independent		control		experimenter
	dependent		randomly		single
			placebo		

Matching Self-Test 6

1. random assignment	4. independent variable	7. control group
2. placebo	5. experimenter effects	
3. double-blind study	6. experiment	

---

7. Evaluating the Findings

7.1. descriptive
arithmetic mean
variance
Inferential
statistically significant

7.2. meta-analysis
cross-sectional
longitudinal

Matching Self-Test 7

1. variance
2. meta-analysis

3. statistical-significance
4. descriptive statistics

5. longitudinal study

ANSWERS TO MULTIPLE CHOICE PROGRESS TESTS

Item No.	Answer(s)	Page(s) in Textbook
1.	d. All of the above	4
2.	d. None of the above	4
3.	a. introspection	6
4.	b. Joseph Gall; William James	5-6
5.	c. environmental conditions; unconscious dynamics	7
6.	b. a psychiatrist	10
7.	d. employing the principle of falsifiability	14-15
8.	b. arguing by anecdote	16
9.	a. case study	18
10.	b. reliability; validity	20
11.	b. survey	21
12.	d. -0.75	23
13.	c. those with lower incomes tend to suffer from higher rates of mental illness and those with higher incomes tend to suffer from lower rates of mental illness.	22-23
14.	d. none of the above	23
15.	b. experiment	24
16.	c. independent; dependent	25
17.	b. double-blind study	28
18.	b. descriptive	30
19.	a. chance; low	31
20.	b. declines; does not decline	32

CHAPTER 2

Theories of Personality

CHAPTER OVERVIEW

Chapter two begins with a description of the trait perspective on personality. The theories of Allport and Cattell are discussed along with a description of the five fundamental personality traits, known as the "Big Five." The biological perspective on personality is discussed next, covering such issues as innate temperament, genes, and heritability of personality. Means of determining heritability are discussed, including studies comparing monozygotic twins to dizygotic twins.

The learning perspective, which includes the behavioural school and cognitive social learning theory is examined. This includes a brief discussion of such terms as radicalism, operant conditioning, and reinforcers. With respect to the cognitive social learning perspective, concepts such as self-fulfilling prophecy and locus of control are introduced. Following the discussion of the learning perspective, the cultural perspective is considered. Differences in personality across cultures are examined, including differences in individualist versus collectivist cultures and differences in monochronic versus polychronic cultures.

Freud's theory and other psychodynamic approaches to the study of personality are examined. Such topics as psychoanalysis, defense mechanisms, psychosexual stages of personality development, Jungian theory, and the object-relations school are covered. Several criticisms of the psychodynamic approach are also noted. Lastly, the humanist perspective is examined. The humanist ideas of Maslow, Rogers, and May are presented including such terms as self-actualization, unconditional positive regard, and the existential approach.

GUIDED STUDY

1. The Elements of Personality

Read the section "The Elements of Personality" and then answer the following questions. If you have trouble answering any of the questions, re-study the relevant material before going on to the review of key terms and the matching test.

1-1.   Each individual has a distinctive pattern of behaviour, thoughts, motives, and emotions that characterizes them over time. This is known as their _____. Personality consists of characteristics known as _____ that supposedly describe the individual over many situations.

1-2.   One of the first trait theorists was _____ _____, who proposed three different types of traits. _____ traits are the most noticeable in some individuals. Allport, however, felt that few people actually possessed this type of trait. Most individuals instead have what are known as _____ traits, which encompass the individual's general personality. These traits are fairly fixed, _____ traits, on the other hand, are more apt to change over time. A second trait theorist, _____ _____, used a statistical method known as _____ _____ to identify personality traits. Cattell believed that there were two different types of traits. The types of traits that we are able to see in an individual are called _____ traits. These traits stem from underlying traits which Cattell called _____ traits. Today, researchers discuss what are called the "Big Five" personality traits. These consist of introversion versus _____; neuroticism; _____; conscientiousness; and openness to _____.

Review of Key Terms

The following is a list of the Key Terms from the section "The Elements of Personality." Make sure you are familiar with each term before taking the matching test on these terms.

personality	surface traits	secondary traits
Allport	"Big Five"	Cattell
central traits	trait	source traits
factor analysis	cardinal traits	

Matching Self Test 1

Match the appropriate term with its definition or description.

1. _____ A descriptive characteristic of an individual, assumed to be stable across situations and time.

2. _____ A statistical method used by Cattell for analyzing the intercorrelations among various measures of test scores.

3. _____ According to Allport, each of us has about ten of these fairly fixed traits that encompass an individual's personality.

4. _____ A distinctive and relatively stable pattern of behaviour, thoughts, motives, and emotions that characterizes an individual.

2. The Biological Tradition

Read the section "The Biological Tradition" and then answer the following questions. If you have trouble answering any of the questions, re-study the relevant material before going on to the review of key terms and the matching test.

2-1.   According to biological psychologists, personality is influenced by an individual's
_____, the individual's consistent style of responding to the environment. Most
individuals' temperaments appear in infancy or early childhood, and because of this, many
psychologists believe it is based on the basic units of heredity or _____. Jerome
Kagan has been studying two extreme temperaments which he calls _____ and
_____. He has found that inhibited 5-year-old children show increased activity
in the _____ nervous system during mildly stressful mental tasks. In white
children inhibition has been associated with having _____ _____
and _____. Steven Suomi has found similar results with infant
_____ _____. He also found that a highly inhibited infant monkey
may overcome their inhibition if raised by a very _____ foster mother.

2-2.   A method used by al geneticists to study the biological basis of personality involves
estimating the _____ of traits. This involves estimating the proportion of the
total variation in a particular trait that is attributable to genetic variation among individuals
within a group. Heritability gives an estimate of how much of the variability for a trait
within a _____ is based on genes. It does not give us the impact of genetics on
any particular _____ traits. Heritability is typically studied using either adopted
children or by comparing identical or _____ twins with fraternal or
_____ twins. Researchers also frequently study identical twins who were
separated at birth. This allows them to make a better estimate of heritability as these twins
are genetically _____, yet reared in different _____. Heritability
estimates based on twin research are typically between _____ and
_____ percent. In other words, within a group of people, 40 to 60 percent of
the variability in a trait is attributable to genetic differences among the individuals in the
group.

2-3.   There are several problems with measures of heritability. These include underestimating
the influence of the _____ and problems with studies of twins that have been
separated at birth being raised in similar settings.

Review of Key Terms

*The following is a list of the Key Terms from the section "The Biological Tradition." Make sure
you are familiar with each term before taking the matching test on these terms.*

temperaments   monozygotic twins   genes

behavioural genetics   heritability   dizygotic twins

Matching Self Test 2

Match the appropriate term with its definition or description.

1. _____ Twins that develop when a fertilized egg divides into two parts that become separate embryos.

2. _____ Characteristic styles of responding to the environment that are present in infancy and are assumed to be innate.

3. _____ A statistical estimate of the proportion of the total variance in some trait within a group that is attributable to genetic differences among individuals within the group.

4. _____ The functional units of heredity; composed of DNA.

3. The Learning Tradition

Read the section "The Learning Tradition" and then answer the following questions. If you have trouble answering any of the questions, re-study the relevant material before going on to the review of key terms and the matching test.

3-1. John B. Watson argued that psychologists would have to avoid terms such as mental state and mind and study observable behaviour, or give up mentalism for _____. B.F. Skinner studied behaviour by focusing on voluntary behaviour rather than reflexive behaviour, in an approach he referred to as _____ _____. This form of conditioning emphasized that behaviours followed by pleasant consequences, known as _____, would be more likely to be repeated. For behavioural psychologists, personality is a collection of acquired behavioural patterns.

3-2. Some psychologists began to doubt that the behavioural explanation was adequate to explain human behaviour and personality. This lead to an outgrowth of behaviourism known as _____ theory. This viewpoint differs from that of behaviourism on three dimensions: _____ learning; _____ processes; and motivating _____, and _____. Julian Rotter studied the extent to which people felt they had control over their lives. He concluded that people learn that certain behaviours will be punished and others rewarded, and they therefore develop what he called _____ _____. He also felt that once these expectancies were acquired, they would lead to behaviour that would make the expectation come true. This is know as a _____-_____ prophecy. Rotter also studied people's feelings or beliefs about the factors that govern their behaviour, referring to these beliefs as an individual's _____ ___ _____. According to Rotter, some people have an _____ locus of control, meaning they tend to believe that they are responsible for what happens to them. Others have an _____ locus of control, meaning they feel what happens to them is frequently the result of luck, fate, or another person's actions.

23

Review of Key Terms

The following is a list of the Key Terms from the section "The Learning Tradition." Make sure you are familiar with each term before taking the matching test on these terms.

B.F. Skinner   locus of control   behaviourism

reinforcer   self-fulfilling prophecy   operant conditioning

generalized expectancies   cognitive social learning theory

Matching Self Test 3

Match the appropriate term with its definition or description.

1. _____ A stimulus or event that strengthens or increases the probability of the response it follows.

2. _____ A general expectation about whether the results of your actions are under your own control, or beyond your control

3. _____ An approach to psychology that emphasizes the study of observable behaviour.

4. _____ The process by which a response becomes more likely to occur or less so, depending on its consequences.

4. The Cultural Tradition

Read the section "The Cultural Tradition" and then answer the following questions. If you have trouble answering any of the questions, re-study the relevant material before going on to the review of key terms and the matching test.

4-1.   Psychologists representing the _____ tradition are interested in how culture affects the factors contributing to personality. A culture is defined as (1) a program of _____ _____ that govern the behaviour of members of a community or society; and (2) a set of _____ , _____. and _____ shared by most members of that community. Cultures that emphasize the independence of the individual over the needs of the group are considered _____ cultures. On the other hand, cultures that emphasize group harmony over the wishes of the individual are known as cultures. We often attribute another's actions to personality traits when in fact they may really be due to cultural norms. How close people stand to one another when speaking, known as _____ _____ is an example of this. Another example involves whether you come from a culture that runs on a linear time schedule, known as a _____ culture, or from a culture where people do many things at once and the needs of friends and family take precedence over a time schedule, known as a _____ culture.

4-2.   One problem for cultural psychologists is how to describe cultural influences on personality without _____.

Review of Key Terms

The following is a list of the Key Terms from the section "The Cultural Tradition." Make sure you are familiar with each term before taking the matching test on these terms.

culture   monochronic cultures   conversational distance

collectivist cultures   individualist cultures   polychronic cultures

Matching Self Test 4

Match the appropriate term with its definition or description.

1. _____   Cultures in which the self is regarded as embedded in relationships and harmony with one's group is prized above individual goals and wishes.

2. _____   Cultures in which time is organized horizontally; people tend to do several things at once and value relationships over schedules.

3. _____   Cultures in which the self is regarded as autonomous, and individual goals and wishes are prized above duty and relations with others.

4. _____   Cultures in which time is organized sequentially; schedules and deadlines are valued over people.

5. The Psychodynamic Tradition

Read the section "The Psychodynamic Tradition" and then answer the following questions. If you have trouble answering any of the questions, re-study the relevant material before going on to the review of key terms and the matching test.

5-1.   Psychodynamic theory, which emphasizes the movement of psychological energy within the person, was originated by _____ _____. Freud believed that the unconscious may reveal itself when an individual talks about anything that pops into their head. This technique was called _____ _____. Freud identified three structures of personality. The _____ is present at birth and is responsible for psychological energies and instincts. It is said to operate based on the _____ principle. The _____ is a referee between the needs of instincts and the demands of society and it operates based on the _____ principle. Lastly, the _____ represents one's conscience or morality. The weapons used by the ego to aid in reducing anxiety are known as _____ _____. For example, _____ is a defense mechanism in which people direct their emotions, such as anger, toward things, animals, or other people that are not

25

the source of these emotions. Another defense mechanism, _____, occurs when a feeling that produces unconscious anxiety is transformed into its opposite in consciousness. When someone refuses to admit that something unpleasant is happening or that they are experiencing a "forbidden" emotion, they are experiencing the defense mechanism of _____. Freud also developed a psychosexual theory of personality development that had five stages to it. The first is the _____ stage in which infants take in the world through their mouths. The second, the _____ stage, marks the start of _____ development. Thirdly, the _____ stage involves the child wishing to possess the parent of the opposite sex and to get rid of the parent of the same sex. Freud called this phenomenon the _____ _____. The fourth stage, in which the child settles down somewhat is called the _____ stage. Lastly, the fifth stage, which begins at puberty, is called the _____ stage. Freud's ideas were positively received by many. Others, however, feel that many of Freud's ideas were _____ but liked the overall framework of his theory. Still others think that psychoanalytic theory is _____, with little _____ support.

5-2.   Other psychologists from the psychodynamic perspective broke away from Freud. In _____ _____'s theory, a _____ unconscious that contained universal memories, symbols and images which are the legacy of human history was proposed. Jung studied myths and folklore from which he identified common themes that he referred to as _____. He felt that two of the most important archetypes were those of _____ and _____. The female archetype is called the _____ and the male is called the _____. In a more recent approach, the _____-_____ _____, which was developed in Great Britain, holds that the first two years of life are the most critical for development of the inner core of personality.

5-3.   Empirical psychologists criticize psychodynamic approaches to personality for failing scientifically on three dimensions. Firstly, they feel that it violates the principle of _____. Secondly, the principles were outlined based on observations of a few _____ patients. Lastly, psychodynamic theories of development were based on _____ accounts. This creates an _____ of causality between events. In other words, people assume that if A preceded B, then A must have caused B.

Review of Key Terms

The following is a list of the Key Terms from the section "The Psychodynamic Tradition." Make sure you are familiar with each term before taking the matching test on these terms.

Sigmund Freud	anal stage	superego
psychodynamic theory	latency stage	repression
psychic reality	Oedipus complex	displacement
id	Carl Jung	reaction formation
libido	archetypes	denial
reality principle	illusion of causality	oral stage
defense mechanisms	psychoanalysis	phallic stage
projection	intrapsychic dynamics	genital stage
sublimation	free association	Karen Horney
regression	pleasure principle	collective unconscious
psychosexual stages	ego	object-relations school

Matching Self Test 5

Match the appropriate term with its definition or description.

1. _____ In psychoanalysis, the part of personality that represents reason, good sense, and rational self-control.

2. _____ In psychoanalysis, a conflict in which a child desires the parent of the opposite sex and views the same-sex parent as a rival.

3. _____ Methods used by the ego to prevent unconscious anxiety or threatening thought from entering consciousness.

4. _____ In psychoanalysis, the part of the personality containing inherited psychological energy, particularly sexual and aggressive instincts.

5. _____ A psychodynamic approach that emphasizes the importance of the infant's first two years of life and the baby's formative relationships.

6. _____ To Carl Jung, the universal memories and experiences of humankind, represented in the unconscious images and symbols or all people.

6. The Humanist Tradition

Read the section "The Humanist Tradition" and then answer the following questions. If you have trouble answering any of the questions, re-study the relevant material before going on to the review of key terms and the matching test.

6-1.   The humanist approach to personality is defined by the human abilities that separate us from other animals, _____ of choice and _____ will. The main figure heads in the humanist movement were Abraham _____, Rollo _____, and Carl _____. Maslow emphasized the positive aspects of human nature, which he called _____ _____. The traits that he thought were important to personality were not the Big Five, but those he saw as pertaining to a _____-_____ person. This is a person who strives for a life that is meaningful, challenging, and productive. Carl Rogers coined a similar phrase for an individual whom he felt had attained congruence or harmony. He called these individuals _____ _____ people. To become fully functioning, Rogers claims that we need _____ _____ regard, or love and support without conditions or strings attached. Rollo May differed from other humanists in that he ascribed to the European philosophy of _____, meaning that May believed in freedom of choice for humans, but he also felt that freedom brings with it a burden of responsibility.

Review of Key Terms

The following is a list of the Key Terms from the section "The Humanist Tradition." Make sure you are familiar with each term before taking the matching test on these terms.

humanist psychology	fully functioning	Rollo May
Carl Rogers	unconditional positive regard	self-actualized person
peak experiences	Abraham Maslow	existential psychology

Matching Self Test 6

Match the appropriate term with its definition or description.

1. _____   To Carl Rogers, love or support given to another person with no conditions attached.

2. _____   An approach to psychology that emphasizes free will, personal responsibility, and the inevitable anxieties of existence.

3. _____   To Abraham Maslow, a person who strives for a life that is meaningful, challenging, and productive.

4. _____   A psychological approach that emphasizes personal growth and the achievement of human potential.

28

SAMPLE ANSWERS TO *WHAT'S AHEAD* QUESTIONS FROM TEXTBOOK

After you have completed the "Looking Back" section at the end of the chapter by answering the "What's Ahead" questions that preceded each major section of the chapter, compare your answers to the following sample answers. If your answers are not similar to the sample answers, review the pertinent sections of the chapter. The relevant page(s) for each question is(are) provided in the "Looking Back" section in the text.

How can psychologists tell which personality traits are basic?

Psychologists typically use psychological tests to identify basic personality traits. They use factor analysis, a statistical procedure that identifies clusters of correlated test items that seem to be measuring some common underlying trait. For example, Raymond Cattell developed a personality inventory known as the 16 PF (Personality Factors) Questionnaire, which he felt identified basic personality traits.

Which five dimensions of personality seem to describe people the world over?

The five dimensions identified by psychologists are (I) introversion versus extroversion; (2) neuroticism; (3) agreeableness; (4) conscientiousness; and (5) openness to experience.

Is it possible to be born touchy or easy-going.

According to biological psychologists, the answer is yes. Your temperament, which you are born with, influences subsequent personality development. We must remember, however, that an initial tendency may be strengthened by a child's experience, or diminished. Every child is always part of a context in which biology and experience are inextricably intertwined.

How do psychologists measure the "heritability" of a trait?

Scientists have no way to estimate the heritability of a trait directly, so they must infer it by studying people whose degree of genetic similarity is known. Researchers can compare correlations between adopted children's traits and those of their biological and adoptive parents and use the results to estimate heritability. Another approach is to compare identical and same-sex fraternal twins. The assumption is that if identical twins are more alike than fraternal twins, then the increased similarity must be genetic.

To what extent are personality differences among people influenced by their genetic differences? Heritability has been estimated at 40 to 60 percent. Thus, in a group of people, 40 to 60 percent of the variance in personality traits can be attributed to genetic differences.

Are people who have highly heritable personality traits stuck with them forever?

No, 40 to 60 percent of personality traits would also be based on environmental factors in a group of people. Certain traits are more environmentally influenced than others. There is a nurturing component to most traits.

Why do behaviourists regard a label such as "aggressive" or "shy" as meaningless for explaining behaviour?

Behaviouristis think that personality traits do not explain behaviour, but rather are behaviours to be explained. A behaviourist, such as Skinner, would say that someone who acts aggressively has been reinforced for acting that way. They act that way, not because of an internal personality trait, but because their environment has shaped that behaviour.

Why did cognitive social-learning theorists break away from radical behaviourists in explaining personality?

They broke away because they felt that the behavioural approach was inadequate to explain human behaviour and personality. Cognitive social-learning theorists departed from behaviourists on several issues including: observational learning and the role of models, cognitive processes such as interpretations of events, and emotions and beliefs concerning expectations of success or failure.

What's the difference between people who think they control their destiny—and those who think destiny controls them?

Julian Rotter would say that people who think they control their own destiny have an internal locus of control whereas those who think destiny controls them have an external locus of control. Thus, the people differ in their beliefs about the factors that govern their behaviour.

How does belonging to an individualist or collectivist culture influence your personality—and even whether you think you have a stable "self"?

Individualist and collectivist ways of defining the self (independence of individual or in context of relationships and the larger community) influence which personality traits we value, how we express emotions, how much we value having relationships or maintaining freedom, and even whether we think personality is stable across situations.

Why might an Arab and a Swede agree on everything the other is saying and still feel uncomfortable with each other?

They would feel uncomfortable because the conversational distance is very different between these two cultures. Arabs like to be very close to you when speaking, whereas Europeans prefer a longer conversational distance.

Why are punctuality and tardiness more than just individual personality traits?

The concept of "being on time" varies from one culture to another. Our culture is monochronic, meaning that time is organized in a linear fashion and that people do one thing at a time. Other cultures are polychronic, meaning that people do many things at once and that "running on time" does not supersede the needs of family and friends.

In Freud's theory of personality, why are the id and the superego always at war?

The id operates on the pleasure principle. Thus, the id "wants" all of the time. The superego represents morality, the rules of parents and society, and the power of authority. It includes the conscience. Thus, it is always trying to act in the manner that is best for all, which is in conflict with the id's selfish desires.

When people tell you that you're being "defensive," what defenses might they be thinking of?

They might be thinking of what Freud termed the ego's defense mechanisms. According to Freud, these defenses are necessary to protect us from conflict and the stresses of reality. Freud described 17 defense mechanisms; later other psychologists expanded and modified his list.

How do psychologists regard Freud today—as a genius or a fraud?

Many revere Freud as a hero. Others acknowledge that some of Freud's ideas have proved faulty, but still believe in the overall framework of Freud's theory. Lastly, some think that psychoanalytic theory is nonsense.

What would Carl Jung have to say about Darth Vader?

Carl Jung would most likely say that Darth Vader represents the shadow archetype. This archetype represents the sinister, evil side of human nature.

What are the "objects" in the object-relations approach to personality?

The objects are the numerous representations of the self and others that a child eventually constructs. The psychodynamic interplay among them comprises the relations.

How does the humanist vision of human nature differ from those of behaviourism and psychoanalysis?

The humanists believe in complete freedom of choice and free will. Psychologists representing behaviourism and psychoanalysis do not believe in this.

In the humanist view, what's wrong with saying to a child, "I love you because you've been good"?

According to Carl Rogers, this is an example of conditional positive regard. He felt that love and regard should be unconditional, given with no strings attached.

MULTIPLE-CHOICE PROGRESS TEST

Choose the single best answer for each of the following questions. When you have finished this progress test, check your answers with those at the end of the chapter. You should review the indicated pages in the text for the questions you do not answer correctly.

1. Cardinal, central, and secondary traits were proposed by:
   a. Cattell.
   b. Freud.
   c. Allport.
   d. Jung.

2. Of the following four traits, which would be classified as a source trait?
   a. assertiveness
   b. courage
   c. ambition
   d. dominance

3. Bill is a very anxious person who is unable to control his impulses and who has a tendency to have unrealistic ideas. Which of the Big Five personality traits is most relevant to Bill's ?
   a. conscientiousness
   b. neuroticism
   c. agreeableness
   d. openness to experience

4. Jerome Kagan and his colleagues have found that socially inhibited white children are more likely to _____ than uninhibited white children.
   a. show sympathetic nervous system activity during stressful mental tasks
   b. have blue eyes
   c. have allergies
   d. all of the above

5. Which of the following groups should have the highest heritability for a given trait?
   a. a group of genetically very similar people raised in very dissimilar environments
   b. a group of genetically very similar people raised in very similar environments
   c. a group of genetically very dissimilar people raised in very dissimilar environments
   d. a group of genetically very dissimilar people raised in very similar environments

6. One fertilized egg divided into two parts is to two eggs each fertilized by a different sperm as _____ twins are to _____ twins.
   a. identical; dizygotic
   b. identical; monozygotic
   c. fraternal; monozygotic
   d. fraternal; dizygotic

7. Based on adoption and twin studies, heritability of personality traits is typically between:
   a. .10 and .20.
   b. .20 and .40.
   c. .40 and.60.
   d. .60 and .80.

8. Mary sees personality as only a set of habits and beliefs that have been rewarded over a person's lifetime. She is most likely a _____.
   a. cognitive social-learning theorist
   b. biological psychologist
   c. behaviourist
   d. psychodynamic theorist

9. Which of the following statements best reflects an internal locus of control?
   a. "That was just a fluke; I could never do it again."
   b. "I was lucky; it will never happen again."
   c. "It was fate; I had nothing to do with it."
   d. "I deserve it; I studied very hard for the test."

10. Cultures whose members regard the "self" as defined in the context of relationships and the larger community are _____ cultures.
   a. individualist
   b. collectivist
   c. monochronic
   d. polychronic

11. In Freud's theory of personality, the _____ represents reason, good sense, and rational self-control
   a. ego
   b. superego
   c. libido
   d. id

12. When displacement serves a higher cultural or useful purpose, as in the creation of art or inventions, it is called _____.
   a. projection
   b. reaction formation
   c. sublimation
   d. repression

13. Which of the following is the correct sequence of stages in Freud's theory of personality development?
   a. oral; genital; latency; anal; phallic
   b. anal; latency; genital; oral; phallic
   c. oral; phallic; anal; latency; genital
   d. oral; anal; phallic; latency; genital

14. According to Freud's theory of personality development, the Oedipus complex occurs in the _____ stage.
   a. oral
   b. anal
   c. phallic
   d. genital

15. Psychodynamic theories have been criticized for:
   a. violating the principle of falsifiability.
   b. overgeneralizing from atypical patients to everyone.
   c. being based on the unreliable and retrospective accounts of patients.
   d. all of the above

16. Which of the following statements about object-relations theory is FALSE?
   a. The first two years of life are the most critical for development of personality.
   b. The basic human drive is the need to be in relationships.
   c. Children of both sexes identify first with the mother.
   d. Women develop more rigid ego boundaries between themselves and other people.

17. The idea that fully functioning people experience congruence between their self image and their true feelings, perceptions, and wishes was proposed by:
    a. Carl Rogers.
    b. Karen Horney.
    c. B.F. Skinner.
    d. Carl Jung.

18. Rollo May added the element of _____ to American psychology.
    a. peak experiences
    b. existentialism
    c. archetypes
    d. illusion of causality

19. Which theory of personality takes the most optimistic view of human nature?
    a. humanistic
    b. psychodynamic
    c. behavioral
    d. cultural

20. Which of the following pairs of personality theorists and perspectives is INCORRECT?
    a. Abraham Maslow; humanist
    b. B.F. Skinner; behavioral
    c. Carl Jung; trait
    d. Karen Horney; psychodynamic

ANSWERS

GUIDED STUDY

1. The Elements of Personality

1.1.   personality   traits

1.2.	Gordon Allport	Raymond Cattell	extroversion
	Cardinal	factor analysis	agreeableness
	central	surface	experience
	Secondary	source	

Matching Self-Test 1

1.   trait   3. central traits
2.   factor analysis   4. personality

2. The Biological Tradition

2.1.   temperament   uninhibited   allergies

            genes   sympathetic   rhesus monkeys

            inhibited   blue eyes   nurturant

2.2.   heritability   monozygotic   environments

            group   dizygotic   40

            individual's   identical   60

2.3.   environment

Matching Self-Test 2

1. monozygotic twins   3. Heritability
2. temperaments   4. genes

3. The Learning Tradition

3.1.   behaviourism   reinforcers

            operant conditioning

3.2.   social learning   self-fulfilling

            observational   locus of control

            cognitive   internal

            values, emotions, and beliefs   external

            generalized expectancies

Matching Self-Test 3

1. reinforcer   3. behaviourism
2. locus of control   4. operant conditioning

4. The Cultural Tradition

4 1   cultural   collectivist

            shared rules   conversational distance

            values, beliefs, and attitudes   monochronic

            individualist   polychronic

4.2.   stereotyping

Matching Self-Test 4

1. collectivist cultures   3. individualist cultures
2. polychronic cultures   4. monochronic cultures

---

5. The Psychodynamic Tradition

5.1.   Sigmund Freud   defense   phallic
        free association   mechanisms   Oedipal complex
        id   displacement   latency
        pleasure   reaction formation   genital
        ego   denial   faulty
        reality   oral   nonsense
        superego   anal   empirical
                               ego

5.2.   Carl Jung   femaleness
        collective   anima
        archetypes   animus
        maleness   object-relations school

5.3.   falsifiability
        atypical
        retrospective
        illusion

Matching Self-Test 5

1. ego   4. id
2. Oedipus complex   5. object-relations school
3. defense mechanisms   6. collective unconscious

---

6. The Humanist Tradition

6.1.   freedom   peak experiences   unconditional
        free   self-actualized   positive
        Maslow   fully functioning   existentialism
        May
        Rogers

36

Matching Self-Test 6

1. unconditional positive regard   3. self-actualized person
2. existentialism   4. humanist psychology

ANSWERS TO MULTIPLE CHOICE PROGRESS TEST

Item No.	Answer(s)	Page(s) in Textbook
1.	c Allport	40
2.	d. dominance	40-41
3.	b. neuroticism 41	
4.	d. all of the above 43	
5.	a. a group of genetically very similar people raised in very dissimilar environments	44-45
6.	a. identical; dizygotic	45
7.	c. 40 and .60	46
8.	c. behaviourist	48
9.	d. "I deserve it; I studied very hard for the test."	49-51
10.	b. collectivist	53
11.	a. ego	57
12.	c. sublimation	58
13.	d. oral; anal; phallic; latency; genital	59-60
14.	d. phallic	60
15.	d. all of the above	65
16.	d. Women develop more rigid ego boundaries between themselves and other people.	63-64
17.	a. Carl Rogers	65-66
18.	b. existentialism	66
19.	a. humanistic	66
20.	c. Carl Jung; trait	61

CHAPTER 3

Development over the Life Span

CHAPTER OVERVIEW

The chapter begins with a discussion of prenatal development including a description of the three stages of prenatal development. In addition, a discussion of possible harmful influences to the embryo and fetus are discussed. These include German measles, radiation, sexually transmitted diseases, cigarette smoking, alcohol, and drugs. The physical abilities of the infant are considered next. Key concepts such as motor reflexes and preferences are described. A discussion of attachment in infancy follows. This includes a description of stranger anxiety, separation anxiety, and research by the Harlows and Mary Ainsworth.

Piaget's stages of cognitive development in childhood are detailed. Terms central to Piaget's theory including assimilation, accommodation, object permanence, conservation, and egocentrism are described. Several criticisms of Piaget's theory of cognitive development are also presented. A discussion of language development follows. The basic progression of language development is described, along with Chomsky's theory of language acquisition.

The biological, learning, and cognitive viewpoints on gender development are considered next. This includes a description of such phenomena as gender roles, gender identity, gender socialization, and gender schemas. Kohlberg's three levels of moral reasoning are presented, along with Carol Gilligan's criticism of this theory. A discussion of developing a moral conscience in children follows. This includes the presentation of two approaches to parenting and Baumrind's three parenting styles.

The time period known as adolescence is discussed next. Key terms such as puberty, menarche, and secondary sex characteristics are covered along with a discussion of the effects of early maturation and late maturation during adolescence. The final topic in the chapter is adulthood. The physical and emotional effects of menopause in women are presented. The work of gerontologists is also presented, including a discussion of crystallized versus fluid intelligence and cross-sectional versus longitudinal research. Lastly, Erik Erikson's eight-stage theory of development is presented along with the concept of a social clock.

GUIDED STUDY

From Conception to the First Year

Read the section "From Conception to the First Year" and then answer the following questions. If you have trouble answering any of the questions, re-study the relevant material before going on to the review of key terms and the matching test.

1-1   The first stage of prenatal development, in which the male sperm unites with the female egg, is called the _____ stage. The fertilized egg is called a _____. When the zygote becomes implanted in the wall of the uterus, the second stage of prenatal development, called the _____ stage, begins. The last stage, the _____ stage, begins at eight weeks. Several things can pass the placental barrier and damage the embryo and fetus. One substance that is damaging to the fetus is alcohol, which can lead to _____ _____ syndrome. This syndrome causes facial deformities, smaller brains, lack of coordination, and mental retardation.

1-2.   A newborn is equipped with automatic s that are necessary for survival and are known as _____ _____. For example, when touched on the side of the face or near the mouth the infant will turn their head in search of something to suck on. This is known as the _____ reflex. Infants also form attachments very early in life. The Harlows' first demonstrated the importance of touching, or _____ _____ in an experiment with rhesus monkeys. The monkeys spent more time with the _____ cloth mother than with the mother that provided _____. Between 7 and 9 months, alter babies are emotionally attached to their primary caregivers, they will frequently be frightened of strangers, experiencing what is called _____ _____, and also be upset if their primary caregiver leaves them, showing what is called _____ _____. Ainsworth developed an experimental situation, known as the _____ situation, to identify different styles of attachment between mothers and infants. Based on children's reactions to the strange situation, Ainsworth classified them as having one of two styles of attachment. The children that were most attached to their mothers were said to have a _____attachment. Other children were described as displaying an _____ attachment which had two forms. Some insecurely attached infants were said to be _____; they did not seem to care where the mother was. Others were described as being _____ or _____; resisting contact with the mother, acting angry with her, and protesting loudly when she left them. Ainsworth further determined that insecurely attached infants often grow into children who have _____ and _____ problems, may have low _____-_____ and are at an increased risk for _____.

Review of Key Terms

The following is a list of the Key Terms from the section "From Conception to the First Year." Make sure you are familiar with each term before taking the matching test on these terms.

maturation	insecure attachment	separation anxiety
embryonic stage	anxious/ambivalent attachment	secure attachment
fetal alcohol syndrome	germinal stage	avoidant attachment
contact comfort	fetal stage	
stranger anxiety	motor reflexes	

Matching Self Test 1

Match the appropriate term with its definition or description.

1. _____ Automatic behaviours that are necessary for survival and with which newborns begin life.

2. _____ The stage in prenatal development that begins with the implantation of the zygote.

3. _____ The sequential unfolding of genetically influenced and physical characteristics.

4. _____ Anxiety displayed when the primary caregiver temporarily leaves the infant.

Cognitive Development

Read the section "Cognitive Development" and then answer the following questions. If you have trouble answering any of the questions, re-study the relevant material before going on to the review of key terms and the matching test.

2-1. The Swiss psychologist who proposed a theory of cognitive development in the 1920s was _____ _____. According to Piaget, we use two processes to organize and adapt information throughout our lives. The first, _____, allows us to fit new information into a present network of knowledge. He referred to this network of knowledge as a _____. The second, _____, allows us to change or modify existing schemas. Piaget further proposed that all children go through four stages of cognitive development. The first, from birth to 2 years of age, is called the _____ stage. In this stage children learn through coordinating sensory information with motor movements. A major accomplishment during this stage is the development of _____ _____, understanding that something continues to exist even if you cannot see or touch it. In the second or _____ stage, from age 2 to 7 years, the use of symbols and language increases. However, Piaget felt that children in this stage were lacking in other mental abilities such as reasoning.

Piaget referred to these mental abilities as _____. One characteristic of the preoperational child is that they cannot take another person's perspective or point of view. In other words, the preoperational child is described as being _____. Another limitation of the preoperational child is that they believe that physical properties change when their appearances change. In other words, they do not understand _____. In the third or _____ _____ stage, from age 7 to 11, children master many of the skills they were lacking in the preoperational stage. Their thinking abilities, however, are still limited to concrete experiences and concepts. Lastly, the fourth or _____ _____ stage, from age 12 to adulthood, signals the beginning of abstract reasoning abilities.

2-2.   Although Piaget's theories contributed tremendously to the field of developmental psychology, there are some criticisms of his findings. Firstly, the movement from one stage to another is not as _____-_____ as Piaget claimed. Secondly, children understand far more than Piaget gave them credit for. Thirdly, preschoolers are not as _____ as Piaget claimed. Fourthly, _____ plays more of a role in development than Piaget claimed. Lastly, Piaget _____ the cognitive abilities of many adults in that not all adults develop formal reasoning abilities.

2-3   According to linguists who study language acquisition, by 4 to 6 months babies have learned many consonant and vowel sounds, called _____. They can distinguish the phonemes of their native language from those of a foreign language. They start to _____ between the ages of 6 months and 1 year and at about 1 year they will typically begin to name things. The two or three word brief communications used by the 18-month to 2-year-old child is referred to as _____ speech. Psychologists first thought that children learn to speak by imitating adults. Many now believe, however, that the human brain possesses a _____ _____ device. This mental module that allows children to develop language when they are exposed to it was proposed by _____. Evidence supporting this notion comes from children's understanding of not only the _____ structure of a sentence, but also their understanding of the underlying meaning of the sentence or the _____ structure of the sentence. Chomsky also noted, as further evidence for a language acquisition device, that children everywhere go through similar stages of linguistic development; that children combine words in ways that adults never would, called _____; and that children learn to speak in a grammatically correct manner even though adults are not consistently correcting them. It does appear, however, that nurture also plays a role in language acquisition, as evidenced by children who are not exposed to language for years and then have trouble mastering language skills. The idea that language has to be learned at a certain time period in life is know as a _____ _____ in language development.

Review of Key Terms

The following is a list of the Key Terms from the section "Cognitive Development." Make sure you are familiar with each term before taking the matching test on these terms.

Jean Piaget	surface structure	conservation
accommodation	universal grammar	egocentric thinking
object permanence	critical period	telegraphic speech
representational thought	language acquisition device	syntax
preoperational stage	assimilation	deep structure
concrete operations stage	sensorimotor stage	overregularizations
formal operations stage	operations	

Matching Self Test 2

Match the appropriate term with its definition or description.

1. _____ The understanding, that develops late in the first year, that an object continues to exist even when you cannot see it or touch it.

2. _____ A child's first combination of words, which omits (as a telegram does) unnecessary words.

3. _____ In Piaget's theory, the process of absorbing new information into existing cognitive structures.

4. _____ Seeing the world from only your own point of view; the inability to take another person's perspective.

5. _____ In Piaget's theory, the process of modifying existing cognitive structures in response to experience and new information.

6. _____ The understanding that the physical properties of objects can remain the same even when their form or appearance changes.

7. _____ A mental module in the brain that allows children to develop language if they are exposed to an adequate sampling of conversation.

3. Gender Development

Read the section "Gender Development" and then answer the following questions. If you have trouble answering any of the questions, re-study the relevant material before going on to the review of key terms and the matching test.

3-1.   The term _____ is used to refer to cultural and psychological attributes that children learn are appropriate for the sexes. _____ , on the other hand, is used to refer to the physiological or anatomical attributes of the sexes. Although most children are able to distinguish between the sexes very early in life, it takes them longer to learn their _____ _____, the rules and expectations governing male and female attitudes and behaviour. At the age of about 4 or 5 years, most children begin to develop a secure _____ _____, a fundamental sense of maleness or femaleness. Biological psychologists feel that differences between the sexes may be due to prenatal _____, _____ and brain _____. These psychologists also point out that gender differences will exist no matter how parents treat their children. They feel that toy and play preferences have a _____ basis.

3-2.   According to learning theorists, differences between boys and girls are a result of _____ _____. This is the psychological process through which children learn what it means to be masculine or feminine. Observational research has demonstrated that when preschool boys acted aggressively, they were paid attention to ____ percent of the time versus only ____ percent when preschool girls acted aggressively. Preschool girls received more attention when they acted _____.

3-3.   A final approach to gender development investigates cognitive abilities and gender development. According to this approach, children develop a _____ _____, a mental network of beliefs, metaphors, and expectations about what it means to be male or female. The period between 2 and 4 years of age is very important in the development of a gender schema. At this point in time, boys express stronger preferences for "masculine" toys than girls do for "feminine" toys. In one study, preschoolers believed that a rabbit that was deferent, had its opinions overruled, and was less likely to have its advice followed was a _____.

Review of Key Terms

The following is a list of the Key Terms from the section "Gender Development." Make sure you are familiar with each term before taking the matching test on these terms.

gender role   gender identity

gender socialization   gender schema

Matching Self Test 3

Match the appropriate term with its definition or description.

1. _____ The process by which children learn the behaviours, attitudes, and expectations associated with being masculine or feminine in their culture.

2. _____ A social position governed by rules and standards for male or female attitudes and behaviour.

3. _____ A mental network or knowledge, beliefs, metaphors, and expectations about what it means to be male or female.

4. Moral Development

Read the section "Moral Development" and then answer the following questions. If you have trouble answering any of the questions, re-study the relevant material before going on to the review of key terms and the matching test.

4-1.   In order to study moral reasoning, _____ _____ used Piaget's ideas to develop a stage theory of moral reasoning. By looking at the reasoning behind decisions given to moral dilemmas, Kohlberg proposed three levels of moral development, each with _____ stages. In the first or _____ level, young children base their decisions to moral dilemmas on obeying rules in order to avoid punishment (Stage 1) and because they feel it is in their best interest to obey the rules (Stage 2). This level of moral reasoning is based on self-centered decisions. The second or _____ level begins at about age _____ or _____. This involves reasoning based on conformity (Stage 3) and _____ and _____ (Stage 4). The highest level of moral reasoning, according to Kohlberg, is attained in the _____ level. This level of moral reasoning involves understanding that laws are important, but that they can be changed (Stage 5) and developing a moral standard based on universal _____ _____. Most studies testing Kohlberg's theory have confirmed that Stages 5 and 6 are _____, but that the other four stages do develop somewhat sequentially. An alternative theory was put forth by _____ _____, who cited gender differences in moral reasoning. She claimed that men tend to base their decisions on abstract principles of _____ and _____, whereas women tend to base their decisions on principles of _____ and _____. Some studies have supported Gilligan's ideas, but most have not. Many psychologists view any stage theory to moral development as limited for three reasons. Firstly, stage theories tend to overlook _____ and _____ influences on moral reasoning. Secondly, moral reasoning is frequently _____ across situations. Thirdly, one's moral _____ is often not related to one's moral _____. Because of these criticisms, many psychologists have begun focusing on the emergence of _____ and not on moral reasoning.

44

4-2. One method frequently used by parents in an attempt to encourage and enforce moral standards is _____ _____. This involves threatening some sort of punishment in order to encourage the child to act in a moral way. Power assertion, however, seems to promote a _____ of moral feeling and behaviour and a failure to _____ moral values. A better approach to teaching moral behaviour is _____. When using this method, parents appeal to the child's sense of responsibility and affection for others. Children reared in this manner tend to feel _____ if they hurt others. They also tend to internalize standards of _____ and _____. Baumrind has investigated the effects of the use of power assertion and induction in her research on parenting styles. She has identified three basic parenting styles. _____ parents tend to provide little _____ and wield too much _____. _____ parents on the other hand, are very nurturant, but have too little _____. They do not expect either _____ or _____ from their children. Lastly, _____ parents are somewhat in between authoritarian and permissive parents. They know when and how to _____ children, set high but reasonable _____, and encourage two-way _____.

Review of Key Terms

The following is a list of the Key Terms from the section "Moral Development.. " Make sure you are familiar with each term before taking the matching test on these terms.

Lawrence Kohlberg	justice-based moral reasoning
preconventional level of moral reasoning	power assertion
conventional level of moral reasoning	induction
postconventional level of moral reasoning	authoritarian parenting style
Carol Gilligan	permissive parenting style
care-based moral reasoning	authoritative parenting style

Matching Self Test 4

Match the appropriate term with its definition or description.

1. _____ The level in Kohlberg's theory on moral reasoning in which individuals base their moral decisions on personal ethical principles rather than on strict laws.

2. _____ A method of child rearing in which the parent uses punishment and authority to correct the child's misbehaviour.

3. _____ One of the parenting styles identified by Baumrind in which the parents are very nurturant but have very little control over their children.

4· _____ A method of child rearing in which the parents appeal to the child's own resources, abilities, sense of responsibility, and feelings for others in correcting the child's misbehaviour.

5. Adolescence

Read the section "Adolescence" and then answer the following questions. If you have trouble answering any of the questions, restudy the relevant material before going on to the review of key terms and the matching test.

5-1. The point at which a person becomes capable of sexual reproduction is known as _____. The interval of time between puberty and adulthood is referred to as _____. From puberty on, boys have a higher level of the hormones called and girls have a higher lever of the hormones called _____. During puberty, the sex organs in the male (the _____). and the female (the _____) mature. Signs of sexual maturity, include the onset of menstruation, called _____ in girls, and the growth of the _____, _____, and _____ in boys. In addition, boys develop a deepened voice and facial and chest hair, and both boys and girls develop pubic hair. These changes are called _____ _____ characteristics. The length and onset of puberty varies tremendously across individuals due to _____ and _____ differences. Research has found that early maturing boys tend to have a more _____ view of their bodies; however, they also tend to be more likely to _____, drink, use _____, and break the law. Early maturing girls tend to have more _____ with their parents, have behavioural and emotional problems, drop out of school, and have a _____ body image.

5-2. During adolescence, boys tend to _____ problems by acting aggressively or antisocial in nature. Girls, on the other hand, tend to _____ problems and display more _____ and eating disorders. Most conflicts between adults and adolescents tend to focus on the adolescent's increasing desire for _____.

Review of Key Terms

The following is a list of the Key Terms from the section "Adolescence." Make sure you are familiar with each term before taking the matching test on these terms.

puberty   secondary sex characteristics   ovaries

androgens   menarche

testicles   estrogens

46

Matching Self Test 5

Match the appropriate term with its definition or description.

1. _____   The onset of menstruation.

2. _____   "Male" hormones, which boys have a higher level of from puberty on.

3. _____   The age at which a person becomes capable of sexual reproduction.

4. _____   The reproductive glands in girls.

6. Adulthood

Read the section "Adulthood" and then answer the following questions. If you have trouble answering any of the questions, restudy the relevant material before going on to the review of key terms and the matching test.

6-1.   When the ovaries stop producing estrogen and progesterone and menstruation ends, this is called _____. Although menopause does produce negative side effects in some women, only about _____ percent of women have severe physical symptoms. Recent research has found that contrary to the myth that menopause is a syndrome that brings on depression and other emotional reactions, most educated women find their mid-life years the _____ and _____. The study of aging and the old is called _____ . Gerontologists are changing our understanding of old age and our view of aging in a positive manner. There are certain aspects of aging, however, that are not entirely positive. For example, the capacity for deductive reasoning and the ability to use new information to solve problems, _____ intelligence, appears to decline in the later years. _____ intelligence, or the knowledge and skills that are built up over a lifetime, does not decline. There is some controversy concerning the evidence on the decline of fluid intelligence. The decline of fluid intelligence is most notable in _____-_____ studies. In _____ studies, which compare the same people as they age, the decline in fluid intelligence is not as notable.

6-2.   A comprehensive stage theory on development was put forth by _____ _____, who felt that we all go through eight stages in our lives and that we face a crisis at each stage. According to Erikson, the crisis of middle adulthood is one of _____ versus _____, and the crisis of old age is one of _____ versus _____. Although comprehensive, Erikson's theory does have some problems. For example, the _____ _____ is not limited to adolescence as Erikson claimed. In addition, Erikson omitted _____ from his original work. When women were finally studied, it was found that they do not go through the stages in the same order as do men. Researchers today do not focus as much on inflexible stages as they do on _____, changes and milestones that mark adult life. Many individuals, however, still evaluate their transitions based on a _____ _____ that supposedly determines whether they are "on

47

time" or not. When you are experiencing life events at the same time as your peers, this is referred to as transitions. You may have to face events that happen without warning, _____ transitions, or changes you expect to happen that don't, _____ transitions.

Review of Key Terms

The following is a list of the Key Terms from the section "Adulthood." Make sure you are familiar with each term before taking the matching test on these terms.

menopause	social clock	longitudinal study
fluid intelligence	nonevent transition	identity crisis
cross-sectional study	gerontology	anticipated transition
Erik Erikson	crystallized intelligence	unanticipated transition

Matching Self Test 6

Match the appropriate term with its definition or description.

1. _____ A way to evaluate transitions in life to determine whether you are "on time" or "off time."

2. _____ A study that compares people of different ages at the same time.

3. _____ The knowledge and skills that are built up over a lifetime, such as the ability to solve math problems or define words.

4. _____ The cessation of menstruation and of the productions of ova.

5. _____ An event (transition) that happens without warning, such as being fired from a job.

SAMPLE ANSWERS TO *WHAT'S AHEAD* QUESTIONS FROM TEXTBOOK

After you have completed the "Looking Back" section at the end of the chapter by answering the "What's Ahead" questions that preceded each major section of the chapter, compare your answers to the following sample answers. If your answers are not similar to the sample answers, review the pertinent sections of the chapter. The relevant page(s) for each question is(are) provided in the "Looking Back" section in the text.

How can a pregnant woman reduce the risk of damage to the embryo or fetus?

A pregnant woman should abstain from smoking, avoid alcohol and x-rays, and take no drugs unless they are necessary. A pregnant woman should also be vaccinated against rubella at least three months before pregnancy.

Given a choice, what do newborns prefer to look at?

Infants enjoy looking at and listening to unfamiliar things. For example, babies will stop nursing if someone new enters their range of vision. They also have a preference for faces over other stimuli in the environment.

Why is cuddling so important for infants (not to mention adults)?

According to research by the Harlows, infant monkeys formed attachments to artificial mothers that provided contact comfort, or cuddling. In addition, research by Ainsworth has demonstrated that infants whose mothers are the most responsive develop the most secure attachments. Depriving infants of affection and cuddling may lead to behavioural and cognitive problems, low self-esteem and increased risk of depression later in life.

If you have a 1-year-old, why shouldn't you worry if your baby cries when left with a new baby-sitter?

The infant is displaying separation anxiety (fear or anxiety when separated from the primary caregiver) and stranger anxiety (fear or anxiety in the presence of new faces). These are both normal anxieties for children of this age and nothing to worry about.

How does culture affect how a baby matures physically and socially?

In some cultures crawling is discouraged and hence children walk sooner than they do in our culture. In other cultures, children form attachments with many people very early in life. In these cultures, stranger and separation anxiety are not experienced as frequently as they are in our culture. Cultural differences such as these show that infants can thrive in many kinds of environments.

What important accomplishment are infants revealing when they learn to play "peekaboo"?

These infants are revealing an understanding of object permanence. At about 1 year of age they begin to enjoy playing this game, indicating that they now have the capacity to use mental imagery and symbolic systems, or what we refer to as representational thought.

Why will most 5-year-olds choose a tall, narrow glass of lemonade over a short, fat one containing the same amount?

Most 5-year-olds do not understand conservation. They believe that when something changes form or appearance, it also changes in quantity or amount. Thus, the 5-year-old in this example believes that the tall narrow glass contains more lemonade than does the short fat glass.

Can a 4-year-old understand that others experience the world from a different perspective?

According to Piaget, no. Piaget claimed that the typical 4-year-old is egocentric, cannot see things from another's perspective. More recent research has not concurred. In several studies it has been demonstrated that children as young as 3 and 4 years old can take another's perspective. For example, 3 and 4 year olds will typically simplify their speech when playing with a 2-year-old child.

How are a toddler's first word combinations similar to the language in a telegram?

Children drop unnecessary articles such as "a", "an" or "the". When people are paying for a telegram they do the same thing. The meaning of the message is still conveyed, but it is in a very abbreviated form.

Why do many psychologists believe that children's brains are equipped with a "language acquisition device"?

There are several reasons that they believe this. Firstly, children everywhere go through similar stages of linguistic development. They use what appears to be a universal grammar, with which the brain is disposed to notice the features common to all languages. Secondly, children use overregularizations; they combine words in ways that adults never would. Thus, they are not just imitating adults. Lastly, adults are not consistent in correcting children's syntax. In fact, they often reward young children for grammatically incorrect statements; but at a very young age, children still master the intricacies of grammar.

How would a biologically oriented psychologist explain why little boys and girls are often so "sexist" in their choice of toys?

Biological psychologists believe that differences between the sexes are largely a matter of prenatal hormones, genes, and possibly brain organization. They feel that gender differences will surface no matter what parents or teachers do. Even when parents and teachers attempt to treat girls and boys in the same manner, many find that boys still prefer mechanical toys and girls still prefer more "feminine" toys.

How do teachers often unintentionally reinforce aggressiveness in boys?

In one observational study, teachers responded far more to boys when they acted aggressively. On the other hand, they responded far more to girls when they acted dependently. Thus, boys receive more attention from teachers, parents, and peers when they act aggressively than do girls. When girls call for help from a teacher, they receive more attention than do boys who engage in the same.

If a little girl "knows" that girls can't be doctors, does this mean she will never go to med school?

No. With increasing age, experience, knowledge, and cognitive sophistication, children become aware of the exceptions to their rigid gender schemas—for instance, that girls can be doctors. Some, however, carry fairly rigid gender schemas into adulthood and feel uncomfortable when they encounter an exception to their schemas.

According to a leading theory, why is moral reasoning based on law, justice, and duty not the pinnacle of moral development?

According to Kohlberg, the pinnacle of moral reasoning involves an understanding that laws are important but relative, and that they can be changed. In addition, those operating at Kohlberg's last stage of moral reasoning develop a moral standard based on universal human rights. These individuals follow their conscience, even at great personal risk. Kohlberg felt that basing moral reasoning on the law, justice, and duty to society was a lower form of moral reasoning.

When reasoning about moral dilemmas, are women more concerned with compassion and caring than men are?

Carol Gilligan claimed that women were more concerned with compassion and caring than men. Some studies have supported Gilligan's theory, but most have found no gender differences. Both sexes tend to use "justice" reasoning when they are thinking about abstract ethical dilemmas and "care" reasoning when they are thinking about intimate personal dilemmas.

Are college students more moral than young children?

Those with a college education tend to give higher level explanations of Kohlberg's moral dilemmas than those who have not attended college. So based on Kohlberg's testing method, yes, college students are more moral. Critics of Kohlberg argue that college students score higher on the moral reasoning test because they are more verbally sophisticated and not because they are more moral.

What's wrong with "because I say so" as a way of getting children to behave?

This method, called power assertion, is based on a child's fear of punishment and is associated with a lack of moral feeling and in children, poor self-control, and a failure to internalize moral values. In addition, longitudinal studies show that when paired with intermittent discipline, power assertion can lead to aggressiveness and poor impulse control in children.

What are the advantages and disadvantages of experiencing puberty earlier than most of your classmates do?

Early developing boys have a more positive body image and have an advantage in sports. Early maturing girls will frequently have the prestige of being more popular. Both sexes usually encounter problems when there is early maturation. Boys who mature early are more likely to use drugs, drink, smoke, break the law, and have less self-control. Girls who mature early are more likely to have behavioural and social problems, drop out of school, have conflicts with their parents, and have a negative body image.

During adolescence, are extreme turmoil and unhappiness the exception or the rule?

Results from most studies have indicated that only a minority of teenagers conform to the stereotype of the troubled, angry, unhappy adolescent. The majority of teenagers have supportive families, a sense of purpose and self-confidence, good friends, and coping skills.

When teenagers and their parents quarrel, what is it typically about?

Most conflicts between teenagers and their parents center on autonomy. Teenagers who have conflicts with their parents over autonomy are trying to develop their own opinions and values. They are not trying to sever the connection completely between themselves and their parents.

Does menopause make most women depressed or irrational?

No, only 10 percent of women have serious problems associated with menopause. Menopause for most women is no big deal and appears to have no effect on most women's mental and emotional health.

Do men experience a male version of menopause?

No, men lack a biological equivalent to menopause. Testosterone never drops as sharply in men as estrogen does in women. In addition, men do not lose their fertility.

What intellectual skills often decline in old age—and which ones don't?

Fluid intelligence declines in old age. This includes the capacity for deductive reasoning and the ability to use new information to solve problems. It is relatively independent of education and experience. Crystallized intelligence, on the other hand, does not decline with age. This includes the knowledge and skills that are built up over a lifetime and allows us to engage in such behaviours as solving math problems and defining words.

What's wrong with thinking of life as a series of predictable stages?

Stage theories have the problem of not being universal. In other words, the stages do not always occur in all cultures and in the same order for everyone within a culture. Today, theories of development emphasize transitions, milestones that mark adult life, rather than having a rigid developmental sequence of stages.

What feelings are common when people fail to marry, start working, or have children at the "right" time?

When people fail to be "on time" in terms of life events, it creates pressures for them. These individuals suffer from nonevent transitions, changes they expect to happen that do not for one reason or another. This may lead to feelings of inadequacy, depression, and anxiety.

MULTIPLE-CHOICE PROGRESS TEST

Choose the single best answer for each of the following questions. When you have finished this progress test, check your answers with those at the end of the chapter. You should review the indicated pages in the text for the questions you do not answer correctly.

1. Which of the following is the correct order of the three stages of prenatal development?
   a. germinal; embryonic; fetal
   b. germinal; fetal; embryonic
   c. embryonic; germinal; fetal
   d. fetal; embryonic; germinal

2. Which of the following is (are) potentially harmful to fetal development?
   a. cigarette smoking
   b. father's cocaine use
   c. lead
   d. all of the above

3. In response to touch on the bottom of the foot, an infant's toes will splay outward and then curl in. This is the ___ reflex.
   a. Moro
   b. Babinski
   c. rooting
   d. stepping

4. Which of the following statements about an infant's physical abilities is FALSE?
   a. Newborns begin life with several motor reflexes, such as the "rooting reflex."
   b. Newborns cannot discriminate their mother or other primary caregiver until they are two or three months old.
   c. Newborns have a preference for faces.
   d. None of the above

5. In Ainsworth's Strange Situation, a child who does not care whether the mother leaves the room, makes little effort to seek contact with her on return, and treats the stranger about the same as the mother is categorized as:
   a. securely attached.
   b. avoidant.
   c. anxious.
   d. ambivalent.

6. In Piaget's theory, the process of modifying existing cognitive structures in response to experience and new information is called _____.
   a. assimilation
   b. accommodation
   c. egocentric thinking
   d. conservation

7 According to Piaget, object permanence is a major accomplishment of the _____ stage.
   a. formal operations
   b. concrete operations
   c. preoperational
   d. sensorimotor

8. Abstract reasoning is to an understanding of conservation as the _____ stage is to the _____ stage.
   a. sensorimotor; preoperational
   b. preoperational; sensorimotor
   c. concrete operations; formal operations
   d. formal operations; concrete operations

9. With respect to the text's evaluation of Piaget's theory, which of the following statements is FALSE?
   a. The changes from one stage to another are neither as clear-cut nor as sweeping as Piaget implied.
   b. Preschoolers are more egocentric than Piaget thought.
   c. Piaget overestimated the cognitive abilities of many adults.
   d. None of the above

10. With respect to language development, which of the following statements is FALSE?
   a. Infants are responsive to the pitch, intensity, and sound of language.
   b. By 4 to 6 months, babies can distinguish phonemes of their native language from those of a foreign language.
   c. From age 6 months to 1 year, babies begin to speak in two- or three-word telegraphic sentences.
   d. None of the above

11. Consider the two sentences "The professor praised Mary" and "Mary was praised by the professor." The surface structure of the two sentences is ___; the deep structure is ___.
   a. the same; the same
   b. the same; different
   c. different; the same
   d. different; different

12. Which of the following kinds of evidence supports Chomsky's argument for a language acquisition device?
    a. Children everywhere go through similar stages of linguistic development.
    b. Children simply imitate adults in their use of language.
    c. Adults consistently correct their children's syntax.
    d. All of the above

13. Gender socialization is to gender schemas as _____ psychologists are to _____ psychologists.
    a. biological; learning
    b. learning; biological
    c. learning; cognitive
    d. cognitive; learning

14. According to Kohlberg, if you obey a rule because you fear being punished if you disobey, then you are in the _____ level of moral development.
    a. preconventional
    b. conventional
    c. postconventional
    d. "principled"

15. With respect to moral reasoning, which of the following statements is FALSE?
    a. Stage theories tend to overlook educational and cultural influences on moral reasoning.
    b. People's moral reasoning is often inconsistent across situations.
    c. Moral reasoning is often unrelated to moral behaviours.
    d. Most studies find gender differences in moral reasoning.

16. Which of the following is NOT a result of the induction method of teaching moral?
    a. acceptance of responsibility for one's s
    b. failure to internalize moral values
    c. acting considerately toward others
    d. none of the above

17. The children of _____ parents tend to have high self-esteem, to be independent yet cooperative, and to do better than average in school.
    a. authoritative
    b. authoritarian
    c. permissive
    d. power assertive

18. _____ intelligence is relatively independent of educational experience and tends to _____ over the life span.
    a. Fluid; not decline.
    b. Fluid; decline
    c. Crystallized; not decline
    d. Crystallized; decline

19. Which of the following statements about our understanding of old age is FALSE?
    a. Old age is no longer just a matter of chronological years, but of how well a person is able to function.
    b. Aging has been separated from illness.
    c. The biology of aging has been separated from its psychology.
    d. None of the above

20. According to Erik Erikson, _____ is the crisis of adolescence, when teenagers must decide what they are going to be and what they hope to make of their lives.
    a. autonomy versus shame and doubt
    b. trust versus mistrust
    c. identity versus role confusion
    d. intimacy versus isolation

ANSWERS

GUIDED STUDY

1. From Conception to the First Year

1.1. germinal   embryonic   fetal alcohol
       zygote   fetal

1.2. motor reflexes   separation anxiety   ambivalent
       rooting   strange   behavioural
       contact comfort   secure   cognitive
       terry   insecure   self-esteem
       milk/food   avoidant   depression
       stranger anxiety   anxious

Matching Self-Test 1

1. motor reflexes
2. embryonic

3. maturation
4. separation anxiety

___

2. Cognitive Development

2.1.   Jean Piaget
      assimilation
      schema
      accommodation
      sensorimotor
      object permanence

preoperational
operations
egocentric
conservation
concrete operations
formal operations

2.2.   clear-cut
      egocentric

culture
overestimated

2.3.   phonemes
      babble
      telegraphic

language
acquisition
Chomsky
surface

deep
overregularizations
critical period

Matching Self-Test 2

1. object permanence
2. telegraphic speech
3. assimilation
4. egocentric thinking

5. accommodation
6. conservation
7. language acquisition device

___

3. Gender Development

3.1.   gender
      sex
      gender roles

gender identity
hormones
genes

organization
biological

3.2.	gender socialization	24
	81	dependently
3.3.	gender schema	female

Matching Self-Test 3

| 1. gender socialization | 2. gender role | 3. gender schema |

4. Moral Development

4.1.	Lawrence Kohlberg	order	compassion
	two	postconventional	caring
	preconventional	human rights	educational
	conventional	rare	cultural
	10	Carol Gilligan	inconsistent
	11	law	reasoning
	law	justice	conscience
4.2.	power assertion	wrong	mature
	lack	Authoritarian	responsible
	internalize	nurturance	authoritative
	induction	power	discipline
	guilty	Permissive	standards
	right	control	communication

Matching Self-Test 4

| 1. postconventional level | 3. permissive parenting |
| 2. power assertion | 4. induction |

58

5. Adolescence

5.1.	puberty	menarche	environmental
	adolescence	testes	positive
	androgens	scrotum	smoke
	estrogens	penis	drugs
	testes	secondary sex	conflict
	ovaries	genetic	negative

5.2.	externalize	depression
	internalize	autonomy

Matching Self-Test 5

1. menarche
2. androgens

3. puberty
4. ovaries

---

6. Adulthood

6.1.	menopause	happiest	Crystallized
	10	gerontology	cross-sectional
	best	fluid	longitudinal

6.2.	Erik Erikson	despair	social clock
	generativity	identity crisis	anticipated
	stagnation	women	unanticipated
	ego integrity	transitions	nonevent

Matching Self-Test 6

1. social clock
2. cross-sectional studies

3. crystallized intelligence
4. menopause

5. unanticipated transition

ANSWERS TO MULTIPLE CHOICE PROGRESS TEST

Item No.	Answer(s)	Page(s) in Textbook
1.	a. germinal; embryonic; fetal	76-77
2.	d. all of the above	77-78
3.	a. Moro	78
4.	b. Newborns cannot discriminate their mother or other primary caregiver until they are two or three months old.	78
5.	b. avoidant	80-81
6.	b. accommodation	83
7.	d. sensorimotor	83
8.	d. formal operations; concrete operations	84
9.	b. Preschoolers are more egocentric than Piaget thought.	85-86
10.	c. From age 6 months to 1 year, babies begin to speak in two- or three-word telegraphic sentences.	87
11.	c. different; the same	88
12.	a. Children everywhere go through similar stages of linguistic development	88
13.	c. learning; cognitive	92
14.	a. preconventional	95-96
15.	d. Most studies find gender differences in moral reasoning.	96-97
16.	b. failure to internalize moral values	98
17.	a. authoritative	98
18.	b. Fluid; decline	106
19.	d. None of the above	107s
20.	c. identity versus role confusion	107

CHAPTER 4

Neurons, Hormones, and the Brain

CHAPTER OVERVIEW

The chapter begins with an overview of the nervous system. This includes coverage of the central versus peripheral nervous systems. In addition, the various subsystems within the peripheral nervous system are outlined including the somatic versus autonomic and the sympathetic versus parasympathetic nervous systems. Communication within the nervous system is covered next. This includes discussion of the types of cells found in the nervous system, the basic structure of a neuron, how an action potential is generated, and how neurons communicate with each other at the synapse via neurotransmitters. Several different neurotransmitters and their functions are described. The role of hormones in the endocrine system and the difference between hormones and neurotransmitters are also discussed.

Various methods of viewing or studying the brain are detailed. These include an EEG (electroencephalogram), a PET (positron emission tomography) scan, and MR/(magnetic resonance imaging). In the section entitled *A Tour Through the Brain,* various brain structures are identified. This includes a discussion of their locations and functions. The structures discussed include those in the brain stem (medulla, pons, and reticular activating system), the cerebellum, the thalamus, the hypothalamus, the pituitary gland, the limbic system (amygdala and hippocampus), and the two cerebral hemispheres. The structure and functioning of the cerebral hemispheres is described in some detail, including coverage of the four lobes within each hemisphere, the visual, auditory, motor, and somatosensory cortices, and Broca's and Wernicke's areas.

The differences in specialization between the two hemispheres are presented next. These differences are explained via research on split-brain patients who have had their corpus callosums severed. Lastly, the issues of why we dream and whether there are sex differences in the brain are discussed.

GUIDED STUDY

1. The Nervous System: A Basic Blueprint

Read the section "The Nervous System: A Basic Blueprint" and then answer the following questions. If you have trouble answering any of the questions, re-study the relevant material before going on to the review of key terms and the matching test.

1-1 The human nervous system is divided into two parts. The _central ne_____ nervous system (CNS) contains the brain and the _spinal____ cord_____. The _peripheral_ nervous system contains all portions of the nervous system outside of the brain and spinal cord. The spinal cord is an extension of the brain and can produce some behaviours on its own without the brain, called _spinal____ reflexes____.

1-2. The peripheral nervous system is responsible for handling input into the CNS and output from the CNS. The neurons that carry information to the CNS are known as _sensory_____ neurons. _Motor_____ neurons carry information away from the CNS to muscles, glands, and internal organs. The peripheral nervous system is further divided into the skeletal nervous system also called the _somatic_____ nervous system and the self-governing or _autonomic____ nervous system. The somatic nervous system permits _voluntary_____ actions whereas the autonomic nervous system works in an _automatic_ fashion. Some researchers claim that people can control their autonomic responses through a process called _biofeedback____, but this procedure is somewhat controversial. The autonomic nervous system is subdivided into two parts. One subsystem, the _sympathetic___ nervous system, mobilizes the body for action. The other subsystem, the _parasympathetic_ nervous system, calms your system down.

Review of Key Terms

The following is a list of the Key Terms from the section "The Nervous System: A Basic Blueprint." Make sure you are familiar with each term before taking the matching test on these terms.

central nervous system   autonomic nervous system   sensory neurons

spinal reflex   sympathetic nervous system   motor neurons

peripheral nervous system   parasympaihetic nervous system   biofeedback

somatic nervous system spinal cord

Matching Self Test 1

Match the appropriate term with its definition or description.

1. _autonatic_ _nervous system_   The subdivision of the peripheral nervous system that regulates the internal organs and glands.

2. _Spinal_ _cord_   A collection of neurons and supportive tissue running from the base of the brain down the center of the back.

3. _Sensory_   Neurons that carry information to the central nervous system.

4. _parasymp_   The subdivision of the autonomic nervous system that acts as a brake, operates during relaxed states, and conserves energy.

5. _____Peripheral_____ All portions of the nervous system outside the brain and spinal cord; including sensory and motor neurons.

2. Communication in the Nervous System

Read the section "Communication in the Nervous System" and then answer the following questions. If you have trouble answering any of the questions, re-study the relevant material before going on to the review of key terms and the matching test.

2-1. The nervous system is made up of two types of cells. The communication specialist cells are called _____. The _____ cells, which greatly outnumber neurons, act as a type of glue and provide nutrients and insulation to the neurons. A neuron has three main parts to it. The _____ receive incoming information. The _____ _____ is responsible for keeping the neuron alive, and it also acts as a mini-decision maker. Lastly, the _____ carries information away from the cell body and toward other neurons. Most axons divide at their ends into _____. In addition, some axons are insulated with a fatty substance called a _____ _____. When axons (and sometimes dendrites) are bundled together, they make up _____.

2-2. The billions of neurons in the nervous system are not physically connected end to end. The space between the axon terminal of one neuron and the dendrites of another neuron is referred to as the _____ _____. This whole area, the axon terminal, the synaptic cleft, and the receiving dendrite, is called the _____. The communications system for neurons is both electrical and _____ in nature. When a neuron is stimulated, an electrical potential called an _____ _____ occurs between the inside and the outside of the cell. This involves the inflow of positively charged _____ ions and the out flow of positively charged ions. In an unmyelinated axon the action potential travels at a _____ speed than it does in a myelinated axon. The sacs that are located in the axon terminal and contain the chemicals used by the nervous system are called _____ _____. The chemicals used by the nervous system to carry information from one neuron to another are called _____. These neurotransmitters bind to _____ _____ on the next neuron. Depending on which receptor sites have been activated, the effect in the receiving neuron is either _____, a voltage shift in a positive direction, or _____, a voltage shift in a negative direction. Only when the neuron's voltage reaches a certain threshold will it fire. A single neuron either fires or does not fire. In other words, neural messages are sent in an _____- _____-_____ fashion.

2-3. As there are many different kinds of neurotransmitters, they only work when they bind to a receptor site that can interpret the specific neurotransmitter's message. Although the understanding of neurotransmitters is somewhat fuzzy, several neurotransmitters and their suspected effects have been identified. For example, _____ affects neurons involved in sleep, appetite, sensory perception, temperature regulation, pain suppression, and mood. _____ affects neurons involved in muscle action, cognitive

63

functioning, memory, and emotion. In addition, when the level of a neurotransmitter is either too high or too low, this can have a negative impact. Low levels of _____ and _____ have been associated with depression. People with Alzheimer's disease lose brain cells responsible for producing _____. Those with Parkinson's disease lose brain cells that produce _____. Substances that sometimes act as a neurotransmitter and sometimes as a neuromodulator are _____. This natural opiate was discovered in the 1970s. The endorphin level seems to increase when an animal or person is _____ or under _____. Another class of chemical messengers, _____, are produced in one part of the body and affect another part of the body. They originate primarily in the _____ _____. The hormone that helps regulate daily biological rhythms and promotes sleep is _____. The organs above the kidneys, the _____ _____, produce a group of hormones called _____ hormones. The outer part of the adrenal gland produces _____, the inner part produces _____ (also known as _____), and _____ (also known as _____). Adrenal hormones activate the _____ nervous system increasing your arousal level. There are three types of sex hormones. Masculinizing hormones such as testosterone, are referred to as _____. Feminizing hormones include _____, which bring on physical changes in females at puberty, and _____, which contributes to the growth and maintenance of the uterine lining.

Review of Key Terms

The following is a list of the Key Terms from the section "Communication in the Nervous System." Make sure you are familiar with each term before taking the matching test on these terms.

neuron	melatonin	synapse
dendrites cortisol	epinephrine	synaptic vesicles
axon	norepinephrine	receptor sites
myelin sheath	androgens	neuromodulators
synaptic cleft	progesterone	endocrine glands
action potential	glial cells	adrenal hormones
neurotransmitter	cell body	sex hormones
endorphins	axon terminals	estrogens
hormones	nerve	

Matching Self Test 2

Match the appropriate term with its definition or description.

1. _Neurotransmitter_   A chemical substance that is released at the synapse by a transmitting neuron and that alters the activity, of a receiving neuron.

2. _Hormones_   Chemical substances, secreted by organs called glands, that affect the functioning of other organs.

3. _Dendrites_   A neuron's branches that receive information from other neurons and transmit it toward the cell body.

4. _Nerves_   A bundle of nerve fibers (axons and sometimes dendrites) in the peripheral nervous system.

5. _Endorphins_   Chemical substances in the nervous system that are similar in structure and action to opiates.

6. _Melatonin_   A hormone secreted by the pineal gland that is involved in the regulation of daily biological rhythms.

7. _Myelin sheath_   A fatty insulation that may surround the axon of a neuron.

8. _Synapse_   The site where transmission of a nerve impulse from one nerve cell to another occurs; it includes the axon terminal, the synaptic cleft, and the receptor sites in the membrane of the receiving cell.

3. Mapping the Brain

Read the section "Mapping the Brain" and then answer the following questions. If you have trouble answering any of the questions, re-study the relevant material before going on to the review of key terms and the matching test.

3-1.   The brain can be studied using several different methods. One method is to remove sections of brain tissue from animals and observe the effects. This is called the _____ method. An alternative method utilizes electrodes that are either pasted to the scalp or inserted into the brain. The electrodes allow measurement of brainwaves in a recording called an _____. More recent techniques for studying the brain involve injecting a radioactive, glucoselike substance into the brain to determine which areas of the brain are active during certain tasks. This is called a _____-_____ tomography scan. Another recent technique, _____ _____ imaging, utilizes magnetic fields and radio frequencies to produce vibrations in the nuclei of atoms making up body organs. These vibrations are picked up as signals that a computer analyzes and converts into a picture.

Review of Key Terms

The following is a list of the Key Terms from the section "Mapping the Brain." Make sure you are familiar with each term before taking the matching test on these terms.

electrodes   positron emission tomography (PET)

electroencephalogram (EEG)   scan magnetic resonance imaging (MRI)

Matching Self Test 3

Match the appropriate term with its definition or description.

1. _____ A method for analyzing biochemical activity in the brain, using injections of a glucoselike substance containing a radioactive element.

2. _____ A method for studying body and brain tissue, using magnetic fields and special radio receivers.

3. _____ A recording or neural activity detected by electrodes.

4. A Tour through the Brain

Read the section "A Tour through the Brain" and then answer the following questions. If you have trouble answering any of the questions, re-study the relevant material before going on to the review of key terms and the matching test.

4-1.   Joseph Gall was one of the first brain researchers to propose that different brain parts perform different tasks. This is known as _____ of _____. The two main structures in the brain stem are the _medulla_ and the _pons_. The medulla is responsible for basic bodily functions such as _breathing_ and heart rate. The pons is involved in _sleeping_, waking, and _dreaming_. At the core of the brain stem, the _____R_____ _____A_____ system is found. This system has connections with higher areas in the brain. Without it we would not be _____ or _____.

4-2.   The structure at the top of the brain stem and toward the back of the brain is called the _____ or lesser brain. This structure plays a role in _____ and in coordinating the _____.

4-3.   The traffic officer of the brain, deep in the brain's interior, is called the _____. The thalamus acts as a sensory relay center, relaying sensory messages received from the body to higher centers in the brain for interpretation. The thalamus relays all sensory information, except that for the sense of _____, which is relayed by the _____ _____.

4-4.   Underneath the thalamus is a structure involved in drives such as hunger, thirst, emotion, sex, and reproduction. This is called the ~~pituary~~ *hypothalamus*. Hanging from the hypothalamus is the _pituary_ gland, which secretes hormones that affect your endocrine glands. The functioning of this gland is regulated by the hypothalamus.

4-5.   The set of structures that form a border between higher and lower brain areas and that have connections to the hypothalamus is called the _____ _____. One structure in the limbic system that plays a role in emotions involved in either approaching or withdrawing is the _____. This structure also appears to be important in mediating _____ and _____. A second structure in the limbic system that enables us to form new memories about facts and events is the _____. One of the most well studied cases of hippocampal damage is the case of H.M. H.M. had his hippocampus removed as a treatment for _____. As a result of this surgery, H.M. has memories for events that happened prior to the surgery (in 1953), but can no longer remember new experiences for much longer than _____ minutes. Recent research has indicated that the hippocampus plays a role in the _____ of long-term memories.

4-6.   The largest part of the brain is known as the _____ and is divided into two _____ _____. The two hemispheres are connected by the _____ _____, a band of neural fibers. The brain and the body operate in a contralateral fashion. The right hemisphere controls the _____ side of the body, and the left hemisphere controls the _____ side of the body. In addition, the two hemispheres control somewhat different functions. This phenomenon is known as _____. The layers of neurons covering the cerebrum are known as the _____ _____. The cortex is often referred to as _____ matter as the neurons here are _____. The brain's _____ matter consists of neurons that are _____. Each of the hemispheres is divided into four distinct regions called lobes. The lobes that contains the visual cortex and are located at the back of the head are the _____ lobes. The lobes that contain the _____ cortex, which receives the input that allows us to interpret body sensations, are the _____ lobes. The lobes are at the sides of the head, just above the ears. They contain the _____ cortex, which allows us to process sounds. Lastly, the _____ lobes, located at the front of the brain contain the _____ cortex, which initiates muscle movements. The frontal lobes are also involved in making plans and thinking creatively. The left frontal lobe contains _____ area, which handles speech production. The areas in the cortex that appear to be responsible for higher mental processes are called _____ cortex. An area of the frontal lobes that is more pronounced in humans than in other animals is the _____ cortex. This structure appears to play a role in _____, as evidenced by the sad case of _____ _____, a railroad worker who had an iron rod pass clear through his head, destroying most of the prefrontal cortex.

Review of Key Terms

The following is a list of the Key Terms from the section "A Tour through the Brain.." Make sure you are familiar with each term before taking the matching test on these terms.

localization of function	somatosensory cortex	consolidation
medulla	auditory cortex	cerebrum
reticular activating system	motor cortex	lateralization
thalamus	prefrontal cortex	occipital lobes
hypothalamus	Wernicke's area	temporal lobes
limbic system	brain stem	frontal lobes
hippocampus	pons	association cortex
cerebral hemispheres	cerebellum	Broca's area
corpus callosum	olfactory bulb	
cerebral cortex	pituitary gland	
visual cortex	amygdala	

Matching Self Test 4

Match the appropriate term with its definition or description.

1. _____ A structure in the brain stem responsible for certain automatic functions, such as breathing and heart rate.

2. _____ A brain structure that regulates movement and balance and is involved in the learning of certain kinds of simple responses.

3. _____ A small endocrine gland at the base of the hypothalamus, that releases many hormones and regulates other endocrine glands.

4. _____ A brain structure involved in the storage (consolidation) of new information in memory.

5. _____ Specialization of particular brain areas for particular functions.

6. _____ A dense network of neurons found in the core of the brain stem; it arouses the cortex and screens incoming information.

7. _____ A brain structure that relays sensory messages to the cerebral cortex.

8. _____ A brain structure involved in the arousal and regulation of emotion and the initial emotional response to sensory information.

9. _____ Specialization of the two cerebral hemispheres for particular psychological operations.

10. _____ An area in the left temporal lobe involved in language comprehension.

5. The Two Hemispheres of the Brain

Read the "The Two Hemispheres of the Brain" and then answer the following questions. If you have trouble answering any of the questions, re-study the relevant material before going on to the review of key terms and the matching test.

5-1. The two halves of the brain are connected by the corpus callosum which allows the two hemispheres to communicate with each other. Researchers have investigated what happens when the corpus callosum is severed. The first studies addressing this issue utilized _____ as subjects. Results from these studies indicated that the cats responded as if they had _____ minds in _____ body. Later research involved human subjects who had had their corpus callosums severed as a treatment for _____. This surgery is called _____-_____ surgery. Patients who had this type of surgery afford brain researchers the ability to study the capabilities of the two hemispheres.

5-2. Results from split-brain research indicate that all right-handed people and a majority of left-handers process language in the _____ hemisphere. The left hemisphere is also more active on tasks such as solving _____ problems and understanding _____ material. Some researchers have concluded that the left hemisphere is _____, exerting control over the right hemisphere. One of the leading researchers supporting this idea is _____. On the other hand, researchers such as _____ have defended the right hemisphere, noting abilities in which is it superior such as _____-_____ ability and _____ recognition. It is important to note that in real-life activities, the two hemispheres work together and that each makes a valuable contribution.

Review of Key Terms

The following is a list of the Key Terms from the section "The Two Hemispheres of the Brain." Make sure you are familiar with each term before taking the matching test on these terms.

corpus callosum   cerebral dominance   split-brain surgery

Matching Self Test 5

Match the appropriate term with its definition or description.

1. _____ The surgery in which the bundle of nerve fibers connecting the two hemispheres is severed.

2. _Corpus Callosum_ The bundle of nerve fibers connecting the two cerebral hemispheres.

3. _____ The idea that one hemisphere (the left) is dominant.

6. Two Stubborn *Issues* in Brain Research

Read the section "Two Stubborn Issues in Brain Research" and then answer the following questions. If you have trouble answering any of the questions, re-study the relevant material before going on to the review of key terms and the matching test.

6-1. During sleep, periods of _____ _____ movement alternate with periods of fewer eye movements, or _____-_____ sleep. During REM sleep, the pattern of electrical activity from the sleeper's brain changes to resemble that of alert _____; _____ rate, _____ pressure, and _____ all increase. Small twitches in the _____ and _____ may occur. In men, the _____ becomes somewhat erect; and in women, the _____ enlarges. In addition, most of your _____ muscles go limp preventing your aroused brain from producing physical movement. Most dreaming occurs during REM. One theory on why we dream is called the _____-_____ theory and states that dreams are the result of the _____ synthesizing and interpreting spontaneous neural signals in the lower part of the brain.

6-2. One of the first differences reported between the brains of men and women was the size and shape of the _____, a small section at the end of the corpus callosum. The researchers concluded that women's brains are less _____ for certain tasks than men's are. Other research concerning differences in the splenium, however, has been inconsistent with these findings. Conclusions concerning differences between the brains of men and women should be taken with caution. Although some researchers have noted brain differences, using these findings to help explain differences between men and women poses several problems. Firstly, the supposed gender differences between men and women are _____. Secondly, a _____ difference does not necessarily have _____ implications. Lastly, sex differences in the brain could be the _____ rather than the _____ of behavioural differences.

Review of Key Terms

The following is a list of the Key Terms from the section "Two Stubborn Issues in Brain Research." Make sure you are familiar with each term before taking the matching test on these terms.

rapid eye movement (REM) sleep   activation-synthesis theory   splenium

Matching Self Test 6

Match the appropriate term with its definition or description.

1. ___Activation Synthesis theory___ The theory that dreaming results from the cortical synthesis and interpretation of neural signals triggered by activity in the lower part of the brain.

2. ___REM sleep___ Sleep periods characterized by eye movement, loss of muscle tone, and dreaming.

SAMPLE ANSWERS TO *WHAT'S AHEAD* QUESTIONS FROM TEXTBOOK

After you have completed the "Looking Back" section at the end of the chapter by answering the "What's Ahead" questions that preceded each major section of the chapter, compare your answers to the following sample answers. If your answers are not similar to the sample answers, review the pertinent sections of the chapter. The relevant page(s) for each question is(are) provided in the "Looking Back" section in the text.

Why do you automatically pull your hand away from something hot, "without thinking"?

This is based on spinal reflex actions. These reflexes are automatic, requiting no conscious effort. Sensory neurons bring the message to the spinal cord and the spinal cord quickly sends out a command via motor neurons telling the muscles in your arm to contract. All of this takes place without input from the brain; hence you are able to do this "without thinking."

Is it possible to consciously control your heartbeat or blood pressure?

Yogis from India have been able to slow their heartbeats and metabolisms so that they can survive in a sealed booth long after most people would have died of suffocation. Neal Miller developed a technique called biofeedback in the 1960s that showed that other people can also learn to control their autonomic responses. This technique involves devices that track bodily processes and produce signals. The individual attempts to alter a signal's frequency. Through biofeedback some people have learned to control blood pressure, blood flow, heart rate, and skin temperature. There is, however, controversy surrounding the efficacy of biofeedback techniques. Researchers are also not sure exactly what is being controlled—the actual autonomic responses or responses that can be voluntarily produced and in turn affect the autonomic system.

If you have to deal with a sudden emergency, which part of your nervous system whirls into action?

The sympathetic nervous system is responsible for accelerating your body. It can make you blush, sweat, increase respiration, increase heart rate, and increase blood pressure.

Which nervous-system cells are "communication specialists"—and how do they "talk" to each other?

The neurons are the communication specialists. They talk to each other via chemicals called neurotransmitters. An electrical impulse travels down the length of a single neuron. When the impulse reaches the axon terminal, the synaptic vesicles open and release neurotransmitters into the synaptic cleft.Some of these neurotransmitters bind to the receptor sites on the dendrite of the next neuron. If that neuron receives enough excitatory information from incoming neurotransmitters, then it will reach action potential and fire an electrical impulse.

How do learning and experience alter the brain's circuits?

New learning and experience lead to new synaptic connections, with stimulating environments producing the greatest changes. Conversely, some unused synaptic connections are lost as cells or their branches die and are not replaced.

Why do neural impulses travel more slowly in babies than adults?

Some neurons are able to transmit messages more quickly than others due to the fact that their axons are myelinated. This means they are covered with a fatty substance that serves as an insulator. The neural impulses in babies travel more slowly because their myelin sheaths are not yet fully developed.

What happens when levels of brain chemicals called neurotransmitters are too low or too high?

The effects of neurotransmitters being too high or too low will depend on the neurotransmitter in question. For example, low levels of serotonin and norepinephrine have been associated with depression. Elevated levels of serotonin have been associated with childhood autism. The loss of brain cells responsible for producing acetylcholine has been implicated in Alzheimer's disease. The lack of the neurotransmitter dopamine plays a role in Parkinson's disease. Pinning down the relationship between neurotransmitter abnormalities and behavioural abnormalities, however, is very difficult as neurotransmitters play multiple roles.

What substances in the brain mimic the effects of morphine by dulling pain and promoting pleasure?

Endogenous opioid peptides or endorphins mimic the effects of morphine. Some function as neurotransmitters but most act primarily as neuromodulators which alter the effects of neurotransmitters.

Which hormones can improve your memory?

The adrenal hormones enhance memory. These include cortisol, produced by the outer part of the adrenal glands, and epinephrine and norepinephrine, produced by the inner part of the adrenal glands. When subjects were given a drug that prevented their adrenal glands from producing these hormones, they remembered less about emotional stories they had heard than did control subjects. In addition, when animals were given epinephrine right after learning, their memories improved. This effect, however, is only present when the hormones are at a moderate level.

Why are patterns of electrical activity in the brain called "brain waves"?

In order to measure brain waves, electrodes are attached either to the scalp or inserted into the brain. The electrodes detect electrical activity in neurons in specific regions of the brain. The electrodes are connected by wires to a machine that translates the electrical activity of the brain into wavy lines (brain waves) on a piece of paper. The wave patterns vary depending on the activity in which one is engaging.

What two techniques allow psychologists to view changes in the brain while people listen to music or solve math problems?

The PET scan, which involves injecting a glucoselike radioactive substance into an individual, allows researchers to assess which areas of the brain are active when we engage in different activities. MRI allows us to evaluate the same types of activities using magnetic fields and radio frequencies to produce vibrations in the nuclei of atoms making up body organs (in this case, the brain.) The vibrations are received as signals analyzed by a computer and eventually converted into a picture of brain activity.

Which brain part acts as a "traffic officer" for incoming sensations?

The thalamus acts as a "traffic officer." It is responsible for relaying incoming sensory information to the appropriate places in the cerebrum. For example, visual information would be routed by the thalamus to the visual cortex in the occipital lobes. The only sense that is not relayed by the thalamus is olfaction, which has its own switching station called the olfactory bulb.

Which brain part is the "gateway to memory"—and what cognitive catastrophe occurs when it is damaged?

The hippocampus is considered the "gateway to memory." This structure allows us to form new memories. It appears to be responsible for consolidating information into long-term memories. When this structure is damaged as in the case of H.M., new memories cannot be formed. H.M. has long-term memories for events prior to his operation but can hold no new information for periods much longer than 15 minutes.

Why is it a good thing that the outer covering of the human brain is so wrinkled?

The cortex or outer layers of neurons is wrinkled in order to allow for more surface space. The cortex contains almost three-fourths of all the cells in the human brain. Thus, it is important to have a large surface area. At the same time, we would not want our skulls to be too large; hence the wrinkled surface of the cortex. This allows for a large surface area (cortex) compressed into a small container (your skull.)

How did a bizarre nineteenth-century accident illuminate the role of the frontal lobes?

The role of the prefrontal cortex was illuminated by the case of Phineas Gage. Gage was a railroad worker involved in an accident in which an iron rod entered his left cheek and exited through the top of his head destroying most of the prefrontal cortex. The accident seemed to affect mainly Gage's personality. Prior to the accident he was known as a likable fellow; yet after the accident he was ill-tempered, foul-mouthed, and undependable.

If the two cerebral hemispheres were out of touch, would they feel different emotions and think

different thoughts?

Studies of split-brain patients, who have had their corpus callosum cut, show that the two cerebral hemispheres have somewhat different talents. In most people, language is processed mainly in the left hemisphere, which generally is specialized for logical, symbolic, and sequential tasks. The right hemisphere is associated with spatial-visual tasks, facial recognition, and the creation and appreciation of art and music. Therefore, if the two hemispheres were "out of touch," they would feel and think differently.

Why do researchers often refer to the left hemisphere as "dominant"?

Researchers refer to the left hemisphere as dominant because it is more active during logical, symbolic, and sequential tasks. It is also the center for language abilities in most people. Some also believe that the left hemisphere exerts control over the right hemisphere. These researchers have argued that without help from the left side, the right side's mental skills would probably be "vastly inferior to the cognitive skills of a chimpanzee."

Should you sign up for a program that promises to perk up the right side of your brain?

No, programs that make these claims typically oversimplify and exaggerate hemispheric differences. The differences between the hemispheres are relative, not absolute. In most activities the two hemispheres work together with each making a valuable contribution.

How do biological theories of dreaming differ from the familiar Freudian view?

Biological theories propose that dreams originate not in the psyche as Freud claimed, but rather in the physiological workings of the brain. For example, Crick and Mitebison argue that during REM sleep, synaptic connections that are unneeded are weakened, making memory more efficient and accurate. In this view, dreams are merely mental garbage, and there's no point in trying to remember them or analyze them for their "meanings." Another biological theory proposed by Hobson, the activation-synthesis theory, also assumes that, contrary to Freud, unconscious wishes do not cause dreams and there are no underlying hidden meanings of dreams. However, Hobson assumes that the brain attempts to at least create surface meaning for the spontaneous signals from the pons. Dreams then are merely this cortical synthesis and interpretation of the random signals.

Do men talk about sports and women about feelings because their brains are different?

Some studies have noted brain differences between men and women. Many, however, have found few consistent differences. Any brain differences found should be interpreted with caution. Firstly, behavioural differences between men and women are based on stereotypes. Secondly, biological differences do not ways have behavioural implications. Lastly, sex differences in the brain could be the result rather than the cause of behavioural differences.

Multiple-Choice Progress Test

Choose the single best answer for each of the following questions. When you have finished this progress test, check your answers with those at the end of the chapter. You should review the indicated pages in the text for the questions you do not answer correctly.

1. _____ nerves carry messages to the CNS from the PNS, and _____ nerves carry messages from the PNS to the CNS.
    a. Sensory; motor
    b. Motor; sensory
    c. Somatic; autonomic
    d. Autonomic; somatic

2. The _____ nervous system divides into the sympathetic and parasympathetic nervous systems.
    a. somatic
    b. autonomic
    c. central
    d. peripheral

3. Which of the following is NOT an action of the sympathetic nervous system, which is active during emergencies?
    a. accelerates heartbeat
    b. inhibits digestion
    c. constricts pupils
    d. stimulates sweat glands

4. Which of the following statements about glial cells is FALSE?
    a. Glial cells greatly outnumber neurons.
    b. The myelin sheath is derived from glial cells.
    c. Glial cells provide neurons with nutrients.
    d. None of the above

5. The normal path for neural transmission within a neuron is:
    a. cell body; dendrites; axon.
    b. dendrites; cell body; axon.
    c. axon; cell body; dendrites.
    d. axon; dendrites; cell body.

6. Loss of myelin surrounding axons causes _____.
    a. Alzheimer's disease
    b. epilepsy
    c. multiple sclerosis
    d. Parkinson's disease

7.   Excitatory neurotransmitters _____ the probability of an action potential in the receiving neuron, and inhibitory neurotransmitters _____ this probability.
      a. increase; increase
      b. increase; decrease
      c. decrease; increase
      d. decrease; decrease

8.   Which of the following statements about neural communication is FALSE?
      a. The firing of a neuron is an all-or-none event.
      b. Conduction of a neural impulse beneath the myelin sheath is impossible.
      c. Each neuron only has synaptic connections with one other neuron.
      d. Chemical communication between neurons occurs at the synapse.

9.   The major inhibitory neurotransmitter in the brain is:
      a. GABA.
      b. acetylcholine.
      c. norepinephrine.
      d. serotonin.

10.   The degeneration of brain cells that produce and use _____ appears to cause the symptoms of Parkinson's disease.
      a. acetylcholine
      b. norepinephrine
      c. dopamine
      d. GABA

11.   Some substances such as _____ serve as both neurotransmitters and hormones.
      a. norepinephrine
      b. melatonin
      c. endorphins
      d. L-dopa

12.   Which of the following hormones helps to regulate daily biological rhythms and promote sleep?
      a. testosterone
      b. epinephrine
      c. melatonin
      d. cortisol

13. A patient is injected with a glucoselike substance that contains a harmless radioactive element. The patient's brain is then scanned. This type of brain probe is called:
   a. an EEG.
   b. a PET scan.
   c. MRI.
   d. the lesion method.

14. "Traffic officer" is to "gateway to memory" as _____ is to _____.
   a. reticular activating system; cerebellum
   b. cerebellum; reticular activating system
   c. thalamus; hippocampus
   d. hippocampus; thalamus

15. Which of the following pairs of lobes and types of cortex is INCORRECT?
   a. occipital lobes and visual cortex
   b. temporal lobes and motor cortex
   c. parietal lobes and somatosensory cortex
   d. none of the above

16. Cases such as the Phineas Gage accident indicate that the _____ lobes have something to do with personality.
   a. frontal
   b. parietal
   c. temporal
   d. occipital

17. Information in a person's left visual field goes to the _____ half of each eye and _____ hemisphere; information in a person's right visual field goes to the _____ half of each eye and _____ hemisphere.
   a. tight, tight; left, left
   b. left, left; right, tight
   c. right, left; left, right
   d. left, tight; right, left

18. The right hemisphere is superior to the left hemisphere in all of the following EXCEPT:
   a. solving problems requiting spatial-visual ability.
   b. facial recognition.
   c. appreciation of art and music.
   d. explaining actions and emotions.

77

19.   If a picture of a spoon is flashed quickly in the left visual field of a split-brain patient, then the patient can:
       a.   use the right hand to identify the spoon.
       b.   use the left hand to identify the spoon.
       c.   say that a spoon was shown.
       d.   a and c

20.   Which of the following statements about sex differences in the brain is FALSE?
       a.   Most studies have found an average sex difference in the size and shape of the splenium.
       b.   A biological difference does not necessarily have behavioural implications.
       c.   Sex differences in the brain could be the result rather than the cause of differences.
       d.   None of the above

ANSWERS

GUIDED STUDY

1.   The Nervous System: A Basic Blueprint

1.1   central   peripheral
       spinal cord   spinal reflexes

1.2.   sensory   autonomic   biofeedback
       Motor   voluntary   sympathetic
       somatic   automatic   parasympathetic

Matching Self-Test 1

1. autonomic nervous system   4. parasympathetic nervous system
2. spinal cord   5. peripheral nervous system
3. sensory neurons

---

2.   Communication in the Nervous System

2.1.   neurons   cell body   myelin sheath
       glial   axon   nerves
       dendrites   axon terminals

2.2.	synaptic cleft	potassium	excitatory
	synapse	slower	inhibitory
	chemical	synaptic vesicles	all-or-none
	action potential	neurotransmitters	
	sodium	receptor sites	

2.3.	serotonin	stress	adrenalin
	Acetylcholine	hormones	norepinephrine
	serotonin	endocrine glands	noradrenalin
	norepinephrine	melatonin	sympathetic
	acetylcholine	adrenal glands	androgens
	dopamine	adrenal	estrogens
	endorphins	cortisol	progesterone
	afraid	epinephrine	

Matching Self-Test 2

1. neurotransmitter	4. nerves	7. myelin sheath
2. hormones	5. endorphins	8. synapse
3. dendrites	6. melatonin	

---

3. Mapping the Brain

| 3.1. | lesion | positron emission |
| | electroencephalogram | magnetic resonance |

Matching Self-Test 3

| 1. PET scan | 2. MRI | 3. EEG |

---

4. A Tour Through the Brain

4.1.	localization of function	dreaming
	medulla	reticular activating
	pons	alert
	breathing	conscious
	sleeping	

4.2.	cerebellum	4.3.	thalamus	4.4.	hypothalamus
	balance		olfaction		pituitary
	muscles		olfactory bulb		

4.5.	limbic system	depression	15
	amygdala	hippocampus	consolidation
	anxiety	epilepsy	

4.6.	cerebrum	grey	auditory
	cerebral	unmyelinated	frontal
	hemispheres	white	motor
	corpus callosum	myelinated	Broca's
	left	occipital	association
	right	somatosensory	prefrontal
	lateralization	parietal	personality
	cerebral cortex	temporal	Phineas Gage

Matching Self-Test 4

1. medulla	5. localization of function	8. amygdala
2. cerebellum	6. reticular activating	9. lateralization
3. pituitary gland	system	10. Wernicke's area
4. hippocampus	7. thalamus	

5. The Two Hemispheres of the Brain

5.1.	cats	one	split-brain
	two	epilepsy	

5.2.	left	dominant	spatial-visual
	math	Gazzaniga	facial
	technical	Sperry	

Matching Self-Test 5

1. split-brain surgery	2. corpus callosum	3. cerebral dominance

6. Two Stubborn Issues in Brain Research

6.1.   rapid eye   respiration   skeletal
        non-REM   face   activation-synthesis
        wakefulness   fingers   cortex
        heart   penis
        blood   clitoris

6.2.   splenium   biological   cause
        REM sleep   al
        stereotypes   result

Matching Self-Test 6

1. activation-synthesis theory   2. REM sleep

ANSWERS TO MULTIPLE CHOICE PROGRESS TEST

Item No.	Answer	Page(s) in Textbook
1.	a. Sensory; motor	119-120
2.	b. autonomic	120
3.	c. constricts pupils	120
4.	d. None of the above	121
5.	b. dendrites; cell body; axon	123
6.	c. multiple sclerosis	123
7.	b. increase; decrease	125
8.	c. Each neuron only has synaptic connections with one other neuron.	126
9.	a. GABA.	126
10.	c. dopamine	126
11.	a. norepinephrine	128
12.	c. melatonin	128
13.	b. a PET scan	131
14.	c. thalamus; hippocampus	133-134
15.	b. temporal lobes and motor cortex	137
16.	a. frontal	137-138
17.	a. right, right; left, left	140
18.	d. explaining actions and emotions.	141
19.	b. use the left hand to identify the spoon	141-142
20.	a. Most studies have found an average sex difference in the size and shape of the splenium.	141-142

CHAPTER 5

Sensation and Perception

CHAPTER OVERVIEW

The chapter opens with a description of the difference between sensation and perception. The functioning of sense receptors is covered, along with types of neural coding (anatomical versus functional). Psychophysics is discussed next. This includes coverage of absolute and difference thresholds (jnds) and signal detection theory. This is followed by a description of sensory adaptation versus sensory deprivation.

The visual system is covered in detail, including the structure and functioning of the eye. The psychological characteristics of hue, brightness, and saturation are related to the physical characteristics of wavelength, intensity, and complexity. The Nobel Prize winning work of Hubel and Wiesel is discussed along with two theories of vision. The Gestalt view of perception is presented. Coverage includes discussion of Gestalt principles of perceptual organization such as figure and ground and grouping. Descriptions of other aids to perception such as the various constancies and binocular versus monocular cues to depth follow.

The properties related to the processing of sound waves are presented along with the structure and functioning of the ear. This includes descriptions of the outer, middle, and inner ear. Following this is a description of the other senses—taste, olfaction, body senses, kinesthesis, and equilibrium.

The perceptual abilities of the newborn are covered along with a description of various methods used to test newborns. A discussion of cultural influences on perception is followed by a look at subliminal perception and various types of ESP. ESP is critically analyzed based on a consideration of empirical studies.

GUIDED STUDY

1. Our Sensational Senses

Read the section "Our Sensational Senses" and then answer the following questions. If you have trouble answering any of the questions, re-study the relevant material before going on to the review of key terms and the matching test.

1-1   The detection of physical energy emitted or reflected by physical objects is
_____, whereas the organization of sensory impulses into meaningful patterns
is _____. The cells that detect sensory information are called _____
_____. Sense receptors convert the energy of the stimulus into an
_____ _____ that travels along nerves to the brain. Johannes Muller
proposed in his doctrine of specific nerve energies that the code used by the sense
receptors was _____. This means that different sensory moralities exist because
signals received by the sense organs stimulate different nerve pathways leading to different
areas of the brain. An anatomical code is not sufficient, however, to explain all differences
in sensations. Another type of code, _____, is necessary to help explain these
differences. Functional coding explains perceived differences based on which cells are
firing, how _____ cells are firing, the _____ of firing, and the
_____ of firing.

1-2.   Measurement of the sensitivity of our senses is accomplished by psychologists in the area
of _____ who are concerned with how the _____ properties of a
stimulus are related to our _____ experiences of them. One measurement that
psychophysicists make is based on the smallest amount of energy that a person can
reliably detect, an _____ threshold. Another measurement studied by
psychophysicists is a just noticeable difference or _____ threshold. This is the
smallest difference in stimulation that a person can detect reliably. In one experiment,
students tested the difference threshold for different types of _____. They
found that the difference between the taste of the two colas exceeded the students'
difference threshold. There are limitations, however, to measuring absolute and difference
thresholds. Thus, researchers will frequently use _____-_____
theory for sensory measurements. Signal-detection theory states that a subject's response
in a detection task can be divided into a _____ process that depends on the
intensity of the stimulus and a process that is influenced by the observer's response bias.

1-3.   When receptors or nerve cells higher up in the sensory system get tired and fire less
frequently, the decline in responsiveness is called _____ _____. In
_____ _____ studies, researchers investigated what would happen if
our senses adapted to most incoming stimuli. Although participants responded negatively
to sensory deprivation in the initial studies, flaws were found in this research. In later
research using better methods, _____ were less dramatic and less disorienting
than at first thought.

1-4.   The opposite of sensory adaptation is sensory _____. When this occurs people
often cope by blocking out unimportant sights and sounds and focusing on interesting and
useful information, a phenomenon referred to as "the _____ party
phenomenon." This capacity for _____ _____ protects us in daily
life from being overwhelmed by too many sensory signals.

Review of Key Terms

The following is a list of the Key Terms from the section "Our Sensational Senses." Make sure you are familiar with each term before taking the matching test on these terms.

sensation	psychophysics	sensory deprivation
sense receptors	absolute threshold	selective attention
perception	difference threshold	signal-detection theory
anatomical codes	jnd	doctrine of specific nerve energies
functional codes	sensory adaptation	

Matching Self Test 1

Match the appropriate term with its definition or description.

1. _____ The area of psychology concerned with the relationship between physical properties of stimuli and sensory experience.

2. _____ A psychophysical theory that divides the detection of a sensory signal into a sensory process and a decision process.

3. _____ Specialized cells that convert physical energy in the environment or the body to electrical energy that can be transmitted as nerve impulses to the brain.

4. _____ The absence of normal levels of sensory stimulation.

5. _____ The process by which the brain organizes and interprets sensory information.

6. _____ The smallest quantity of physical energy that can be reliably detected by an observer.

2. Vision

Read the section "Vision" and then answer the following questions. If you have trouble answering any of the questions, re-study the relevant material before going on to the review of key terms and the matching test.

2-1. The stimulus for vision is _____ which travels in the form of _____. The characteristics of light waves affect the way we see the world. The wavelength of light, the distance between the crests of a light wave, specifies the colour or _____.

84

The intensity or amplitude of the light wave corresponds to _____. The complexity of the wavelengths, how wide or narrow the range of wavelengths, relates to the dimension of _____. Hue, brightness, and saturation are all _____ dimensions of visual experience, whereas wavelength, intensity, and complexity are all _____ properties of the visual stimulus light.

2-2.   Light waves enter the visual system through the eyes. The front covering of the eye is the transparent _____ which protects the eye and sends incoming light waves toward the _____. The lens focuses the light on the back of the eye. The amount of light let into the eye is controlled by the coloured _____. This structure surrounds the round opening of the eye, the _____. The visual sense receptors are located at the back of the eye in the _____. The more numerous visual receptors are called _____. They enable us to see in _____ levels of light and at _____. Rods cannot distinguish different wavelengths of light and therefore are not sensitive to _____. The less numerous visual receptors in the retina are the _____, which are located primarily in the center of the retina, the _____. Cones are sensitive to specific wavelengths of light and allow us to see _____. They also need much more light than do rods to respond and therefore do not allow us to see well in _____ levels of light. The amount of time to adapt to darkness varies for rods and cones. The cones, which do not operate well in dim levels of illumination, dark adapt in about _____ minutes. The rods, which are more sensitive in dim levels of illumination, dark adapt in about _____ minutes. Rods and cones are connected via synapses to _____ neurons, which in turn connect to _____ cells via synapses. The axons of the ganglion cells converge to form the _____ nerve, which exits the eye at the _____ disc. As there are no rods and cones at this point of the retina, a _____ spot is produced in the field of vision.

2-3.   The visual system is not a passive recorder of the external world as is a camera. Different cells in the visual system respond to different features in the environment, building up a picture of the world. For example, ganglion cells and cells in the _____ respond to simple features in the environment, such as spots of light and dark. Special _____-_____ cells in the visual cortex respond to more complex features. This was demonstrated by the Nobel Prize winning researchers _____ and _____.

2-4.   The Young-Helmholtz, or _____ theory of colour vision assumed that three mechanisms in the visual system worked together to bring about our sensations of different colours. Another approach to colour vision posited that the visual system treated particular pairs of colours as opposing. The trichromatic approach appears to explain how colour processing works at the level of the _____. The retina contains three types of _____, each of which responds to differing ranges of light wavelengths (different colours). The opponent process theory appears to explain how colour processing works at the level of _____ cells in the retina and in neurons in the

_____ and visual cortex of the brain. One pair of opponent cells is responsible for seeing red versus _____, another for _____ versus yellow, and the last for _____ versus black. The opponent process theory can explain why we are susceptible to negative _____, why we see for example red after staring at green.

2-5.   The ability to detect where one thing begins and another ends is called _____ perception. The _____ psychologists were among the first to study how people organize the world visually into meaningful units and patterns. One principle identified by the Gestalt psychologists was known as _____ and ground. Other Gestalt strategies to aid interpretation are grouping things that are near each other together, _____; filling in the gaps in order to perceive complete forms, _____; grouping things that are alike in some way, _____; and perceiving lines and patterns in a continuous manner, _____. In order to perceive depth and distance we rely on cues that involve both eyes, _____ cues, and cues that involve only one eye, _____ cues. There are two binocular cues. _____ involves the turning in of the eyes when they focus on a nearby object— the closer the object the _____ the convergence. A second binocular cue is _____ disparity—the slight difference in lateral separation between two objects as seen by the left eye and the right eye. Binocular cues aid us in estimating distances up to about _____ feet. For objects that are far away, we rely on monocular cues. The ability to perceive objects as stable or unchanging even though the sensory patterns they produce are constantly shifting is called _____ constancy. The best-studied visual constancies include: perceiving objects as having a constant shape even though the shape of the retinal image changes when our point of view changes—_____ constancy; perceiving stationary objects as remaining in the same place even though the retinal image moves about as we move our eyes, heads, and bodies—_____ constancy; continuing to see an object as having a constant size even when its retinal image becomes smaller or larger—_____ constancy; continuing to see objects as having a relatively constant brightness even though the amount of light they reflect changes as the overall level of illumination changes—_____ constancy; and seeing an object as maintaining its hue despite the fact that the wavelength of light reaching our eyes may change—_____ constancy. Even though we regularly use all of these constancies, we can occasionally be fooled by a perceptual _____.

Review of Key Terms

The following is a list of the Key Terms from the section "Vision." Make sure you are familiar with each term before taking the matching test on these terms.

hue	ganglion cells	binocular cues
brightness	optic nerve	convergence

saturation	feature detectors	retinal disparity
complexity of light	trichromatic theory	monocular cues
retina	Gestalt principles	perceptual constancy
rods	opponent-process theory	
cones	figure and ground	
dark adaptation	negative afterimage	

Matching Self Test 2

Match the appropriate term with its definition or description.

1. _____ A process by which visual receptors become maximally sensitive to dim light.

2. _____ Vividness or purity of colour ; the dimension of visual experience related to the complexity of light waves.

3. _____ A theory of colour perception that assumes that the visual system treats pairs of colours as opposing or antagonistic.

4. _____ Cells in the visual cortex that are sensitive to specific features of the environment.

5. _____ Visual receptors that respond to dim light but are not involved in colour vision.

6. _____ The dimension of visual experience specified by colour names and related to the wavelength of light.

7. _____ An erroneous or misleading perception of reality.

8. _____ The slight difference in lateral separation between two objects as seen by the left eye and the right eye.

9. _____ Neural tissue lining the back of the eyeball's interior, which contains the receptors for vision.

10. _____ Visual cues to depth or distance which can be used by one eye alone.

3. Hearing

Read the section "Hearing" and then answer the following questions. If you have trouble answering any of the questions, restudy the relevant material before going on to the review of key terms and the matching test.

3-1.   The stimulus for sound is a wave of _____. The intensity of a wave's pressure is related to the psychological dimension of _____. The intensity of a sound is measured in _____. The frequency of a sound wave is related to the psychological experience of _____. Frequency refers to the number of times per second the wave cycles through a peak and low point. Frequency is measured in _____. The complexity of a sound wave is related to the psychological experience of _____.

3-2.   The ear is divided into outer, middle and inner sections. The outer ear consists of the funnel-shaped outer ear, an inch-long canal at the end of which is the _____. The eardrum vibrates at the same rate as the sound wave and causes three bones in the middle ear to vibrate. The bones are the _____, _____, and _____. The stirrup pushes on a membrane that opens into the inner ear. The inner ear consists of a snail-shaped structure, the _____, inside of which is the organ of _____. The organ of Corti contains the sense receptors for audition, the hair cells or _____. The hair cells are embedded in the _____ membrane. As the fluid in the cochlea moves, the hair cells move, initiating a signal that is passed along to the _____ nerve and eventually to the brain.

Review of Key Terms

The following is a list of the Key Terms from the section "Hearing." Make sure you are familiar with each term before taking the matching test on these terms.

audition	timbre	hair cells (cilia)
loudness	eardrum	basilar membrane
pitch	cochlea	auditory nerve
frequency	organ of Corti	

Matching Self Test 3

Match the appropriate term with its definition or description.

1. _____   The distinguishing quality of a sound; the dimension of auditory experience related to the complexity of the pressure wave.

2. _____ The sense receptors for audition that are embedded in the basilar membrane.

3. _____ The dimension of auditory experience related to the intensity of a pressure wave.

4. _____ A snail-shaped, fluid-filled organ in the inner ear, containing the receptors for hearing.

5. _____ The oval-shaped membrane at the end of the outer ear canal.

4. Other Senses

Read the section "Other Senses" and then answer the following questions. If you have trouble answering any of the questions, re-study the relevant material before going on to the review of key terms and the matching test.

4-1. The sense receptors for taste or _____ are located inside the _____ _____ that line the sides of _____ on the tongue. The four basic tastes are: _____, _____, _____, and _____. Each of these tastes is produced by a different type of _____. Some differences in taste sensations are due to _____. For example, people who are "supertasters" for bitter substances have more _____ than do others. In addition a certain type of _____ are smaller, more densely packed, and look different than those in nontasters. Certain foods like chocolate and vanilla would have little taste if we could not also _____ them.

4-2. The sense of smell is called _____. The sense receptors for smell are located in a tiny patch of mucous membrane in the upper part of the nasal passage, just below the eyes. Signals from the sense receptors are carried to the brain's olfactory _____ by the olfactory _____. One activity that researchers have found damages your sense of olfaction is _____.

4-3. The four skins senses include: _____, _____, _____, and _____. There are not, however, four distinct kinds of receptors to process these four senses. Recent research has focused on _____ codes involved in the skin senses. One of the most studied skin senses is _____. The first theory on pain was the _____-_____ theory, that stated that the experience of pain depends on whether pain impulses get past a gate in the spinal cord and reach the brain. The gate-control theory helps to explain pain and can also explain the pain an amputee feels, _____ pain.

4-4. Two senses that keep us informed about the movements of our own bodies are _____ and _____. Kinesthesis tells us where our body parts are _____ and lets us know when they _____. Equilibrium, our sense of _____, relies primarily on three fluid-filled _____ canals in the inner ear.

89

Review of Key Terms

The following is a list of the Key Terms from the section "Other Senses." Make sure you are familiar with each term before taking the matching test on these terms.

gustation   olfaction   kinesthesis

papillae   gate-control theory   equilibrium

taste buds   phantom pain   semicircular canals

Matching Self Test 4

Match the appropriate term with its definition or description.

1. _____ The theory that the experience of pain depends in part on whether pain impulses get past a neurological "gate" in the spinal cord and thus reach the brain.

2. _____ The sense of body position and movement of body parts.

3. _____ Sense organs in the inner ear that contribute to equilibrium by responding to rotation of the head.

4. _____ Knoblike elevations on the tongue, containing the taste buds.

5. Perceptual Powers: Origins and Influences

Read the section "Perceptual Powers: Origins and Influences" and then answer the following questions. If you have trouble answering any of the questions, re-study the relevant material before going on to the review of key terms and the matching test.

5-1.   Researchers studying inborn perceptual abilities have used cats as subjects in experiments testing _____ periods of development. They have found that without certain early experiences, perception develops _____. For example, cats allowed to view only vertical stripes for the first few months of life seemed blind to all _____ contours later in life. It appears that brain cells sensitive to the horizontal (or vertical) orientation _____ when not used. Human infants also seem to be equipped at birth to detect and discriminate edges and angles. One procedure that demonstrates this in human infants is to place infants on a device called a _____ _____. Experimenters utilizing the visual cliff device have shown that babies as young as 6 months of age refuse to crawl over the "cliff."

5-2.   Because human beings care about what they see, hear, taste, smell, and feel, psychological factors can influence what we perceive and how we perceive it. These factors include: _____, beliefs, _____, and expectations. The tendency to perceive what we expect is called _____ set. Culture also affects our needs, beliefs, emotions, and expectations. In one study on the Mueller-Lyer illusion, it was found that people living in a carpentered society were _____ susceptible to the illusion than those living in a non-carpentered society.

Review of Key Terms

The following is a list of the Key Terms from the section "Perceptual Powers: Origins and Influences." Make sure you are familiar with each term before taking the matching test on these terms.

critical periods   perceptual set   visual cliff

Matching Self Test 5

Match the appropriate term with its definition or description.

1. _____   A habitual way of perceiving, based on expectations.

2. _____   A device used in experiments to determine whether infants can detect and discriminate edges and angles.

6. Puzzles of Perception

Read the section "Puzzles of Perception" and then answer the following questions. If you have trouble answering any of the questions, re-study the relevant material before going on to the review of key terms and the matching test.

6-1.   Although some researchers have found support for visual _____ perception, subliminal _____ is quite another matter. Empirical research has uncovered no basis whatsoever for believing that advertisers can seduce us into buying certain products by the use of _____ messages.

6-2.   ESP, _____ perception experiences, fall into four general categories—direct communication from one mind to another, _____; the perception of an event or fact without normal sensory input, _____; the perception of an event that has not yet happened, _____; and perception of one's own body from "outside," as an observer might see it, _____-_____ experience. ESP has been studied by those in the field of _____. Most studies have found no evidence for the existence of ESP and those that have found some evidence have typically been flawed in some way.

Review of Key Terms

The following is a list of the Key Terms from the section "Puzzles of Perception." Make sure you are familiar with each term before taking the matching test on these terms.

ESP   subliminal persuasion   parapsychology

subliminal perception   clairvoyance   out-of-body experience

telepathy   precognition

Matching Self Test 6

Match the appropriate term with its definition or description.

1. _____ The study of purported psychic phenomena such as ESP and mental telepathy.

2. _____ The perception of one's own body from "outside," as an observer might see it.

3. _____ Direct communication from one mind to another.

4. _____ Perceiving and responding to messages that are below the threshold.

SAMPLE ANSWERS TO *WHAT'S AHEAD* QUESTIONS FROM TEXTBOOK

After you have completed the "Looking Back" section at the end of the chapter by answering the "What's Ahead" questions that preceded each major section of the chapter, compare your answers to the following sample answers. If your answers are not similar to the sample answers, review the pertinent sections of the chapter. The relevant page(s) for each question is(are) provided in the "Looking Back" section in the text.

What kind of "code" in the nervous system helps explain why a pinprick and a kiss feel different?

The first explanation for this difference was based on an anatomical coding system. This was specified in the *doctrine of specific nerve energies* by Johannes Muller and stated that different sensory modalities exist because signals received by the sense organs stimulate different nerve pathways leading to different areas of the brain. Anatomical coding, however, does not completely answer the question. Linking different skin senses to distinct nerve pathways has been difficult and the *doctrine of specific nerve energies* does not explain variations of experience within a sense. A functional coding system offers a better explanation. This coding system provides information about which cells are firing, how many cells are firing, the rate at which cells are firing, and the patterning of each cell's firing.

Why does your dog hear a "silent" doggie whistle when you can't?

Our senses are tuned in to only a narrow band of physical energies. Dogs are able to pick up signals that we cannot and thus, can detect high frequency sound waves that are beyond our range.

What kind of bias can influence whether you think you hear the phone ringing in the other room?

According to signal-detection theory, a response bias can influence your ability to hear the phone ringing in the other room. A response bias is one's tendency to be either a yea-sayer (a gambler) or a nay-sayer (cautious and conservative.)

What happens when people are deprived of all external sensory stimulation?

In initial studies of sensory deprivation, subjects were edgy and disoriented within a few hours. Those who participated for longer than this were confused, restless, and grouchy. Some reported having hallucinations. The methodology in these studies was questionable, and in more recent studies, the response of the subjects included hallucinations that were less dramatic and less disorienting. In fact, many people enjoy limited time periods of deprivation. It is clear, however, that the human brain requires a minimum amount of sensory stimulation in order to function normally.

How does the eye differ from a camera?

A camera lens focuses incoming light by moving closer to or farther from the shutter opening. The lens of the eye works by changing shape. It becomes more or less curved to focus light from objects that are close by or far away. The visual system is not a passive recorder of information as is a camera. Neurons in the visual system build up a picture of the world by detecting its meaningful features.

Why can we describe a colour as bluish green but not as reddish green?

Based on the opponent process theory of colour vision, there are three pairs of opposing colours. These are blue/yellow, red/green, and white/black. Thus, we would be able to see a bluish green when cells responsible for these colours fire; however, as red and green represent an opposing pair, they cannot both fire at the same time and we would not be able to see a reddish green.

If you were blind in one eye, why might you misjudge the distances of different objects on a nearby table, but not of buildings in the distance?

You might misjudge the distances of objects nearby as we typically rely on binocular cues to judge the distance of objects that are close by. Binocular cues to depth and distance involve the use of both eyes and include convergence (the turning of the eyes inward when they focus on a nearby object) and retinal disparity (the slight difference in lateral separation between two objects as seen by the left eye and the right eye.) When judging the depth or distance of a building in the distance we rely on monocular cues, involving one eye. Thus, if you were blind in one eye you would still be able to use monocular cues, but not binocular cues.

As a friend approaches, her image on your retina grows larger, then why do you continue to see her as the same size?

This is due to a perceptual constancy known as size constancy. Size constancy depends in part on familiarity with objects and on the apparent distance of an object. As the friend approaches, we know she does not change in size and thus correctly perceive that she is getting closer.

Why are perceptual illusions so fascinating?

For psychologists, they are fascinating because they are systematic errors that provide us with hints about the perceptual strategies of the mind. Many illusions are cultural in nature. The Muller-Lyer illusion in particular seems to have a cultural basis. The illusion works best for people from carpentered societies. It does not work well for people from rural, less carpentered environments.

Why does a note played on a flute sound different from the same note on an oboe?

The difference is due to the timbre or complexity of the sound waves produced by each instrument. A pure tone consists of only one frequency. A flute produces relatively pure tones, whereas an oboe produces very complex sounds, not pure tones.

If you habitually listen to loud music through headphones, what kind of hearing impairment are you risking?

You are risking impairment to the cilia or hair cells located on the basilar membrane. The hair cells are the sense receptors for audition. Exposure to extremely loud noise can damage these fragile cells and cause them to flop over like broken blades of grass.

To locate the source of a sound, why does it sometimes help to turn or tilt your head?

If the sound originates from either the right or left side, turning or tilting your head is not necessary as the sound waves will reach one ear first and aid in localization. However, when the sound originates from directly above or behind your head, it is hard to localize because such sounds reach both ears at the same time. In this case, when you turn or tilt your head, you are actively trying to overcome this problem.

Why do saccharin and caffeine taste bitter to some people but not to others?

Saccharin and caffeine taste bitter to "supertasters" for bitter substances. Supertasters have more taste buds on their tongues than do "nontasters." In addition, in supertasters papillae of a certain type are smaller, more densely packed, and look different than those in nontasters.

Why do you have trouble tasting your food when you have a cold?

A food's odor is important to a food's taste. Very subtle flavors such as vanilla and chocolate would have little taste if we could not also smell these foods. Thus, when your nose is stuffy and you are having trouble with your sense of smell, your sense of taste will also be inhibited.

Why do people often continue to "feel" limbs that have been amputated?

According to the gate-control theory of pain, although sense receptors that were in the body part no longer exist, the pain can nonetheless be severe. This may be due to the fact that the impulses normally responsible for closing the pain "gate" are reduced or eliminated by the amputation or operation. Without these inhibitory impulses, pain fibers near the spinal cord are able to get their messages through. In addition, the level of activity in certain brain circuits may increase, generating pain sensations that continue on their own in the absence of normal sensory input from the missing limb.

Do babies see the world the way adults do?

Based on research findings, it appears that human infants are probably born with an ability to detect and discriminate between the edges and angles of objects. They can also discriminate between sizes and colours very early, possibly at birth. They can distinguish contrasts, shadows, and complex patterns after only a few weeks. They may even have some depth perception at birth. Thus, many fundamental perceptual skills are inborn or acquired shortly after birth; but not all are. In addition, perception also depends upon one's needs, beliefs, emotions, and expectations. Therefore, babies do not see the world in the same way that adults do.

Why does one person think a cloud is a cloud, and another think it's a spaceship?

Our beliefs about the world can affect our interpretations of ambiguous sensory signals. Hence, if you believe in extraterrestrials and spaceships, you will be more likely to view an ambiguous object (for example, a cloud) as a spaceship versus what it is, a cloud).

Can "subliminal perception" tapes help you lose weight or reduce you stress?

Although subjects in some studies have demonstrated visual subliminal perception, subliminal persuasion (to lose weight or reduce stress) is quite another matter. Empirical research has uncovered no basis whatsoever for believing that advertisers can seduce us into buying certain products, voting in a particular way, losing weight, or reducing stress. In every study, "placebo" tapes have been just as effective as subliminal tapes.

Why are most psychologists skeptical about ESP?

Most psychologists are skeptical about ESP because there have been no reliable findings under controlled conditions supporting its existence. In any study supporting ESP claims, researchers have ultimately found flaws. After an exhaustive review, the National Research Council concluded that there was "no scientific justification.., for the existence of parapsychological phenomena." In addition, all of the so called "Psi" phenomena produced by psychics such as Uri Geller have been reproduced by magicians such as James Randi.

Multiple-Choice Progress Test

Choose the single best answer for each of the following questions. When you have finished this progress test, check your answers with those at the end of the chapter. You should review the indicated pages in the text for the questions you do not answer correctly.

1.   Our ability to perceive differences within a particular sense (e.g., differentiating red from pink) depends upon _____.
        a. the doctrine of specific nerve energies
        b. anatomical coding
        c. functional coding
        d. response bias

2.   The smallest amount of energy that a person can detect 50% of the time is known as the _____ threshold.
        a. absolute
        b. difference
        c. attention
        d. response

3.   In a detection task, yea-sayers will have _____ "hits" than nay-sayers when a weak stimulus is present and _____ "false alarms" when there is no stimulus present.
        a. more; more
        b. more; less
        c. less; more
        d. less; less

4.   The reduction or disappearance of sensory responsiveness that occurs when stimulation is unchanging or repetitious is called _____.
        a. selective attention
        b. sensory deprivation
        c. sensory adaptation
        d. sensory overload

5.   Which of the following is NOT a psychological dimension of visual experience?
        a. hue
        b. intensity
        c. brightness
        d. saturation

6. Which of the following statements about rods and cones is FALSE?
   a. There are more rods than cones.
   b. At the optic disc, there are no rods or cones.
   c. Rods are more sensitive to light than cones are.
   d. Only rods are sensitive to colour.

7. Which of the following sequences represents the correct order of processing in the visual pathways?
   a. receptor cells-bipolar cells-feature detector cells-ganglion cells
   b. bipolar cells-receptor cells-ganglion cells-feature detector cells
   c. receptor cells-bipolar cells-ganglion cells-feature detector cells
   d. bipolar cells-ganglion cells-feature detector cells-receptor cells

8. According to the opponent-process theory of colour vision, if you stare at a patch of red on a white screen and then the patch is taken away, you should see a _____ afterimage where the patch had been located.
   a. blue
   b. green
   c. yellow
   d. grey

9. You perceive two groups of circles: three red circles and three blue circles. Your perception illustrates which of the following Gestalt principles of perceptual organization?
   a. proximity
   b. closure
   c. continuity
   d. similarity

10. If you are standing between railroad tracks and staring down the tracks, the tracks appear to converge in the distance. This is an example of a _____ cue called _____.
    a. monocular; convergence
    b. binocular, convergence
    c. monocular; linear perspective
    d. binocular; linear perspective

11. The dimension of auditory experience related to the complexity of a sound wave is
    _____.
    a. loudness
    b. timbre
    c. pitch
    d. intensity

12. The function of the _____ in the ears is analogous to the function of the rods
    and cones in the eyes.
    a. cochlea
    b. cilia (hair cells)
    c. eardrum
    d. organ of Corti

13. To discriminate low-pitched sounds, we use _____; to discriminate high-
    pitched sounds, we use _____.
    a. the location of the activity along the basilar membrane; the frequency of the basilar
       membrane's activity
    b. the frequency of the basilar membrane's activity; the location of the activity along the
       basilar membrane
    c. the location of the activity along the basilar membrane; the location of the activity
       along the basilar membrane
    d. the frequency of the basilar membrane's activity; the frequency of the basilar
       membrane's activity

14. Which of the following statements about our sense of taste is FALSE?
    a. There are four basic tastes—salty, sour, bitter, and sweet.
    b. A different area of the tongue is sensitive to each of the four basic tastes.
    c. The center of the tongue contains no taste buds.
    d. None of the above

15. With respect to our olfactory and skin senses, which of the following statements is (are)
    FALSE?
    a. Researchers do not agree on which smells, if any, are basic.
    b. There is a distinct kind of receptor for each of the four skin senses.
    c. According to the gate-control theory of pain, larger fibers that respond to pressure
       close the gate.
    d. All of the above

16. Which of the following senses depends upon the three semicircular canals in the inner ear?
    a. audition
    b. kinesthesis
    c. equilibrium
    d. none of the above

17. The visual cliff is a device used to test _____ in infants.
    a. size perception
    b. depth perception
    c. perception
    d. shape perception

18. Which of the following psychological factors can influence what we perceive and how we perceive it?
    a. our needs
    b. our beliefs
    c. our emotions
    d. all of the above

19. Mind-to-mind communication is to perception of a future event as _____ is to
    _____.
    a. precognition; clairvoyance
    b. clairvoyance; precognition
    c. precognition; telepathy
    d. telepathy; precognition

20. Which of the following phenomena is (are) supported by reliable empirical evidence?
    a. visual subliminal perception
    b. subliminal persuasion
    c. ESP
    d. all of the above

ANSWERS

GUIDED STUDY

1. Our Sensational Senses

1.1.
sensation	electrical impulse	many
perception	anatomical	rate
sense receptors	functional	pattern

1.2.
psychophysics	cola	sensory deprivation
physical	signal-detection	hallucinations
psychological	sensory	overload
absolute	decision	cocktail
difference	sensory adaptation	selective attention

Matching Self-Test 1

1. psychophysics	3. sense receptors	5. perception
2. signal detection theory	4. sensory deprivation	6. absolute threshold

---

2. Vision

2.1.
light	brightness	physical
waves	saturation	
hue	psychological	

2.2.
cornea	night	20
lens	colour	bipolar
iris	cones	ganglion
pupil	fovea	optic
retina	colour	optic
rods	low	blind
low	10	

2.3.
thalamus	Hubel
feature-detector	Wiesel

2.4.	trichromatic	ganglion	blue
	retina	thalamus	white
	cones	green	afterimages

2.5.	form	binocular	shape
	Gestalt	monocular	location
	figure	Convergence	size
	proximity	greater	brightness
	closure	retinal	illusion
	similarity	50	
	continuity	perceptual	

Matching Self-Test 2

1. dark adaptation
2. saturation
3. opponent-process theory
4. feature detectors

5. rods
6. hue
7. perceptual illusion
8. retinal disparity

9. retina
10. monocular cues

3. Hearing

| 3.1. | pressure | decibels | hertz |
| | loudness | pitch | timbre |

3.2.	eardrum	stirrup	cilia
	hammer	cochlea	basilar
	anvil	Corti	auditory

Matching Self-Test 3

1. timbre
2. hair cells (cilia)

3. loudness
4. cochlea

5. eardrum

4. Other Senses

4.1.	gustation	sour	genetics
	taste buds	bitter	taste buds
	papillae	sweet	papillae
	salty	chemical	smell

4.2.	olfaction	nerve	
	bulb	smoking	

4.3.	touch	pain	gate-control
	warmth	neural	phantom
	cold	pain	

4.4.	kinesthesis	located	balance
	equilibrium	move	semicircular

Matching Self-Test 4

1. gate control theory	3. semicircular canals
2. kinesthesis	4. papillae

5. Perceptual Powers: Origins and Influences

5.1.	critical	horizontal	visual cliff
	abnormally	deteriorate	

5.2.	needs	perceptual	
	emotions	more	

Matching Self-Test 5

1. perceptual set	2. visual cliff

6. Puzzles of Perception

6.1.	subliminal	persuasion	subliminal

6.2.	extrasensory	precognition	half
	telepathy	out-of-body	
	clairvoyance	parapsychology	

Matching Self-Test 6

1. parapsychology	3. telepathy
2. out-of-body experience	4. subliminal perception

ANSWERS TO MULTIPLE CHOICE PROGRESS TEST

Item No.	Answer	Page(s) in Textbook
1.	c. functional coding	157
2.	a. absolute threshold	157
3.	a. more; more	159
4.	c. sensory adaptation	159
5.	b. intensity	161-162
6.	d. Only rods are sensitive to	163
7.	c. receptor cells-bipolar cells ganglion cells-feature detector cells	164
8.	b. green	165
9.	d. similarity	168
10.	c. monocular; linear perspective	169
11.	b. timbre	173
12.	b. cilia (hair cells)	174-175
13.	b. the frequency of the basilar membrane activity; the location of the activity along the basilar membrane	176
14.	b. A different area of the tongue is sensitive to each of the four basic tastes	170-171
15.	b. There is a distinct kind of receptor for each of the four skin senses.	178-180
16.	c. equilibrium	182
17.	b. depth perception	183
18.	d. all of the above	184
19.	d. telepathy; precognition	187
20.	a. visual subliminal perception	185-187

CHAPTER 6

Thinking and Intelligence

CHAPTER OVERVIEW

The chapter opens with a discussion of concepts and concept formation. This includes explanations of such terms as prototype, propositions, cognitive schemas, and mental images. Subconscious and nonconscious processes are covered and related to mindlessness. Formal versus informal reasoning is considered next. This involves a description of deductive versus inductive reasoning, algorithms versus heuristics, dialectical reasoning, and reflective judgment. Barriers to rational reasoning such as using the availability heuristic, framing effects, confirmation bias, mental set, hindsight bias, and cognitive dissonance are covered in some detail.

A history of intelligence testing and theories of intelligence follow. The discussion of the psychometric approach includes the gfactor, factor analysis, achievement tests, aptitude tests, and intelligence quotients. The Binet test is discussed along with the Stanford-Binet Intelligence Scale, and Wechsler's adult intelligence scale and intelligence scale for children. Group tests are compared to individualized tests and attempts to develop culture-free and culture-fair tests are described. Recent cognitive theories of intelligence are also introduced. These include Sternberg's triarchic theory and Gardner's theory of multiple intelligences.

The heritability of intelligence is discussed with respect to twin and adoption studies. Included in this discussion is a description of how to interpret intellectual differences within groups versus between groups. Several environmental factors impacting intelligence are presented. In addition, the effects of attitudes and motivation on intelligence are emphasized through the description of a study comparing Asian and American children. Lastly, a discussion of animal intelligence follows. The area of cognitive ethology is introduced and various studies on language in animals are described.

GUIDED STUDY

1. Thought: Using What We Know

Read the section "Thought: Using What We Know" and then answer the following questions. If you have trouble answering any of the questions, re-study the relevant material before going on to the review of key terms and the matching test.

1-1   Thinking involves the _____ manipulation of internal representations of objects, activities, and situations. One type of mental representation that summarizes information about the world so that it is manageable and so that we can make decisions quickly and efficiently is a _____. An especially representative example of a concept is called a _____. One way in which we represent the relationship of concepts to one another is through the use of _____, units of meaning that express singular ideas. Propositions are linked together in networks of knowledge, associations, beliefs, and expectations called _____ schemas. Another important aspect of thinking is the use of _____ images, especially visual images. It is also believed that people use _____ images and _____ images when thinking.

1-2.   Not all mental processing takes place at a conscious level. _____ processes lie outside of awareness but can be brought into consciousness with little effort. _____ processes on the other hand remain outside of awareness, but can affect our behaviour. Thinking that takes place at a conscious level when we are not thinking very hard or analyzing what we are doing is called _____. Although mindlessness can be beneficial (if we stopped to think about everything that we do we would never get anything done) it can also lead to errors (e.g., driving carelessly while on automatic pilot).

Review of Key Terms

The following is a list of the Key Terms from the section "Thought: Using What We Know." Make sure you are familiar with each term before taking the matching test on these terms.

thinking	proposition	subconscious processes
concept	cognitive schema	mindlessness
prototype	mental image	nonconscious processes

Matching Self Test 1

Match the appropriate term with its definition or description.

1. _____   Mental processes occurring outside of conscious awareness but accessible to consciousness when necessary.

2. _____   An especially representative example of a concept.

3. _____   An integrated mental network of knowledge, beliefs, and expectations concerning a particular topic or aspect of the world.

4. _____   A unit of meaning that is made up of concepts and expresses a single idea.

2. Reasoning Rationally

Read the section "Reasoning Rationally" and then answer the following questions. If you have trouble answering any of the questions, re-study the relevant material before going on to the review of key terms and the matching test.

2-1.   Purposeful mental activity that involves operating on information in order to reach conclusions is referred to as _____. When the information to solve a problem is specified clearly and there is a one correct answer to the problem, the problem is one involving _____ reasoning. Many times formal reasoning problems may be solved by applying a set of procedures guaranteed to produce a solution, an _____. At other times formal reasoning requires that you apply the processes of inductive and _____ reasoning. When a conclusion necessarily follows from certain propositions or premises we are using _____ reasoning; however, when a conclusion *probably* follows from certain propositions or premises, we are using _____ reasoning.

2-2.   Contrary to formal reasoning problems, _____ reasoning problems may involve no clearly correct solution. Sometimes it helps to apply a rule of thumb, a _____, that suggests a course of action without guaranteeing an optimal solution. A person must also be able to evaluate opposing points of view. This involves the ability to reason _____ as juries should.

2-3.   Kitchener and King have studied our ability to use _____ judgment. This involves our ability to _____ and integrate evidence, relate that evidence to a theory or _____, and reach a conclusion that can be defended as _____ or plausible. According to these researchers people in the early stages of reflective thought are said to be _____, they assume a correct answer always exists and that it can be obtained directly through the senses. During the _____-_____ stages people recognize that some things cannot be known with absolute certainty but they are not sure how to deal with these situations. Lastly, when an individual becomes capable of reflective judgment, they understand that although some things can never be known with certainty, some judgments are more valid than others.

Review of Key Terms

The following is a list of the Key Terms from the section "Reasoning Rationally." Make sure you are familiar with each term before taking the matching test on these terms.

reasoning	deductive reasoning	dialectical reasoning
algorithm	inductive reasoning	prereflective judgment
heuristic	formal reasoning	quasi-reflective judgment
premise	informal reasoning	reflective judgment

Matching Self Test 2

Match the appropriate term with its definition or description.

1. _____   A rule of thumb that suggests a course of action or guides problem solving but does not guarantee an optimal solution.

2. _____   The drawing of conclusions or inferences from observations, facts, or assumptions.

3. _____   Reasoning when the information needed for drawing a conclusion or a solution is specified clearly, and there is a single fight (or best) answer.

4. _____   Reasoning when a conclusion probably follows from certain propositions or premises, but it could conceivably be false.

5. _____   A problem-solving strategy guaranteed to produce a solution even if the user does not know how it works.

3. Barriers to Reasoning Rationally

Read the section "Barriers to Reasoning Rationally" and then answer the following questions. If you have trouble answering any of the questions, re-study the relevant material before going on to the review of key terms and the matching test.

3-1.   People have a tendency to exaggerate the probability of very rare events. One manner in which they do this is to use the _____ heuristic, which involves a tendency to judge the probability of an event by how easy it is to think of examples or instances.

3-2.   In research studies on avoiding loss it has been found that people have a tendency to _____ risk when they think of the outcome in terms of lives saved, but _____ risk when they think of the outcome in terms of lives lost.

3-3.   When humans pay more attention to information that confirms what they believe and find fault with evidence to the contrary, they are employing the _____ _____.

3-4.   Problem solving is sometimes made more efficient by using the same heuristic, strategy, or rule that has worked in the past, a _____. Mental sets can also cause us to cling rigidly to the same old assumptions, hypotheses, and strategies, _____ us to better or more rapid solutions.

3-5.   According to psychologists, using the statement "I knew it all along" is an example of _____ _____. This is an individual's tendency to overestimate their ability to have predicted an event once the outcome is known.

3-6.   When in a state of tension due to holding two beliefs that are incompatible or a belief that is incongruent with the person's , Festinger said we were in a state of _____

_____. Three conditions under which we are likely to try to reduce dissonance are: (1) when you feel that you have _____ made a decision; (2) when what you do _____ your self-concept; and (3) when you put a lot of effort into a _____, only to find the results less than you had hoped for.

Review of Key Terms

The following is a list of the Key Terms from the section "Barriers to Reasoning Rationally." Make sure you are familiar with each term before taking the matching test on these terms.

availability heuristic	confirmation bias	hindsight bias
avoidance of loss	mental set	cognitive dissonance

Matching Self Test 3

Match the appropriate term with its definition or description.

1. _____ The tendency to look for or pay attention only to information that confirms one's own belief.

2. _____ A state of tension that occurs when a person simultaneously holds two cognitions that are psychologically inconsistent, or when a person's belief is incongruent with his or her behaviour.

3. _____ The tendency to judge the probability of a type of event by how easy it is to think of examples or instances.

4. _____ The tendency to overestimate one's ability to have predicted an event once the outcome is known.

4. Intelligence

Read the section "Intelligence" and then answer the following questions. If you have trouble answering any of the questions, restudy the relevant material before going on to the review of key terms and the matching test.

4-1. Psychologists have a hard time agreeing on what _____ is. Some feel it involves _____ reasoning, while others feel that it involves the ability to learn and profit from _____. Psychologists also disagree over whether intelligence is based on one factor, a _____, or whether it is determined by multiple factors. Researchers use a statistical technique, _____ _____, to identify which basic abilities underlie intelligence. The traditional approach to studying intelligence that focuses on how well people perform on standardized tests is the _____ approach. Two types of tests assessed by psychometricians are: (1) those that are designed to measure skills and knowledge, _____ tests; and (2) those that are designed to measure the ability to acquire skills or knowledge in the future,

_____ tests. The first intelligence test was developed by _____ and Simon in 1904. This test measured a child's age. A scoring system developed later by others used a formula in which a child's mental age was divided by a child's chronological age to yield an _____ _____. There were problems, however, in the derivation of intelligence quotients, and intelligence test scores are now computed from tables based on established norms. Binet and Simon's test was revised by _____ _____ and named the _____-Binet Intelligence Scale. Another set of intelligence tests were developed by _____. The first was the _____, which was designed for adults. This was followed by the _____, designed for children. Some problems with intelligence testing involve the use of the tests to _____ people rather than to help bring slow learners up to average performance. During the 1970s, group intelligence testing was criticized, hence test makers attempted to develop tests that were culture-_____ in an attempt to eliminate the effects of culture on a test score. This was not successful and test makers thus attempted to develop tests that were culture-_____ in an endeavor to develop tests that incorporate knowledge and skills common to many different cultures. This was also not tremendously successful. Today many school systems have begun to use intelligence testing in the manner Binet originally intended, to identify a child's strengths and weaknesses so that teachers can design individualized programs that will boost the child's performance. Educators also use tests to identify a problem with a specific mental skill and no general intellectual impairment, a _____ disability.

4-2.   An alternative approach to the psychometric approach to intelligence is the _____ approach, that emphasizes the strategies people use when thinking about problems and arriving at a solution. One popular cognitive theory, the _____ theory, was proposed by _____ _____. According to Sternberg there are three aspects to intelligence. _____ intelligence involves the information processing strategies that go on inside your head when you are thinking intelligently. Some of these operations require knowledge and awareness of your own cognitive processes, _____. The second aspect of intelligence according to Sternberg is _____ intelligence. This refers to how _____ you are and how well you _____ skills to new situations. The third aspect of intelligence is _____ intelligence. This refers to the _____ application of intelligence and _____ knowledge, action oriented strategies for success that usually are not formally taught but must instead be inferred. Another cognitive approach to intelligence was proposed by _____ _____ in his theory of _____ intelligences. According to Gardner, there are _____ intelligences. Two of Gardner's intelligences, intrapersonal and interpersonal, correspond to what some psychologists call EQ, _____ intelligence. This is the ability to express your emotions deafly and to regulate emotions in yourself and others.

Review of Key Terms

The following is a list of the Key Terms from the section "Intelligence." Make sure you are familiar with each term before taking the matching test on these terms.

intelligence	Stanford-Binet Scale	metacognition
factor analysis	WAIS	componential intelligence
g factor	WISC	tacit knowledge
psychometric approach	culture-free tests	experiential intelligence
achievement tests	culture-fair tests	multiple intelligences
aptitude tests	learning disability	contextual intelligence
mental age	cognitive approaches	emotional intelligence
intelligence quotient	triarchic theory	

Matching Self Test 4

Match the appropriate term with its definition or description.

1. _____ A measure of mental development expressed in terms of the average mental ability at a given age.

2. _____ A statistical method for analyzing the intercorrelations among various measures of test scores.

3. _____ A measure of intelligence originally computed by dividing a person's mental age by his or her chronological age and multiplying by 100.

4. _____ The knowledge or awareness of one's own cognitive processes.

5. _____ A general intellectual ability assumed by some theorists to underlie specific mental abilities and talents.

6. _____ A cognitive theory on intelligence that proposed three aspects of intelligence.

7. _____ A type of intelligence specified by the triarchic theory that refers to the practical application of intelligence.

8. _____ Tests that measure skills and knowledge that have been explicitly taught.

5. The Origins of Intelligence

Read the section "The Origins of Intelligence" and then answer the following questions. If you have trouble answering any of the questions, re-study the relevant material before going on to the review of key terms and the matching test.

5-1. Behavioural geneticist study the _____ of intelligence, that is, the proportion of the total variance in a trait within a group that is attributable to genetic variation within the group. Heritability estimates for intelligence are about _____. For adults, the estimates are usually higher, from _____ to _____. Twin studies have shown that identical twins reared _____ are more similar in their intelligence scores than are fraternal twins reared _____. And in adoption studies, adopted children are more similar in intelligence level to their _____ parents than they are to their _____ parents. Although genetics can explain some _____ differences in intelligence levels, genetics does not necessarily account for differences _____ groups.

5-2. There are several ways in which the environment can negatively affect mental ability. These include: poor _____ care; poor _____; exposure to _____; large family _____.; and _____ family circumstances. Factors in the environment can also raise mental performance. These include such things as mental _____; reading to children; taking _____ trips; and _____ children to do well.

5-3. Other factors related to intellectual ability are one's _____ and _____. One study comparing American school children to Asian school children found the Asian children outperforming the Americans in many academic areas. These differences could not be accounted for by educational _____, income or _____ level of the parents, or intellectual ability in general. The researchers found instead that Asians and Americans were very different in their _____, _____ and _____. Overall, American parents believed that mathematical ability was _____ and had _____ standards for their children's performance. They also found that American students have more stressful, conflicting demands on their _____ and do not _____ education as much as Asian students do.

Review of Key Terms

The following is a list of the Key Terms from the section "The Origins of Intelligence." Make sure you are familiar with each term before taking the matching test on these terms.

heritability	adoption studies	environmental factors
twin studies	genetic factors	

Matching Self Test 5

Match the appropriate term with its definition or description.

1. _____ Heritability estimates account for these factors in intelligence scores.

2. _____ The proportion of the total variance in a trait within a group that is attributable to genetic variation within the group.

6. Animal Minds

Read the section "Animal Minds " and then answer the following questions. If you have trouble answering any of the questions, re-study the relevant material before going on to the review of key terms and the matching test.

6-1.   The study of cognitive processes in nonhuman animals is _____ _____. Cognitive ethologists argue that some animals can _____ future events, make _____ and _____, and coordinate activities with their _____. Others argue that these complex behaviours may be wired.

6-2.   In a variety of studies, researchers have attempted to teach animals to use _____. Early studies involved attempting to teach _____ to use language. Chimpanzees have "communicated" with geometric plastic shapes, by _____ symbols on a computer-monitored keyboard, and by using American _____ language. Many of these early studies, however, were flawed. Today, better controlled experiments have established that with training, chimps can acquire the ability to use _____ to refer to _____. In further studies, _____ have been taught to respond to requests made in two artificial languages and one researcher has even taught an African _____ _____ to count, classify, and compare objects. Scientist are concerned, however, about the tendency to falsely attribute human qualities to nonhuman beings, _____. On the other hand, others warn of _____, the tendency to think that human beings have nothing in common with other animals.

Review of Key Terms

The following is a list of the Key Terms from the section "Animal Minds. " Make sure you are familiar with each term before taking the matching test on these terms.

cognitive ethology   anthropocentrism   anthropomorphism

Matching Self Test 6

Match the appropriate term with its definition or description.

1. _____ The tendency to falsely attribute human qualities to nonhuman beings.

2. _____ The study of cognitive processes in nonhuman animals.

SAMPLE ANSWERS TO *WHAT'S AHEAD* QUESTIONS FROM TEXTBOOK

After you have completed the "Looking Back" section at the end of the chapter by answering the "What's Ahead" questions that preceded each major section of the chapter, compare your answers to the following sample answers. If your answers are not similar to the sample answers, review the pertinent sections of the chapter. The relevant page(s) for each question is(are) provided in the "looking Back" section in the text.

When you think of a bird, why are you more likely to recall a robin than a penguin?

You are more likely to think of a robin because a robin is a prototypical bird, and a penguin is not. Our concepts are organized around the prototypical instances of the concept, and therefore we are more likely to think of these instances when we think of the concept.

How are visual images like images on a television screen?

Visual images are like images on a television screen because we can manipulate them, they occur in a mental "space" of a fixed size, and small ones contain less detail than larger ones.

What's happening mentally when you mistakenly bring your geography notes to your psychology class?

You are engaging in what Ellen Langer terms "mindless" behaviour. This mindlessness keeps people from recognizing when a change in context requires a change in behaviour.

Mentally speaking, why is making a cake—well, a piece of cake?

Making a cake is a piece of cake because all we have to do is apply a recipe, which is an algorithm—a set of procedures guaranteed to produce a solution.

Why can't logic solve all problems?

Logic cannot solve all of life's problems because for informal reasoning problems, there may be no clearly correct solution. In informal reasoning problems, many approaches, viewpoints, or possible solutions may compete, and you may have to decide which one is most reasonable, based on what you know.

What kind of reasoning do juries need to be good at?

Dialectical reasoning is what juries are supposed to do to arrive at a verdict: consider arguments for and against the defendant's guilt, point and counterpoint. Dialectical reasoning is the ability to evaluate opposing points of view.

When people say that all opinions and claims are equally valid, what error are they making?

They are engaging in quasi-reflective thinking in which everyone has a right to their own opinion and all opinions are created equal. They should use reflective thinking in which some judgments are better than others because of their coherence, their fit with the evidence, their usefulness, and so on.

Why do people worry about dying in an airplane crash but ignore dangers that are far more likely?

One reason is the use of the availability heuristic, the tendency to judge the probability of an event by how easy it is to think of examples or instances. Catastrophes stand out in our minds and are therefore more available than other kinds of negative events. Thus, people incorrectly think that the likelihood of dying in an airplane crash (a very available event because such crashes always make the headlines) is greater than for other less available but more probable dangers (e.g., dying from disease).

How might a physician's choice of words affect which treatment you choose?

Our decision may be affected by whether the doctor frames the choice in terms of chances of surviving or chances of dying. When a choice is framed in terms of risk, we respond more cautiously than when the same choice is framed in terms of gain. Thus, the physician should be careful to frame all medical choices in terms of survival rates in order for the patient to make the best choice.

When "Monday morning quarterbacks" say they knew all along who would win Sunday's big game, what bias might they be showing?

They might be showing the hindsight bias, the tendency to overestimate one's ability to have predicted an event once the outcome is known. This bias is also sometimes called the "I knew it all along" phenomenon.

Why will a terrible hazing make you more loyal to the group that hazed you?

You will become more loyal to the group as a result of making your cognition about your behaviour (undergoing the hazing to join the group) consistent with your cognition about your attitude toward the group to eliminate cognitive dissonance. Your cognition about going through the hazing is dissonant with the cognition that you hate the group. Thus, you must really like this group. This mental reevaluation is called the justification of effort and is one of the most popular methods of reducing dissonance.

Is it possible to design intelligence tests that aren't influenced by culture?

Several test-makers have tried to construct culture-free and culture-fair intelligence tests but with little success. Culture affects performance. Cultural values affect a person's attitude toward taking tests, comfort while being tested, motivation, rapport with the test-giver, competitiveness, and experience in solving problems independently rather than with others. Moreover, cultures differ in the problem-solving strategies they emphasize.

Why do some psychologists oppose traditional intelligence testing and others defend it?

Most educators feel that the tests have value, as long as a person's background is kept in mind and the results are interpreted cautiously. IQ tests predict school performance fairly well. Critics argue that when a child's abilities don't match those expected by teachers and testers, the best solution may be to modify the classroom or the test. They also point out that standardized tests don't reveal how a person goes about answering questions and solving problems. Nor do the tests explain why people with low scores often behave intelligently in real life. Intelligence tests put some groups of children at a disadvantage, yet they also measure skills and knowledge useful in school and in the larger society. Thus, there are two sides to this argument.

What kind of intelligence allows you to master the "unspoken rules" for academic success?

That which Robert Steinberg terms "contextual intelligence" allows you to master the "unspoken rules" for academic success. Contextual intelligence refers to the practical application of intelligence. Without it, you won't have the practical savvy that allows you to pick up important tacit knowledge, which is not formally taught but must be inferred.

What's your "EQ—and why is it as important as IQ?

"EQ" refers to your emotional intelligence, the ability to identify your own and other people's emotions accurately, express your emotions clearly, and regulate emotions in yourself and others. It is important because people with high EQ use their emotions to motivate themselves and others, to spur creative thinking, and to deal empathically with others. Emotional intelligence also contributes to academic achievement.

If intelligence is highly heritable, does that mean that group differences in IQ are genetic?

No, it doesn't. Although intellectual differences within groups are at least partially genetic, that does not mean that differences between groups are genetic. The various ethnic groups do not grow up, on the average, in the same environments. This fact greatly limits our ability to judge the genetic contribution to between-group differences.

Is a child with a low IQ destined to have a low score throughout life?

No, a healthy and stimulating environment can raise mental performance. Although heredity may provide the range of a child's intellectual potential, many other factors affect where in that range the child will fall.

Some gifted people are professionally successful and others aren't; what makes the difference?

Based on the results of the study of the gifted "Termites," motivation seems to make the difference. The successful men were ambitious, were socially active, had many interests, and were encouraged by their parents. The least successful drifted casually through life. There was no average difference in IQ between the two groups.

Why do Asian children do so much better in school than American students, even though Asian classes are larger, with worse facilities?

Research has shown that Asians and Americans are worlds apart in their attitudes, expectations, and efforts. For example, Americans are far more likely to believe that ability is innate and that if you don't have it, there's no point in trying. American parents have far lower standards for their children's performance than Asian parents do. American students have more stressful, conflicting demands on their time than their Asian counterparts do. American students do not value education as much as Asian students do and are more complacent about mediocre work. These factors then help account for the differences in academic performance.

Why do some researchers think that animals can think, and others remain skeptical?

Cognitive ethologists argue that some animals can anticipate future events, make plans and choices, and coordinate their activities with those of their comrades. The versatility of these animals in meeting new challenges in the environment suggests to these researchers that the animals are capable of thought. Other scientists are not so sure, noting that even complex behaviour can be genetically prewired. We may be reading too much cognition into an animal's behaviour. In addition, an animal could be aware of its environment and know some things without knowing that it knows and without being able to think about its own thoughts in the way that humans do.

Everyone loves to talk to their pets—but can their pets learn to talk back?

It depends upon what you mean by "talk." It is certainly not possible in the normal sense of the word. Several researchers, however, have used visual symbol systems or American Sign Language to teach primates language skills, and some animals (even some nonprimates) seem able to use simple grammatical ordering rules to convey meaning. However, scientists are still divided as to how to interpret these findings.

Multiple-Choice Progress Test

Choose the single best answer for each of the following questions. When you have finished this progress test, check your answers with those at the end of the chapter. You should review the indicated pages in the text for the questions you do not answer correctly.

1. Which of the following is the correct ordering of units of thought from simplest to most complex?
    a. concepts-propositions-cognitive schemas
    b. propositions-concepts-cognitive schemas
    c. cognitive schemas-concepts-propositions
    d. cognitive schemas-propositions-concepts

2. Intuition is described in the text as an orderly process involving two stages. The first stage involves _____ processes.
    a. subconscious
    b. nonconscious
    c. Freud's unconscious
    d. conscious

3. Deducing that the conclusion *I am mortal* must necessarily follow from the premises *All human beings are mortal* and *I am a human being* is an example of _____ reasoning.
    a. dialectical
    b. informal
    c. deductive
    d. inductive

4. Which of the following is NOT a characteristic of informal reasoning?
    a. There are typically several possible answers that vary in quality.
    b. Established methods often exist for solving the problem.
    c. Some premises are implicit and some are not supplied at all.

116

d. None of the above

5.   According to King and Kitchener, people who assume that a correct answer always exists and that it can be obtained directly through the senses are in the _____ stages of reflective thought.
a. pre-reflective
b. quasi-reflective
c. reflective
d. dialectical

6.   When people overestimate the frequency of deaths from tornadoes and underestimate the frequency of deaths from asthma, they are most likely _____.
a. using the availability heuristic
b. using dialectical thinking
c. demonstrating hindsight bias
d. demonstrating confirmation bias

7.   If a doctor says that there is a 10% chance of survival given Treatment X and a 90% chance of dying given Treatment Y, people usually choose Treatment _____ because _____.
a. X; this alternative is framed in terms of gain
b. Y; this alternative is framed in terms of gain
c. X; they are using the availability heuristic
d. Y; they are using the availability heuristic

8.   The difficulty that people have with the 9-dot problem given in the text illustrates _____.
a. cognitive dissonance
b. confirmation bias
c. hindsight bias
d. mental set

9.   Which of the following conditions is NOT one under which you are likely to try to reduce cognitive dissonance?
a. when you feel that you have freely made a decision
b. when what you do does not violate your self concept
c. when you put a lot of effort into a decision only to find the results less than you had hoped for
d. none of the above

10. Which of the following intelligence test developers devised the Stanford-Binet Intelligence Test?
a. Binet
b. Terman

c. Wechsler

d. Steinberg

11. Using the IQ formula, an eight-year-old child with a mental age of a six-year-old child would have an IQ of _____.

    a. 50

    b. 75

    c. 100

    d. 125

12. Which of the following statements about intelligence testing is FALSE?

    a. Rather than using the IQ formula, intelligence test scores today are computed from tables based on established norms.

    b. Attempts to design culture-free and culture-fair intelligence tests have not been very successful.

    c. To eliminate earlier-observed sex differences on the Stanford-Binet intelligence test, the items leading to these differences were deleted.

    d. None of the above

13. The psychometric approach is to the cognitive approach to intelligence as _____ is to _____.

    a. Terman; Steinberg

    b. Steinberg; Terman

    c. Binet; Terman

    d. Terman; Binet

14. According to the triarchic theory of intelligence, _____ intelligence refers to how creative you are and how well you transfer skills to new situations.

    a. componential

    b. emotional

    c. contextual

    d. experiential

15. Which of the following researchers on intelligence proposes seven "intelligences"?

    a. Binet

    b. Gardner

    c. Steinberg

    d. Wechsler

16. Which of the following statements about emotional intelligence (EQ) is FALSE?

    a. Although important to our personality development, EQ does not contribute to school achievement.

    b. People who have low EQs misread nonverbal signals from others.

c. People who have high EQs use their emotions to motivate themselves and to spur creative thinking.

d. None of the above

17. Which of the following statements about heritability and intelligence test scores is FALSE?

    a. The kind of intelligence that produces high IQ scores is highly heritable.

    b. For adults, the estimates of heritability are higher than for children and adolescents.

    c. If intellectual differences within each of two groups are due to genetics, then the differences between the groups must also be due to genetics.

    d. None of the above

18. Which of the following statements about environmental deficits that hinder intellectual development is FALSE?

    a. Lead can damage the nervous system, producing lower IQ scores.

    b. The average IQ in a family tends to increase as the number of children in the family rises.

    c. On average, each family risk factor reduces a child's IQ score by four points.

    d. None of the above

19. Based on the results of the study of the "Termites," which of the following factors led to success?

    a. high IQ

    b. high EQ

    c. motivation

    d. logical thinking

20. Which of the following statements about Asians and North Americans is FALSE?

    a. North American parents have far lower standards for their children's school performance than Asian parents do.

    b. North American students have more stressful, conflicting demands on their time than their Asian counterparts do.

    c. North American students do not value education as much as Asian students do.

    d. None of the above

ANSWERS

GUIDED STUDY

1. Thought: Using What We Know

1.1.   mental   propositions   auditory

119

| concept | cognitive | kinesthetic |
| prototype | mental | |

1.2.   Subconscious   Nonconscious   mindlessness

Matching Self-Test 1

| 1. subconscious processes | 3. cognitive schema |
| 2. prototype | 4. proposition |

---

2.   Reasoning Rationally

| 2.1. | reasoning | algorithm | deductive |
| | formal | deductive | inductive |

| 2.2. | informal | heuristic | dialectically |

| 2.3. | reflective | opinion | prereflective |
| | evaluate | reasonable | quasi-reflective |

Matching Self-Test 2

| 1. heuristic | 3. formal reasoning | 5. algorithm |
| 2. reasoning | 4. inductive reasoning | |

---

3.   Barriers to Reasoning Rationally

3.1.	availability	3.2.	reject	3.3.	confirmation bias
			accept		
3.4.	mental set	3.5.	hindsight bias		
	blinding				
3.6.	cognitive dissonance	violates			
	freely	decision			

Matching Self-Test 3

| 1. confirmation bias | 3. availability heuristic |
| 2. cognitive dissonance | 4. hindsight bias |

---

4. Intelligence

4.1.
intelligence	aptitude	Wechsler
logical	Binet	WAIS
experience	mental	WISC
g factor	intelligence	categorize
factor analysis	quotient	free
psychometric	Lewis Terman	fair
achievement	Stanford	learning

4.2.
cognitive	experiential	tacit
triarchic	creative	Howard Gardner
Robert Steinberg	transfer	multiple
Componential	contextual	seven
metacognition	practical	emotional

Matching Self-Test 4

1. mental age	4. metacognition	7. contextual intelligence
2. factor analysis	5. g factor	8. achievement tests
3. intelligence quotient	6. triarchic theory	

5. The Origin of Intelligence

5.1.
heritability	apart	individual
.50	together	between
.60	biological	
.80	adoptive	

5.2.
prenatal	size	field
nutrition	stressful	expecting
toxins	enrichment	

5.3.
attitudes	attitudes	lower
motivation	expectations	time
resources	efforts	value
education	innate	

Matching Self-Test 5

1. genetic factors	2. heritability

6. Animal Minds

6.1.   cognitive ethology   plans   comrades
           anticipate   choices   genetically

6.2.   language   symbols   gray
           chimpanzees   objects   anthropomorphism
           punching   dolphins   anthropocentrism
           sign   parrot

Matching Self-Test 6

1. anthropomorphism   2. cognitive ethology

ANSWERS TO MULTIPLE CHOICE PROGRESS TEST

Item No.	Answers	Page(s) in Textbook
1.	a concepts-propositions-cognitive schemas	196-197
2.	b. nonconscious	198
3.	c. deductive	199-200
4.	b. Established methods often exist for solving the problem	200
5.	a. pre-reflective	201-202
6.	a. using the availability heuristic	204
7.	a X; this alternative is framed in terms of gain	205
8.	d. mental set	207
9.	b When what you do does not violate your self concept.	208-209
10.	b. Terman	212
11.	b. 75	211
12.	d. None of the above	212, 215
13.	a. Terman; Sternberg	209, 216
14.	d. experiential	216
15.	b. Gardner	216
16.	a. Although important to our personality development, EQ does not contribute to school achievement.	217
17.	c. If intellectual differences within each of two groups are due to genetics, then the differences between the two groups must also be due to genetics.	219-220
18.	b. The average IQ in a family tends to increase as the number of children in the family rises.	221
19.	c. motivation	222
20.	d. None of the above	223 - 224

CHAPTER 7

Memory

CHAPTER OVERVIEW

The chapter opens with a discussion of the accuracies and inaccuracies of memory. This includes consideration of the reconstructive nature of memory, hypnosis and memory, flashbulb memories, and eyewitness testimony. Various methods of measuring memory are covered, including recall versus recognition tests of memory. The different types of memory tests are also related to explicit versus implicit memory.

The information processing model of memory is covered in some detail. This includes coverage of sensory memories, short-term memory, and long-term memory. The limitations and functioning of each of these memory structures is covered in some detail. Key distinctions such as procedural versus declarative memory and semantic versus episodic memory are also introduced. Mechanisms for remembering information are also presented. These include elaborative encoding, deep processing, and mnemonic strategies.

Theories of forgetting such as decay theory, interference theory, and motivating forgetting are described. There is also a discussion of autobiographical memories, including topics such as childhood amnesia and the "reminiscence bump."

GUIDED STUDY

1. Reconstructing the Past

Read the section "Reconstructing the Past" and then answer the following questions. If you have trouble answering any of the questions, re-study the relevant material before going on to the review of key terms and the matching test.

1-1.   The idea that memory was not like replaying a film but more like watching a few unconnected frames and trying to figure out what the rest of the scene must have been was put forth by _____, who concluded that memory is largely a _____ process. This reconstructive nature of memory is referred to by psychologists as _____. When attempting to recall events, we may have a difficult time separating our original experience from what we added after the fact. This phenomenon is referred to as _____ _____. Misremembering or false memories are most likely to occur under certain circumstances—(1) you have thought about the

123

imagined event _____ times, (2) the image of the event contains a lot of _____, (3) the event is _____ to imagine, and (4) you focus on your _____ reactions to the event rather than on what actually happened.

1-2.   Although hypnosis can sometimes be successful in jogging people's memories, it also frequently leads to an increased number of _____ in memory. In addition, although many therapists believe that it is possible to use age _____, a study by Nash found that most people are basically playing a _____ when they are regressed to either an earlier age or a supposed past life and when they are progressed ahead to an older age. In another study, Spanos attempted to use hypnosis to regress college students to past lives. The descriptions given by the students of their past lives included persons from their _____ lives and were influenced by what the _____ told them.

1-3.   The vivid recollections of surprising, shocking, or tragic events were labeled _____ memories by Brown and Kulik. Research has indicated, however, that these memories are not as accurate as once thought. Facts tend to get mixed up with a little _____.

1-4.   As the accounts of eyewitnesses play a vital role in the justice system, the accuracy of the eyewitness's memory is very important. Because memory is _____, eyewitness testimony is not always reliable. In a classic study by Loftus and Palmer on _____ questions, subjects' estimates of the _____ of two cars involved in an accident varied depending on the way the questions were phrased. More recent research on leading questions and child sexual abuse has addressed whether children's memories are accurate. It was concluded that, children, like adults, can be _____ in what they report; and, also like adults, they can be _____.

Review of Key Terms

The following is a list of the Key Terms from the section "Reconstructing the Past." Make sure you are familiar with each term before taking the matching test on these terms.

Confabulation   age regression   flashbulb memories

reconstructive memory   age progression

source amnesia   leading questions

Matching Self Test 1

Match the appropriate term with its definition or description.

1. _____ The inability to distinguish what you originally experienced from what you heard or were told about an event later.

2. _____ Altering memory in ways that help us make sense of the material based on what we already know, or think we know.

3. _____ Reliving early memories under hypnosis.

4. _____ Memories of shocking, surprising, or tragic events that seem frozen in time with all of the details intact.

2. Measuring Memory

Read the section "Measuring Memory" and then answer the following questions. If you have trouble answering any of the questions, re-study the relevant material before going on to the review of key terms and the matching test.

2-1.   When we consciously recollect a memory, we are using _____ memory. This can be measured using tests that require retrieval of information, _____ tests, or tests that require identification of information, _____ tests. Examples of recall tests include fill-in-the-blank and _____ tests, whereas examples of recognition tests include _____-_____ and multiple-choice tests. In general, _____ tests are easier than _____ tests. This was demonstrated in a study in which people first tried to recall the names of their high school classmates. Recall _____ as age of the participants increased. In contrast, recognition of the classmates names and faces was similar across ages. When information learned previously affects our thoughts and actions and we do not consciously remember it, we are said to be using _____ memory. One way of examining implicit memory is to use a _____ task in which you are presented with information and later tested to see if the information affects your performance on another type of task. Hermann _____ used the _____ method, or savings method, to measure memory. This method requires that you relearn information you have learned at some previous time. If you relearn the information _____ than you learned it initially, you must be remembering something from the prior learning experience. Some researchers consider this an _____ memory task, whereas others consider this an implicit memory task.

Review of Key Terms

The following is a list of the Key Terms from the section "Measuring Memory." Make sure you are familiar with each term before taking the matching test on these terms.

explicit memory   implicit memory   relearning method

recall   priming

recognition   Ebbinghaus

Matching Self Test 2

Match the appropriate term with its definition or description.

1. _____   The ability to retrieve and reproduce from memory previously encountered material.

2. _____   A method for measuring implicit memory in which a person reads or listens to information and is later tested to see whether the information affects performance on another type of task.

3. _____   Conscious, intentional recollection of an event or an item of information.

4. _____   A method for measuring retention that compares the time required to relearn material with the time used in the initial learning of the material.

3. The Three-Box Model of Memory

Read the section "The Three-Box Model of Memory" and then answer the following questions. If you have trouble answering any of the questions, re-study the relevant material before going on to the review of key terms and the matching test.

3-1.   The _____-_____ model of memory borrows from the language of computer programming. According to the information-processing model, we have the capability to encode, _____, and retrieve information. The information-processing model posits three types of memory and is often referred to as the three-_____ model of memory,. _____ memory retains incoming sensory information for one or two seconds. _____-_____ memory holds a limited amount of information for about 3 0 seconds. Lastly, _____-_____ memory holds information for a few minutes to decades. A more recent model of memory, the _____ _____ processing (PDP) model, says that knowledge is represented as connections among thousands of interacting processing units distributed in a vast network and operating in parallel.

3-2.   According to the three-box model of memory, the entryway of memory is _____ memory. As there are many senses, sensory memory is made up of many subsystems or sensory _____. The visual register holds visual images or _____ for about _____ second. The auditory register holds

_____ for about _____ seconds. The process of _____ recognition occurs during the transfer of information from memory to _____-_____ memory.

3-3. Short-term memory (STM) holds information for approximately _____ seconds. In H.M., _____ memory is functioning. He cannot, however, retain _____ information because he cannot transfer explicit memories from _____ to long-term memory (LTM). STM is also referred to as _____ memory because when we retrieve information from LTM, it is held in STM in order for us to "work" on it. STM is often described as a "leaky bucket" because it has a very limited capacity of approximately _____ items. Frequently we can take several pieces of information and _____ them into larger units in order to hold more information in STM.

3-4. The third box in the three-box model is _____. As there is a vast amount of information stored in LTM, it must be organized in some manner. One manner in which it may be organized is based on _____ categories. This idea was supported by the case of M. D., who had a series of strokes that left him with the inability to identify _____ or _____. One description of semantic organization in LTM posits _____ models, conceptual grids for storing related information. We also organize information in LTM based on the way words sound or look. For example, when trying to retrieve information that is on the _____ of the tongue (TOT), we frequently recall not only words with similar _____, but also words that _____ similar. The contents of LTM are stored based on information related to "knowing how" to do something, _____ memories, and information related to "knowing that," _____ memories. Procedural memories are considered to be _____ and declarative memories are considered to be _____. There are two types of declarative memories, _____ memories, internal representations of the world independent of any particular context, and _____ memories, internal representations of personally experienced events. The three-box model can also explain the _____-_____ effect, the retention of any particular item depending on its position in a list. Recall is usually best for information at the beginning of the list, the _____ effect, and for the information at the end of the list, the _____ effect. According to the three-box model, the information at the beginning of the list is remembered because it has the best chance of getting into _____, and the information at the end of the list is well remembered because is it still in _____.

Review of Key Terms

The following is a list of the Key Terms from the section "The Three-Box Model of Memory." Make sure you are familiar with each term before taking the matching test on these terms.

information-processing models   pattern recognition   declarative memories

encoding   short-term memory   semantic memories

storage   working memory   episodic memories

retrieval   chunks   serial-position effect

three-box model   long-term memory   primacy effect

PDP models   semantic categories   recency effect

sensory memory   network models

icons   TOT state

echoes   procedural memories

Matching Self Test 3

Match the appropriate term with its definition or description.

1. _____ A memory system that momentarily preserves extremely accurate images of sensory information.

2. _____ Memories of facts, rules, concepts, and events ("knowing that").

3. _____ A meaningful unit of information; it may be composed of smaller units.

4. _____ An alternative to the information-processing model of memory, in which knowledge is represented as connections among thousands of interacting processing units, distributed in a vast network, and all operating in parallel.5. _____ Memories of general knowledge, including facts, rules, concepts, and propositions.

6. _____ The tendency for recall of the first and last items on a list to surpass recall of items in the middle of the list.

7. _____ In the three-box model of memory, the memory system involved in the long-term storage of information.

8. _____ Memories for the performance of actions or skills ("knowing how").

4. How We Remember

Read the section "How We Remember" and then answer the following questions. If you have trouble answering any of the questions, re-study the relevant material before going on to the review of key terms and the matching test.

4-1. In order to remember information well, it has to be _____. Some information will be encoded _____ without effort, but most information requires _____ encoding, it has to be labeled, associated with personal information, or rehearsed until it is familiar.

4-2. _____ is an important technique for keeping information in STM and for transferring information to LTM. Without rehearsal, the information in STM fades within _____ seconds. There are two types of rehearsal, the rote repetition of material, _____ rehearsal, and associating new items of information with material that has already been stored, _____ rehearsal. This latter type of rehearsal is better for long-term retention. For such retention, it is also important to process information for meaning, _____ processing. This is a better approach than simply processing information based on physical or sensory features, _____ processing.

4-3. Another strategy for improving memory is to use formal strategies and tricks for encoding, storing, and retaining information called _____. Mnemonics can involve rhymes, _____, visual images, or _____ associations.

Review of Key Terms

The following is a list of the Key Terms from the section "How We Remember." Make sure you are familiar with each term before taking the matching test on these terms.

automatic encoding	maintenance rehearsal	mnemonics
effortful encoding	shallow processing	
elaborative rehearsal	deep processing	

Matching Self Test 4

Match the appropriate term with its definition or description.

1. _____ Association of new information with already stored knowledge and analysis of the new information to make it memorable.

2. _____ Strategies and tricks for improving memory, such as the use of a verse or a formula.

3. _____ In the encoding of information, the processing of meaning rather than simply the physical or sensory features of a stimulus.

4. _____ The processing of information involving labeling concepts, associating the information with personal experiences, or rehearsing information until it is familiar.

5. Why We Forget

Read the section "Why We Forget" and then answer the following questions. If you have trouble answering any of the questions, restudy the relevant material before going on to the review of key terms and the matching test.

5-1. There are several explanations of why we forget information. One view, _____ theory, holds that memory traces fade with time if they are not used occasionally. This theory alone, however, cannot explain all forgetting in LTM.

5-2. A second explanation holds that _____ information can replace _____ information. This view was supported by a study in which subjects were misled by the use of _____ questions to think that they had previously seen a stop sign rather than a _____ sign in slides of traffic accidents.

5-3. A third explanation holds that forgetting occurs because similar items of information _____ with one another in either storage or retrieval. When new information interferes with old information, _____ interference has taken place. When old information interferes with new information, _____ interference has taken place.

5-4. What Freud referred to as _____, psychologists today refer to as _____ forgetting, the forgetting of events that are embarrassing, painful, or shocking.

5-5. When trying to remember, we very often rely on retrieval _____. When memory fails due to a lack of cues, we are experiencing _____-_____ forgetting. A mental or physical state can also act as a memory cue. This is called _____-_____ memory. There is also some evidence that _____ may serve as a retrieval cue.

Review of Key Terms

The following is a list of the Key Terms from the section "Why We Forget." Make sure you are familiar with each term before taking the matching test on these terms.

decay theory   proactive interference   cue-dependent forgetting

retroactive interference   motivated forgetting   state-dependent memory

repression   retrieval cues

Matching Self Test 5

Match the appropriate term with its definition or description.

1. _____ Forgetting that occurs when previously stored material interferes with the ability to remember similar, more recently learned material.

2. _____ The theory that information in memory eventually disappears if it is not accessed; it applies more to short-term than to long-term memory.

3. _____ Forgetting that occurs because of a desire to eliminate awareness of painful, embarrassing, or otherwise unpleasant experiences.

4. _____ The tendency to remember something when the rememberer is in the same physical or mental state as during the original learning or experience.

6. Autobiographical Memory

Read the section "Autobiographical Memory" and then answer the following questions. If you have trouble answering any of the questions, re-study the relevant material before going on to the review of key terms and the matching test.

6-1.   Our memories about our own lives are called _____ memories. Most people have no autobiographical memories for events earlier than the _____ or _____ year of life. This is referred to as _____ or infantile _____. Freud thought that childhood amnesia was due to _____. Biological researchers today, however, feel that childhood amnesia is due to the fact that _____ areas involved in the formation or storage of events are not developed enough during the first few years of life. There are also cognitive explanations for childhood amnesia. These include (1) lack of a sense of _____, (2) differences between early and later cognitive _____, (3) impoverished _____, and (4) a focus on the _____.

6-2.   The elderly remember more from _____ and early adulthood then from _____. This phenomenon is known as the _____ bump.

Review of Key Terms

The following is a list of the Key Terms from the section "Autobiographical Memory." Make sure you are familiar with each term before taking the matching test on these terms.

autobiographical memory   infantile amnesia   childhood amnesia

reminiscence bump

Matching Self Test 6

Match the appropriate term with its definition or description.

1. _____   The inability to remember events and experiences that occurred during the first two or three years of life.

2. _____   The tendency for the elderly to remember events from adolescence and early adulthood better than those from midlife.

_____

SAMPLE ANSWERS TO *WHAT'S AHEAD* QUESTIONS FROM TEXTBOOK

After you have completed the "Looking Back" section at the end of the chapter by answering the "What's Ahead" questions that preceded each major section of the chapter, compare your answers to the following sample answers. If your answers are not similar to the sample answers, review the pertinent sections of the chapter. The relevant page(s) for each question is(are) provided in the ''Looking Back" section in the text.

What's wrong with thinking of memory as a mental movie camera?

Unlike a movie camera, human memory is highly selective and largely a reconstructive process. It is more like watching a few unconnected frames and then figuring out what the rest of the scene must have been like rather than replaying a film of an event. People add, delete, and change elements in ways that help them make sense of information and events.

If you have a strong emotional reaction to a remembered event, does that mean your memory is accurate?

Emotional reactions to an imagined event can resemble those that would have occurred in response to a real event, and so they can mislead us. This means that your strong feelings about an event, no matter how strongly you hold them, are not a reliable cue to the event's reality.

Do people remember better when they're hypnotized?

Sometimes, hypnosis can indeed be used successfully to jog people's memories. But in other cases, hypnotized witnesses, despite feeling completely confident about their memories, have been completely mistaken. It turns out that although hypnosis does sometimes boost the amount of information recalled, it also increases errors, perhaps because hypnotized people are more willing to guess or because they mistake vividly imagined possibilities for actual memories.

Why do "flashbulb memories" of surprising or shocking events sometimes have less wattage than we assume?

Despite their intensity, flashbulb memories are not always complete or accurate records of the past. Like other memories, they often grow dim with time. Facts tend to get mixed with a little fiction. Even with flashbulb memories, remembering is an active process, one that involves not only dredging up stored information but also putting two and two together to reconstruct the past.

Can the question a person asks you about a past event affect what you remember about it?

Yes, it certainly can. Eyewitness accounts are heavily influenced by the way in which questions are put to the witness. Research has shown differences in eyewitness accounts due to the particular words used in the questions asked by the researchers. People have even been induced by leading questions to reconstruct complicated personal events that never happened.

In general, which is easier: a multiple-choice item or a short-answer essay item—and why?

A multiple-choice item calls for recognition whereas a short-answer essay item requires recall. Although multiple-choice items can be very difficult when the distractors closely resemble the correct alternative, under most conditions recognition is easier than recall. Thus, multiple-choice items are usually easier than short-answer essay items because they only require recognition and not recall.

Can you know something without knowing that you know it?

Sometimes information that we have encountered affects our thoughts and actions even though we do not consciously or intentionally remember it. This is a phenomenon known as implicit memory. To get at this subtle sort of knowledge, researchers must rely on indirect methods, such as priming in which people show that they know more than they know that they know.

Why is the computer often used as a metaphor for the mind?

Many cognitive psychologists liken the mind to an information processor, along the lines of a computer, though more complex. This metaphor is often used because both the computer and the mind encode, store, and retrieve information. In a computer, when you type something in on your keyboard, the machine encodes the information into an electronic language, stores it on a disk, and retrieves it when you need to use it. Similarly, in information-processing models of memory, we encode information by converting it to a form that the brain can understand, store the information, and retrieve it later when we need to use it. Some cognitive scientists, however, have pointed out a crucial difference between the mind and the computer. Most computers process instructions sequentially and work on a single stream of data whereas the human brain performs many operations in parallel. Because of this difference, recent information-processing models of the mind assume parallel distributed processing.

133

Why is short-term memory like a leaky bucket?

Short-term memory has been called a "leaky bucket" because information in short-term memory is in such a fragile state that if a person is distracted, the information is forgotten (it has leaked from the bucket). If the bucket did not leak, however, it would overflow quickly because the capacity of short-term memory is very small.

When a word is on the tip of your tongue, what errors are you likely to make in recalling it?

When a word is on the tip of your tongue, you are likely to come up with incorrect words that are similar in meaning to the fight one or incorrect guesses that have the correct number of syllables, the correct stress pattern, the correct first letter, or the correct prefix or suffix.

What's the difference between "knowing how" and "knowing that"?

Memories of "knowing how" are procedural memories, which are implicit. Once skills and habits are well learned, they do not require much conscious processing. Memories of "knowing that" are declarative memories, which are explicit and thus require conscious processing. Declarative memories come in two types—episodic memories (personal recollections) and semantic memories (general knowledge).

What's wrong with trying to memorize in a rote fashion when you're studying and what's a better strategy?

Maintenance rehearsal (memorizing in a rote fashion) is fine for keeping information in short-term memory, but it will not always lead to long-term retention. A better strategy is elaborative rehearsal. This involves associating new items of information with material that has already been stored or with other new facts. You should also engage in the related strategy of deep processing, or the processing of meaning.

Memory tricks are fun but are they always useful?

No, they are not always useful. Such tricks are often no more effective than rote rehearsal, and sometimes they are actually worse. Most memory researchers do not use such mnemonics themselves.

How might new information "erase" old memories?

New information might wipe out old information, just as rerecording on an audio tape or videotape will obliterate the original material.

What theory explains why you keep dialing an old area code instead of the one that has replaced it?

The interference theory of forgetting would explain this behaviour. In this case, old information (the old area code) is interfering with the ability to remember new information (your new area code). This type of interference is called proactive interference.

Why is it easier to recall experiences from elementary school if you see pictures of your classmates?

It is easier because the pictures of your classmates provide retrieval cues that can help us find the specific information that we are looking for. Retrieval cues may work by getting us into the general area of memory where an item is stored, or by making a match with information that is linked in memory with the item in question.

Why are the first few years of life a mental blank?

We are victims of childhood amnesia in that we cannot remember any events from earlier than the third or fourth year of our lives. Freud thought that childhood amnesia was due to repression, but biological researchers argue that it occurs because brain areas involved in the formation or storage of events are not well developed until a few years after birth. Cognitive explanations include lack of a sense of self, differences between early and later cognitive schemas, impoverished encoding, and a focus on the routine.

Which periods of life tend to stand out in memory?

As we age, certain periods of our lives tend to stand out; old people remember more from adolescence and early adulthood than from midlife, a phenomenon known as the "reminiscence bump." Perhaps the younger years are especially memorable because they are full of memorable transitions. It is also possible that people are especially likely to weave events from their youth into a coherent story and thus remember them better.

MULTIPLE-CHOICE PROGRESS TEST

Choose the single best answer for each of the following questions. When you have finished this progress test, check your answers with those at the end of the chapter. You should review the indicated pages in the text for the questions you do not answer correctly.

1. Which of the following statements about human memory is (are) TRUE?
    a. Human memory works like a tape recorder.
    b. Human memory usually allows us to recall information by rote.
    c. Human memory is largely a reconstructive process.
    d. Both (a) and (b)

2. The inability to distinguish what you originally experienced from what you heard or were told about an event later is called _____.
    a. motivated forgetting
    b. source amnesia
    c. priming
    d. cue-dependent forgetting

3. Confabulation for the memory of an event is most likely to occur when:
    a. you have thought about the imagined event often.
    b. the image of the event is not very detailed.
    c. the event is difficult to image.
    d. you focus on what actually happened and not your emotional reactions to the event.

4. Which of the following statements about human memory is FALSE?
    a. Pseudomemories and errors are common in hypnotically induced recall.
    b. Flashbulb memories are always complete and accurate records of the past.
    c. Eyewitness memory is heavily influenced by the way in which questions are put to the witnesses.
    d. None of the above

5. In the Loftus and Palmer classic study of leading questions, which of the following words led to the highest estimate of speed for the question, "About how fast were the cars going when they _____?"
    a. smashed
    b. bumped
    c. collided
    d. contacted

6. Essay exams are to multiple-choice exams as _____ is to _____.
    a. long-term memory; short-term memory
    b. short-term memory; long-term memory
    c. recall; recognition
    d. recognition; recall

7. The _____ method of measuring memory straddles the boundary between implicit and explicit memory tests.
    a. recall
    b. recognition
    c. relearning
    d. mnemonic

8. Priming is an illustration of _____.
    a. explicit memory
    b. implicit memory
    c. maintenance rehearsal
    d. elaborative rehearsal

9. Which of the following types of memory has the most limited capacity?
   a. sensory memory
   b. short-term memory
   c. episodic memory
   d. semantic memory

10. Which of the following statements about Sperling's sensory memory experiments using 3 x 4 visual arrays of letters is (are) FALSE?
    a. When people were asked to report the whole array, they recalled most of the letters.
    b. When people were cued to report only one row of the array, they recalled about three letters from the row.
    c. If the tonal cue was delayed more than one second, people remembered little of what they had seen.
    d. All of the above

11. The difficulty with amnesic patients like H. M. is with the flow of information:
    a. from sensory to short-term memory.
    b. from short-term to long-term memory.
    c. from long-term to short-term memory.
    d. all of the above

12. The acronym R.C.M.P. is _____ chunk(s); the date 1867 is _____ chunk(s).
    a. 1; 1
    b. 1; 4
    c. 3; 1
    d. 3; 4

13. Recalling "Siam" or "sarong" when you are trying to recall "sampan" is an example of:
    a. a reminiscence bump.
    b. a TOT state.
    c. the serial position effect.
    d. source amnesia.

14. "Knowing how" is to "knowing that" as _____ memory is to _____ memory.
    a. declarative; procedural
    b. procedural; declarative
    c. semantic; episodic
    d. episodic; semantic

15. The tendency for recall of the first and last items on a list to surpass recall of items in the middle of the list is called _____.
    a. parallel distributed processing
    b. the serial position effect.
    c. chunking
    d. cue-dependent forgetting

16. Which of the following leads to better long-term memory?
    a. maintenance rehearsal
    b. elaborative rehearsal
    c. rote repetition
    d. memorization

17. Which of the following best accounts for H. M.'s exceptional declarative memory of childhood and adolescence?
    a. no decay
    b. no retroactive interference
    c. no proactive interference
    d. no motivated forgetting

18. Suppose you have driven only cars with 5-speed manual transmissions, and then you buy a car with an automatic transmission. The problems you have driving your new car are due to:
    a. decay.
    b. retroactive interference.
    c. proactive interference.

    d. motivated forgetting.

19. Which type of forgetting involves the Freudian notion of repression?
    a. cue-dependent forgetting
    b. retroactive interference
    c. proactive interference
    d. motivated forgetting

20. Which of the following has (have) been proposed to explain childhood amnesia?
    a. Brain areas involved in the formation or storage of events are not developed until a few years after birth.
    b. We lack a sense of self during the first few years of life.
    c. The young child relies on cognitive schemas that differ from the schemas used later on in life.
    d. All of the above

ANSWERS

GUIDED STUDY

1. Reconstructing the Past

1.1.	Bartlett	source amnesia	easy
	reconstructive	many	emotional
	confabulation	details	

| 1.2. | errors | role | hypnotist |
| | regression | present | |

| 1.3. | flashbulb | fiction | |

| 1.4. | reconstructive | speed | misled |
| | leading | accurate | |

Matching Self-Test I

1. source amnesia
2. reconstructive memory
3. age regression
4. flashbulb memories

2. Measuring Memory

2.1.	explicit	recognition	Ebbinghaus
	recall	recall	relearning
	recognition	decreased	faster
	essay	implicit	explicit
	true-false	priming	

Matching Self-Test 2

1. recall
2. priming
3. explicit memory
4. relearning method

3. The Three-Box Model of Memory

3.1.   information-processing   Short-term
             store   long-term
             box   parallel distributed
             Sensory

3.2.   sensory   one-half   pattern
             registers   echoes   sensory
             icons   two   short-term

3.3.   thirty   STM   chunk
             implicit   working
             explicit   seven

3.4.   LTM   sound   serial-position
             semantic   procedural   primacy
             fruits   declarative   recency
             vegetables   implicit   LTM
             network   explicit   STM
             tip   semantic
             meanings   episodic

Matching Self-Test 3

1. sensory memory	4. PDP models	7. LTM
2. declarative memories	5. semantic memories	8. procedural memories
3. chunk	6. serial-position effect	

---

4. How We Remember

4.1.   encoded   automatically   effortful

4.2.   Rehearsal   maintenance   deep
             eighteen   elaborative   shallow

4.3.   mnemonics   formulas   word

Matching Self-Test 4

1. elaborative rehearsal	3. deep processing
2. mnemonics	4. effortful encoding

---

5. Why We Forget

5.1.   decay

5.2.   new   leading
        old   yield

5.3.   interfere   retroactive   proactive

5.4.   repression   motivated

5.5.   cues   state-dependent
        cue-dependent   mood

Matching Self-Test 5

1. proactive interference	3. motivated forgetting
2. decay theory	4. state-dependent memory

---

6. Autobiographical Memory

6.1.   autobiographical   amnesia   schemas
        third   repression   encoding
        fourth   brain   routine
        childhood   self

6.2.   adolescence   midlife   reminiscence

Matching Self-Test 6

1. childhood (infantile) amnesia	2. reminiscence bump

ANSWERS TO MULTIPLE CHOICE PROGRESS TEST

Item No.	Answers	Page(s) in Textbook
1.	c. Human memory is largely a reconstructive process.	236
2.	b. source amnesia	237
3.	a. you have thought about the imagined event often.	237-238
4.	b. Flashbulb memories are always complete and accurate records of the past.	239-242
5.	a. smashed	240-241
6.	c. recall; recognition	233-245
7.	c. relearning	244
8.	b. implicit memory	244
9.	b. short-term memory	245
10.	a. When people were asked to report the whole array, they recalled most of the letters.	247
11.	b. from short-term to long-term memory.	248
12.	a. 1; 1	240
13.	b. a TOT state	250
14.	b. procedural; declarative	251
15.	b. the serial position effect	243-244
16.	b. elaborative rehearsal	254
17.	b. no retroactive interference	258
18.	c. proactive interference	259
19.	d. motivated forgetting	259
20.	d. All of the above	261-262

CHAPTER 8

Learning

CHAPTER OVERVIEW

The chapter opens with a discussion of classical conditioning theory. This includes mention of Pavlov and his original research in physiology in addition to the principles of classical conditioning he developed. Terms essential to classical conditioning such as unconditioned stimulus, unconditioned response, conditioned stimulus, and conditioned response are illustrated. Basic principles of classical conditioning are also covered, including extinction, spontaneous recovery, higher-order conditioning, stimulus generalization, and stimulus discrimination. Various examples of classical conditioning in real life are presented. These include learned fears, taste aversions, and compensatory bodily responses to drugs.

Operant conditioning procedures are compared to classical conditioning procedures. Thorndike's Law of Effect is explained along with the basic premises put forth by Skinner. A description of the differences between positive and negative reinforcement and positive and negative punishment follows. Primary and secondary reinforcers and punishers are also distinguished. Various principles of operant conditioning are presented including extinction, spontaneous recovery, stimulus generalization, stimulus discrimination, and continuous versus partial schedules of reinforcement. A description of how to shape a behaviour and the origins of superstitious behaviours follows. Various examples of operant conditioning in real life are provided. These include a description of behaviour modification, token economies, and possible problems with punishment and reward.

The differences between social learning theories and the learning theories previously described are noted. This includes a description of the cognitive aspects of social learning theories, observational learning, the effect of models, latent learning, and cognitive maps. Lastly, the concept of insight is examined from both the cognitive and behavioural perspectives.

GUIDED STUDY

1. Classical Conditioning

Read the section "Classical Conditioning" and then answer the following questions. If you have trouble answering any of the questions, re-study the relevant material before going on to the review of key terms and the matching test.

1-1.   A relatively permanent change in behaviour that occurs because of experience is referred to by psychologists as _____. Two types of learning studied by behaviourists

143

have been _____ conditioning and _____ conditioning. The person who stumbled upon classical conditioning was _____. Pavlov called the food in the mouth an _____ stimulus and salivation to the food an _____ response. According to Pavlov, learning occurs when a _____ stimulus is regularly paired with the US. The neutral stimulus becomes a _____ stimulus and elicits a _____ response. This procedure of classical conditioning is also known as _____ or _____ conditioning.

1-2. For classical conditioning to be effective, the neutral stimulus, which will become the CS, must _____ the US, as the CS serves as a _____ for the US. According to _____ _____, "Pavlovian conditioning is not a stupid process by which the organism willy-nilly forms associations between any two stimuli that happen to co-occur."

1-3. When the CS is continuously presented without the US, the CR will eventually disappear through the process of _____. The reappearance of the CR during extinction is referred to as _____ recovery. A neutral stimulus can be paired with a CS and become a CS itself through the procedure of _____-_____ conditioning. When a stimulus similar to the CS produces a CR, the organism is displaying stimulus _____. The opposite of generalization, _____, occurs when a stimulus similar to the CS fails to evoke the CR.

Review of Key Terms

The following is a list of the Key Terms from the section "Classical Conditioning." Make sure you are familiar with each term before taking the matching test on these terms.

learning	unconditioned stimulus	higher-order conditioning
behaviourism	unconditioned response	stimulus generalization
conditioning	classical conditioning	stimulus discrimination
conditioned stimulus	extinction	
conditioned response	spontaneous recovery	

Matching Self Test 1

Match the appropriate term with its definition or description.

1. _____ The classical-conditioning term for a stimulus that elicits a reflexive response in the absence of learning

2. _____ A relatively permanent change in behaviour due to experience.

3. _____ The reappearance of a learned response after its apparent extinction.

4. _____ The tendency to respond differently to two or more similar stimuli; in classical conditioning, it occurs when a stimulus similar to the CS fails to evoke the CR.

5. _____ The classical-conditioning term for a reflexive response elicited by a stimulus in the absence of learning.

6. _____ The process by which a previously neutral stimulus acquires the capacity to elicit a response through association with a stimulus that already elicits a similar or related response.

2. Classical Conditioning in Real Life

Read the section "Classical Conditioning in Real Life" and then answer the following questions. If you have trouble answering any of the questions, re-study the relevant material before going on to the review of key terms and the matching test.

2-1. Classical conditioning procedures help to explain why we like or dislike certain _____. By pairing a food we like with one we dislike or with illness, we become conditioned to dislike that food.

2-2. Watson believed that emotions were no more than muscular and glandular _____ to stimuli. Today, psychologists believe that classical conditioning can explain _____ responses to objects and events.

2-3. Classical conditioning can also help explain how we acquire _____. In a classic study, Watson and Rayner conditioned an 11-month-old boy to fear a white _____. In a later study, Watson and Jones reversed a phobia of _____ in a 3-year-old boy through the process of _____.

2-4. Classical conditioning may also have important implications for understanding some components of drug addiction. A drug is the US for a _____ bodily response that opposes the drug's effect in order to restore a normal biological state. This can help explain a drug addict's increasing _____ to drugs.

Review of Key Terms

The following is a list of the Key Terms from the section "Classical Conditioning in Real Life." Make sure you are familiar with each term before taking the matching test on these terms.

phobia   systematic desensitization

counterconditioning   compensatory bodily response

Matching Self Test 2

Match the appropriate term with its definition or description.

1. _____ In classical conditioning, the process of pairing a conditioned stimulus with a stimulus that elicits a response that is incompatible with an unwanted conditioned response.

2. _____ In drug addicts, a response that opposes the drug's effect in order to restore a normal biological state.

3. Operant Conditioning

Read the section "Operant Conditioning" and then answer the following questions. If you have trouble answering any of the questions, re-study the relevant material before going on to the review of key terms and the matching test.

3-1.   Unlike classical conditioning, _____ conditioning is dependent on environmental consequences. One of the first psychologists to study operant conditioning was _____ _____, who placed cats in a _____ _____ in order to observe how they escaped from the box. Thorndike established the law of _____, which stated that the correct response is "_____ in" by satisfying consequences. This idea was elaborated on by B. F. _____. Skinner felt that we have to look _____ the individual in order to explain behaviour. Skinner also felt that we are shaped by our environments and our genetic heritage and that there is no free will. In other words, he held a _____ viewpoint. According to Skinner, a response can have one of three types of consequences. The first consequence, a _____ consequence, neither increases nor decreases the probability of the response occurring again. The second type of consequence strengthens or increases the probability of the response that it follows and involves the use of _____. The third type of consequence weakens a response or makes it less likely to occur and involves _____. Not any response, however, can be trained. There are limitations due to biological constraints. Often an animal's behaviour will drift back to _____ .

3-2.   There are two types of reinforcement and two types of punishment. When using _____ reinforcement, something pleasant follows a response. However, when using _____ reinforcement, a behaviour is strengthened by the _____ of something unpleasant. When using _____ punishment, a response is followed by something _____; but when using _____ punishment, a response is followed by the _____ of something pleasant. It is important to remember that all reinforcers _____ the likelihood of a response, whereas all punishers _____ the likelihood of a response.

3-3.	Reinforcers that satisfy biological needs are _____ reinforcers, whereas reinforcers that are learned are _____ reinforcers. Punishers that are inherently punishing, such as pain, are _____ punishers and punishers that are learned are _____ punishers.

3-4.	One of the most used tools in studies on operant conditioning is the _____ box. A response learned through operant conditioning procedures may be stopped or _____ by removing the reinforcer. We may also see _____ recovery after a rest period. As in classical conditioning, a response may generalize to stimuli that resemble original stimuli, stimulus _____. You can also train for stimulus _____ as in classical conditioning. When an animal or human being learns to respond to a stimulus only in the presence of another stimulus, the second stimulus is a _____ stimulus and is said to exert stimulus _____. The procedure of _____ reinforcement involves reinforcing a response every time it occurs, whereas the procedure of _____ reinforcement involves reinforcing only some responses. _____ reinforcement leads to the fastest learning, but _____ reinforcement leads to responding that is more resistant to extinction. The procedure of successive _____ is used when _____ a behaviour. Human beings and animals often develop _____ behaviour due to being coincidentally reinforced after engaging in certain actions.

Review of Key Terms

The following is a list of the Key Terms from the section "Operant Conditioning." Make sure you are familiar with each term before taking the matching test on these terms.

operant conditioning	positive reinforcement	stimulus generalization
law of effect	secondary reinforcers	stimulus discrimination
free will	negative reinforcement	discriminative stimulus
determinism	primary punishers	continuous reinforcement
reinforcement	secondary punishers	intermittent reinforcement
punishment	Skinner box	shaping
instinctive drift	extinction	successive approximations
primary reinforcers	stimulus control	

Matching Self Test 3

Match the appropriate term with its definition or description.

1. _____ The process by which a stimulus or event strengthens or increases the probability of the response that it follows.

147

2. _____ A stimulus that is inherently punishing.

3. _____ In operant conditioning, the tendency for a response that has been reinforced (or punished) in the presence of one stimulus to occur (or be suppressed) in the presence of other, similar stimuli.

4. _____ A stimulus that has acquired punishing properties through association with other punishers.

5. _____ The tendency of an organism to revert to an instinctive behaviour over time; it can interfere with learning.

6. _____ A reinforcement procedure in which a response is followed by the removal, delay, or decrease in intensity of an unpleasant stimulus; as a result, the response becomes stronger or more likely to occur.

7. _____ The process by which a response becomes more likely to occur or less so, depending on its consequences.

8. _____ An operant-conditioning procedure in which successive approximations of a desired response are reinforced; used when the desired response has a low probability of occurring spontaneously.

9. _____ Control over the occurrence of a response by a discriminative stimulus.

10. _____ A reinforcement schedule in which a particular response is sometimes but not always reinforced.

4. Operant Conditioning in Real Life

Read the section "Operant Conditioning in Real Life" and then answer the following questions. If you have trouble answering any of the questions, re-study the relevant material before going on to the review of key terms and the matching test.

4-1.   When using operant and classical conditioning techniques in real world settings, we are using what psychologists call _____. Most behaviour modification techniques rely on secondary reinforcers and employ a _____ economy. Although punishment can be effective when it immediately follows an unwanted behaviour, it is often ineffective for several reasons. Firstly, punishment is often administered _____. Secondly, the recipient of punishment often responds with _____, fear, or _____. Thirdly, the effects of punishment are sometimes _____. Fourthly, most misbehaviour is hard to punish _____. Fifthly, punishment conveys little _____. Lastly, an action intended to be punishing may instead be _____ due to the fact that it brings _____. An alternative to punishment is _____ of the unwanted responses and reinforcement of alternative responses.

4-2.   Psychologists have found that reinforcers that come from an outside source, _____ reinforcers, are not always as effective as reinforcers that are inherently related to the activity being reinforced, _____ reinforcers. For many people, extrinsic reinforcers are seen as _____.

Review of Key Terms

The following is a list of the Key Terms from the section "Operant Conditioning in Real Life." Make sure you are familiar with each term before taking the matching test on these terms.

behaviour modification   extrinsic reinforcers

token economy   intrinsic reinforcers

Matching Self Test 4

Match the appropriate term with its definition or description.

1. _____   Reinforcers that are inherently related to the activity being reinforced, such as enjoyment of the task and the satisfaction of accomplishment.

2. _____   A behaviour-modification technique in which secondary reinforcers called tokens are used to shape behaviour.

3. _____   Reinforcers that are not inherently related to the activity being reinforced, such as money, prizes, and praise.

5. Social-Learning Theories

Read the section "Social-Learning Theories" and then answer the following questions. If you have trouble answering any of the questions, re-study the relevant material before going on to the review of key terms and the matching test.

5-1.   Social-learning theories differ from traditional behavioural theories in that they emphasize that learning is _____; that is, acquired by _____ other people in a social context. Observational learning or _____ conditioning involves learning by watching a _____ behave in certain ways and experience the consequences. In a study on observational learning, Albert _____ had children watch a film of two adults playing together. One of the adults acted _____ towards the other and took all of the toys. When the children were allowed to play with the same toys, those that had seen the film acted more _____ than those who had not viewed the film.

5-2.   Edward _____ studied _____ learning in rats. He claimed that rats had learned a _____ map, or mental representation of a maze.

149

Review of Key Terms

The following is a list of the Key Terms from the section "Social-Learning Theories." Make sure you are familiar with each term before taking the matching test on these terms.

social-learning theories   modeling   Tolman

Bandura   vicarious conditioning   cognitive map

observational learning   latent learning

Matching Self Test 5

Match the appropriate term with its definition or description.

1. _____ A process in which an individual learns new responses by observing the behaviour of another (a model) rather than through direct experience; sometimes called vicarious conditioning.

2. _____ A mental representation of the environment.

3. _____ Theories that emphasize how behaviour is learned and maintained through observation and imitation of others.

4. _____ A form of learning that is not immediately expressed in an overt response; it occurs without obvious reinforcement.

6. Behaviour and the Mind: The Question of Insight

Read the section " Behaviour and the Mind: The Question of Insight" and then answer the following questions. If you have trouble answering any of the questions, re-study the relevant material before going on to the review of key terms and the matching test.

6-1. The behavioural and cognitive explanations of _____, learning which appears to occur in a flash, are very different. Cognitivists feel that insight is an entirely _____ phenomenon, involving mentally combining previously learned responses in new ways. Behaviourists on the other hand, feel that it is simply a matter of _____.

Review of Key Terms

The following is a list of the Key Terms from the section " Behaviour and the Mind: The Question of Insight." Make sure you are familiar with each term before taking the matching test on these terms.

insight

Matching Self Test 6

Match the appropriate term with its definition or description.

1. _____ A form of problem solving that appears to involve the (often sudden) understanding of how elements of a situation are related or can be reorganized to achieve a solution.

SAMPLE ANSWERS TO *WHAT'S AHEAD* QUESTIONS FROM TEXTBOOK

After you have completed the "Looking Back" section at the end of the chapter by answering the "What's Ahead" questions that preceded each major section of the chapter, compare your answers to the following sample answers. If your answers are not similar to the sample answers, review the pertinent sections of the chapter. The relevant page(s) for each question is(are) provided in the "Looking Back" section in the text.

Why would a dog salivate when it sees a light bulb or hears a buzzer, even though they are inedible?

The dog would salivate because the sight of the light bulb and the sound of the buzzer have become conditioned stimuli for the salivary response. This means that they were paired with an unconditioned stimulus for the salivary response (e.g., food in the dog's mouth) using the classical conditioning procedure. The conditioned salivary responses that were achieved would be like those observed by Pavlov in his dogs.

How can classical conditioning help explain prejudice?

Higher-order conditioning may contribute to the formation of prejudices. Words may acquire their emotional meanings through higher-order conditioning. For example, a person may learn a negative response to ethnic or national labels, such as *Swede, Turk,* or *Jew,* if those words are paired with already disagreeable words, such as *dumb* or *dirty.*

If you have learned to fear collies, why might you also be scared of sheepdogs?

You would fear sheepdogs and other types of dogs similar to collies because of stimulus generalization. After a stimulus becomes a conditioned stimulus for some response, other, similar stimuli may produce a similar reaction.

If you eat licorice and then happen to get the flu, how might your taste for licorice change?

You will likely acquire a taste aversion to it. Many people have learned to dislike a food after eating it and then falling ill, even though the two events were unrelated. The food (in this case, licorice) becomes a conditioned stimulus for nausea or for other symptoms produced by the illness.

Why do advertisers often include pleasant music and gorgeous scenery in ads for their products?

Because we like the music and scenery, the advertisers are hoping that these feelings will be classically conditioned to their products. In classical conditioning terms, the music and scenery are unconditioned stimuli for internal responses associated with pleasure; and the products become conditioned stimuli for similar responses.

How would a classical conditioning theorist explain your irrational fear of heights or mice?

A classical conditioning theorist would say that your irrational fear of heights had been classically conditioned through some earlier experiences in your life. The object of the phobic response (e.g., mice) have come to serve as conditioned stimuli for the fear response. Such phobias can be treated with counterconditioning therapies, usually systematic desensitization.

Why might a drug dose that is ordinarily safe kill you if you take it in a new place?

In the presence of environmental cues associated with drug taking, a compensatory response (a response that opposes the drug's effect in order to restore a normal biological state) occurs, so more and more of the drug is needed to produce the usual effects. The compensatory response is conditioned to the normal circumstances. Thus, a drug dose that would ordinarily be safe, given an addict's tolerance level, may be lethal when the drug is used in novel circumstances (a novel place) because the usual conditioned compensatory response does not occur.

What do praise and the cessation of nagging have in common?

They are both usually reinforcers. Praise is a positive reinforcer (the presentation of something pleasant), and cessation of nagging is a negative reinforcer (the removal of something unpleasant).

What's the best way to discourage a friend from interrupting you while you're studying?

To get rid of a response, you should be careful not to reinforce it intermittently. Thus, you must completely ignore your friend while you are studying. This should extinguish your friend's behaviour.

How to trainers teach guide dogs to do the amazing things they do for their owners?

The trainers use shaping, an operant conditioning procedure in which successive approximations of a desired response are reinforced.

How can operant principles account for the popularity of good-luck charms?

Coincidental reinforcement might account for some human superstitions, such as good-luck charms. Intermittent reinforcement may make the response particularly resistant to extinction. If coincidental reinforcement occurs occasionally, the superstitious behaviour may continue indefinitely.

Why do efforts to "crack down" on wrongdoers often go awry?

There are many reasons for this. People often administer punishment inappropriately or when rage prevents them from thinking through what they are doing and how they are doing it. The recipient of punishment often responds with anxiety, fear, or rage. The effects of punishment are sometimes temporary, depending heavily on the presence of the punishing person or circumstances. Most misbehaviour is hard to punish immediately. Punishment conveys little information. An action intended to punish may instead be reinforcing because it brings attention. Because of these drawbacks, attempts to punish may go awry.

What's the best way to discourage a child from throwing tantrums?

The simplest form of extinguishing this behaviour (ignoring the child) is often not possible. When punishment must be used, it should not involve physical abuse and should be accompanied by information about what kind of behaviour would be appropriate. This more desirable behaviour should be followed, whenever possible, by reinforcement. Thus, extinction and punishment should be combined with reinforcement of desirable behaviour. It is also important to understand the reasons for a child's behaviour before deciding how to respond to it. For example, a child's tantrums may be a call for attention. Once we understand the purpose of a child's behaviour, we will be more effective in dealing with it.

Why does paying children for good grades sometimes backfire?
Because extrinsic reinforcement (in this case, the payment), if the child focuses on it exclusively, can become too much of a good thing. It can kill the pleasure of doing something (getting good grades) for its own sake. Why should extrinsic rewards undermine intrinsic motivation? One possibility is that when we are paid for an activity, we interpret it as work. Another possibility is that extrinsic rewards are seen as controlling, and therefore may reduce a person's sense of autonomy and choice. A third, more behavioural explanation is that extrinsic reinforcement sometimes raises the rate of responding above some optimal, enjoyable level. Then the activity really does become work.

How might watching violence on TV make (some) people more aggressive?
Some people may become more aggressive through observational learning (which behaviourists call vicarious conditioning)—learning by watching what others do and what happens to them for doing it. Sometimes the learner imitates the behaviour shortly after observing it. At other times the learning remains latent until circumstances allow or require it to be expressed in performance. Individual differences in perceptions and interpretations also help to explain why violent television programs do not have the same impact on all children. In general, the more aggressive a person is to begin with, the more likely the person is to seek out violent media and be affected by what they see.

Why do two people often learn different lessons from exactly the same experience?
Social learning theorists would say that this is due to the importance of people's perceptions in what they learn perceptions of the models they observe and also perceptions of themselves. Individuals also bring different knowledge and assumptions to an event, and they notice and pay attention to different aspects of a situation. Thus, all of these individual differences result in people learning different lessons from exactly the same experience.

Can an ape show "insight" into a problem?
Insight is learning that appears to occur in a flash. There is some empirical evidence that chimpanzees demonstrated "insight" in learning how to reach some bananas. If the bananas were outside of the cage for example, the animal might pull them in with a stick. Often, the solution came after the animal had been sitting quietly without actively trying to reach the bananas. To cognitive researchers, this insight seems to be an entirely cognitive phenomenon. But behaviourists do not think this is the case. See the next question and answer for their explanation of so-called "insight."

Can a pigeon show insight? What would a behaviourist say?
Robert Epstein and his colleagues taught pigeons three separate behaviours—to push boxes in a particular direction, to climb onto a box, and to peck at a toy banana in order to obtain grain. They also extinguished flying or jumping responses to the bananas. Then the pigeons were left alone with a banana suspended just out of reach overhead with a box at the edge of the cage. The birds

quickly solved the problem by pushing the box beneath the banana and climbing onto it. The pigeons' behaviour looks like what is often called "insight," but behaviourists would say that it is just a combination of previously learned behaviours and not a product of higher cognitive processes, which the pigeons do not have. Cognitive researchers, however, are not convinced. Just because the behaviour of a pigeon looks something like that of a human being does not mean its origins are the same. Cognitive studies, they maintain, show that in human beings (and possibly chimpanzees), insight requires *mentally* combining previously learned responses in new ways.

MULTIPLE-CHOICE PROGRESS TEST

Choose the single best answer for each of the following questions. When you have finished this progress test, check your answers with those at the end of the chapter. You should review the indicated pages in the text for the questions you do not answer correctly.

1. In Pavlov's classical conditioning research, the ticking of a metronome is to salivation as _____ is to _____.
    a. US;UR
    b. UR; US
    c. CS; CR
    d. CR; CS

2. For effective classical conditioning to occur, the stimulus to be conditioned must reliably _____ the unconditioned stimulus.
    a. precede
    b. follow
    c. occur simultaneously with
    d. All of the above are equally effective procedures.

3. Disappearance of the conditioned response is to reappearance of the conditioned response as _____ is to _____.
    a. stimulus generalization; stimulus discrimination
    b. stimulus discrimination; stimulus generalization
    c. extinction; spontaneous recovery
    d. spontaneous recovery; extinction

4. In classical conditioning, _____ occurs when a stimulus similar to the CS fails to evoke the CR.
    a. acquisition
    b. spontaneous recovery
    c. stimulus generalization
    d. stimulus discrimination

5. Classical conditioning is likely involved in _____.
   a. learning to like and dislike various foods.
   b. acquiring emotional responses to music.
   c. developing a tolerance to addictive drugs.
   d. all of the above

6. Little Albert's fear of the white rat generalized to:
   a. a white rabbit.
   b. cotton wool.
   c. a Santa Claus mask.
   d. all of the above

7. Which of the following is NOT the same as the others?
   a. Pavlovian conditioning
   b. instrumental conditioning
   c. classical conditioning
   d. respondent conditioning

8. Which of the following behaviour would probably be the most difficult to condition?
   a. associating taste with sickness
   b. associating taste with sounds
   c. associating fear with snakes
   d. associating fear with heights

9. An emphasis on the environmental consequences of a behaviour is at the heart of
   _____ conditioning.
   a. operant
   b. respondent
   c. Pavlovian
   d. classical

10. Which of the following researchers regarded himself not as a "self" but as a "repertoire of behaviours"?
    a. Tolman
    b. Skinner
    c. Bandura
    d. Pavlov

11. Increasing the probability of the response it follows is to decreasing the probability of the response it follows as _____ is to _____.
    a. positive reinforcement; negative reinforcement
    b. negative reinforcement; positive reinforcement

c. positive reinforcement; positive punishment

d. positive punishment; positive reinforcement

12. Giving something is to taking something away as _____ is to
_____.
   a. positive reinforcement; negative reinforcement
   b. negative reinforcement; positive reinforcement
   c. positive reinforcement; positive punishment
   d. positive punishment; positive reinforcement

13. Which of the following could NEVER be a primary reinforcer?
   a. food
   b. water
   c. a grade of A+
   d. a comfortable air temperature

14. In operant conditioning, the _____ stimulus exerts stimulus control over a
response by setting the occasion for reinforcement to occur if the response is made.
   a. latent
   b. discriminative
   c. conditioned
   d. unconditioned

15. For rapid learning and greater resistance to extinction, _____ reinforcement
should be used for learning and _____ reinforcement following learning.
   a. continuous; continuous
   b. continuous; partial
   c. partial; continuous
   d. partial; partial

16. The reinforcement of successive approximations of a desired response is involved in
_____.
   a. counterconditioning
   b. higher-order conditioning
   c. shaping
   d. instinctive drift

17. Many behaviour modification programs rely on a technique called _____ in
which secondary reinforcers are used.
   a. the token economy
   b. instinctive drift
   c. higher-order conditioning
   d. stimulus control

18. Which of the following is a reason (are reasons) that punishment fails?
    a. The recipient often responds with anxiety, fear, or rage.
    b. The effect depends heavily on the presence of the punishing person or circumstances.
    c. Punishment conveys little information.
    d. All of the above

19. Observational learning is sometimes called _____ conditioning.
    a. classical
    b. operant
    c. vicarious
    d. higher-order

20. Which of the following learning researchers would NOT agree with the claim that what a learner learns in observational learning is not a specific response but knowledge about responses and their consequences?
    a. Skinner
    b. Mischel
    c. Bandura
    d. Both (b) and (c)

ANSWERS

GUIDED STUDY

1. Classical Conditioning

1.1.	learning	unconditioned	conditioned
	classical	unconditioned	Pavlovian
	operant	neutral	respondent
	Pavlov	conditioned	

| 1.2. | precede | predictor | Robert Rescorla |

| 1.3. | extinction | higher-order | discrimination |
| | spontaneous | generalization | |

Matching Self-Test 1

| 1. unconditioned stimulus | 3. spontaneous recovery | 5. unconditioned response |
| 2. learning | 4. stimulus discrimination | 6. classical conditioning |

2. Classical Conditioning in Real Life

2.1.   foods   2.2.   responses   emotional

2.3.   fears   rabbits
        rat   counterconditioning

2.4.   compensatory   tolerance

Matching Self-Test 2

1. counterconditioning   2. compensatory bodily response

---

3. Operant Conditioning

3.1.   operant   stamped   neutral
        Edward Thorndike   Skinner   reinforcement
        puzzle box   outside   punishment
        effect   deterministic   instinctive

3.2.   positive   positive   removal
        negative   unpleasant   increase
        removal   negative   decrease

3.3.   primary   primary
        secondary   secondary

3.4.   Skinner   control   partial
        extinguished   continuous   (intermittent)
        spontaneous   partial   approximations
        generalization   (intermittent)   shaping
        discrimination   Continuous   superstitious
        discriminative

Matching Self-Test 3

1. reinforcement   5. instinctive drift   9. stimulus control
2. primary punisher   6. negative reinforcement   10. partial (intermittent)
                                                         reinforcement
3. stimulus generalization   7. operant conditioning
4. secondary punisher   8.shaping

4. Operant Conditioning in Real Life

4.1.
modification	rage	reinforcing
token	temporary	attention
inappropriately	immediately	extinction
anxiety	information	

4.2.   extrinsic intrinsic bribes

Matching Self-Test 4

1. intrinsic reinforcers   2. token economy   3. extrinsic reinforcers

---

5. Social-Learning Theories

5.1
social	model	aggressively
observing	Bandura	
vicarious	aggressively	

5.2.   Tolman   latent   cognitive

Matching Self-Test 5

1. observational learning   3. social-learning theories
2. cognitive map   4. latent learning

---

6. Behaviour and the Mind: The Question of Insight

6.1.   insight   cognitive   conditioning

Matching Self-Test 6

1.   insight

ANSWERS TO MULTIPLE CHOICE PROGRESS TEST

Item No.	Answers	Page(s) in Textbook
1.	c. CS; CR	271
2.	a. precede	272
3.	c. extinction; spontaneous recovery	273
4.	d. stimulus discrimination	274
5.	d. all of the above	274-277
6.	d. all of the above	276
7.	b. instrumental conditioning	271
8.	b. associating taste with sounds	277
9.	a. operant	286-288
10.	b. Skinner	278-286
11.	c. positive reinforcement; positive punishment	281
12.	a. positive reinforcement; negative reinforcement	281
13.	c. a grade of A+	282
14.	b. discriminative	284
15.	b. continuous; partial	285
16.	c. shaping	286
17.	a. the token economy	288-289
18.	d. All of the above	289–290
19.	c. vicarious	294-295
20.	a. Skinner	296

CHAPTER 9

Behaviour in Social and Cultural Context

CHAPTER OVERVIEW

The chapter opens with a discussion of social norms and social roles. Several classic studies investigating these issues are described, including the Milgram obedience study and the Zimbardo prison study. The power of roles and the process of entrapment are discussed with respect to these studies. The concept of social identity is discussed with respect to ethnic identity and acculturation. Attribution theory is introduced, detailing the difference between situational and dispositional attributions. In addition, common errors in attribution are covered, including the fundamental attribution error, the serf-serving bias, and the just-world hypothesis. The origin of attitudes is covered next. This includes a discussion of cognitive dissonance theory and effective persuasive techniques.

The issue of conformity is addressed via Asch's famous line-length judgment experiment. A discussion of groupthink and strategies to avoid it follows. The concept of diffusion of responsibility is discussed with respect to the Kitty Genovese murder, social loafing, and deindividuation. Situations in which conformity is avoided and persons dissent or act altruistically are described. Lastly, cross-cultural relations are explored. This involves discussion of ethnocentrism, stereotypes, prejudice, and possible solutions to these problems.

GUIDED STUDY

1. Roles and Rules

Read the section "Roles and Rules" and then answer the following questions. If you have trouble answering any of the questions, re-study the relevant material before going on to the review of key terms and the matching test.

1-1.   The fields of _____ psychology and _____ psychology study human behaviour by emphasizing the _____ environment rather than _____ personality dynamics. Rules about how we are supposed to act from one situation to another are referred to as _____. Norms about how people in certain positions are supposed to act, help comprise one's social _____. The Milgram study on _____ looked at norms and social roles in a situation in which subjects were asked to comply with a request to supposedly deliver _____ _____ to a confederate. Subjects were told that the experiment was on the effects of _____ on learning, when in reality it was on obedience. Milgram found that about _____-_____ of the subjects obeyed to the fullest extent. In later experiments, Milgram identified situations in which fewer subjects obeyed. These included (1) having the _____ leave the room, (2) having the _____ in the room, (3) having two experimenters issuing _____ demands, (4) having an ordinary _____ issuing the orders, and (5) having the subject work with _____ who refused to go further. Some criticisms of the Milgram obedience study are that it was _____ because subjects were unaware of the true nature of the experiment and that subjects may have suffered _____ pain.

1-2.   In an experiment investigating the roles of prisoners and guards, _____ had college students play the roles. Zimbardo found that both the prisoners and the guards fell very easily into their respective roles. In fact, within a short time the guards typically took on one of three roles. Some were _____, others were tough but _____, and about a _____ of the guards were _____. The experiment was supposed to last for _____ weeks, but had to be stopped after _____ days. Some have criticized the study as being _____, but Zimbardo maintains that the study demonstrates how roles can transform people.

1-3.   Social psychologists have identified several factors that lead people to obey even when they would rather not. Some of these factors include feeling that the authority figure has the ultimate _____ for the results of your actions and _____, the process by which individuals increase their commitment to a course of action in order to justify their investment in it.

Review of Key Terms

The following is a list of the Key Terms from the section "Roles and Rules." Make sure you are familiar with each term before taking the matching test on these terms.

social psychology	norms (social)	routinization
cultural psychology	role (social)	entrapment

Matching Self Test 1

Match the appropriate term with its definition or description.

1. _____   A given social position that is governed by a set of norms for proper behaviour.

2. _____   A gradual process in which individuals escalate their commitment to a course of action to justify their investment of time, money, or effort.

3. _____ Social conventions that regulate human life, including explicit laws and implicit cultural standards.

2. Identity, Attribution, and Attitudes

Read the section "Identity, Attribution, and Attitudes" and then answer the following questions. If you have trouble answering any of the questions, re-study the relevant material before going on to the review of key terms and the matching test.

2-1.   According to social psychologists, each of us develops a _____ identity that is based on aspects of our self-concepts which are determined by nationality, ethnicity, religion, and social roles. One's social identity may be based on one's identity, an identification with a religious or ethnic group. It may also be based on one's _____ identity, an identification with a religious or ethnic group. It may also be based on _____, identification with the dominant culture. Individuals who are _____ have strong ties both to their ethnicity and the larger culture, whereas individuals who choose _____ have weak feelings of ethnicity but a strong sense of acculturation. Ethnic _____ have a strong sense of ethnic identity but weak feelings of acculturation, and those who feel _____ are connected to neither their ethnicity nor the dominant culture.

2-2.   How we make explanations about our own behaviour and the behaviour of others is known as _____ theory. Attributions typically fall into two categories, a _____ attribution, which is based on the environment, and a _____ attribution, which is based on an internal trait in the person. One very common error made when making attributions about another's behaviour is the _____ attribution error. This is the tendency to attribute the behaviour of others to _____ factors. This error is more frequently made in _____ nations. Westerners do not always make dispositional attributions. When explaining their own behaviour, they tend to use a _____-_____ bias, taking credit for their _____ actions but letting the situation account for their _____ actions. People's attributions are also influenced by the need to believe that the world is fair and that good people are rewarded and bad people punished, the _____-_____ hypothesis. This can lead to the phenomenon of _____ the victim. When something bad happens to another person, it is reassuring to think that they must have done something to deserve it.

2-3.   A relatively stable opinion concerning beliefs and feelings about a topic is an _____. Attitudes may come from a _____ effect, a generational effect. That is, attitudes may be based on events that occurred in the generation in which one was raised. Our behaviours may also influence our attitudes due to _____ dissonance. Our attitudes may also be altered based on _____ persuasion. Arkes has found that when statements are repeated, people eventually began to believe them. He calls this the _____ effect. Our attitudes are also influenced by the individual presenting the argument. Effective persuaders are _____ and

_____. Another persuasive technique involves using _____. The use of fear is most effective when the level of fear is _____ and information about how to _____ the danger is provided. Some methods used to alter attitudes involve more than friendly persuasion. This is referred to as _____ persuasion by psychologists and as _____ by others. Coercive persuasion has several defining features, including (1) placing the individual under physical or emotional _____, (2) the person's problems are defined in _____ terms and simple answers are offered, (3) the leader offers _____ love, acceptance, and attention, (4) a new identity based on the _____ is created, (5) the person is subjected to _____, and (6) the person's access to information is severely _____.

Review of Key Terms

The following is a list of the Key Terms from the section "Identity, Attributions, and Attitudes."
Make sure you are familiar with each term before taking the matching test on these terms.

social identity	attribution theory	blaming the victim
ethnic identity	self-serving bias	validity effect
acculturation	situational attributions	cognitive dissonance
bicultural identity	attitude	coercive persuasion
assimilation	dispositional attributions	friendly persuasion
ethnic separatism	cohort effect	brainwashing
marginal identity	just-world hypothesis	fundamental attribution error

Matching Self Test 2

Match the appropriate term with its definition or description.

1. _____ A close identification with your own racial, religious, or ethnic group.

2. _____ The theory that people are motivated to explain their own and others' behaviour by attributing causes of that behaviour to a situation or a disposition.

3. _____ The part of a person's self-concept that is based on identification with a nation, culture, or ethnic group, with gender, and other roles in society.

4. _____ The tendency, in explaining one's own behaviour, to take credit for one's good actions and rationalize one's mistakes.

5. _____ The tendency of people to believe that a statement is true or valid simply because it has been repeated many times.

6. _____ The notion that many people need to believe that the world is fair and that justice is served; that bad people are punished and good people rewarded.

7. _____ The process by which members of minority groups in a given society come to identify with and feel part of the mainstream culture.

8. _____ The tendency, in explaining other people's behaviour, to overestimate personality factors and underestimate the influence of the situation.

3. Individuals in Groups

Read the section "Individuals in Groups" and then answer the following questions. If you have trouble answering any of the questions, re-study the relevant material before going on to the review of key terms and the matching test.

3-1. The behaviour of an individual may change when the individual is placed in a group setting, usually due to _____. In a set of classic experiments, Asch had subjects make a simple judgment about the length of three lines while they were in a group setting. Asch found that all but _____ percent of the subjects conformed at some point in time. Asch's work has been replicated in many situations and in many countries. The basic findings are that (1) conformity in the United States has since the original experiment in the 1950s, (2) people from _____ cultures are less likely to conform than are those from group-oriented cultures, and (3) conformity increases as the stimulus becomes _____, as the number of confederates giving the wrong answer _____, and as members of the group become more alike in age, _____, and gender.

3-2. When working in a group, the tendency for all members to think alike and to suppress dissent is called _____. According to Janis, groupthink occurs when a group's need for total _____ overwhelms its need to make the _____ decision and when the members' needs to be _____ and _____ overwhelm their ability to _____ with a bad decision. Two examples of groupthink from recent history include Kennedy's plan to invade _____ and Johnson's involvement in the _____ war. Symptoms of groupthink include (1) an illusion of _____, (2) a lack of _____-_____, (3) pressure on _____ to conform, and (4) and illusion of _____.

3-3. The phenomenon of _____ of responsibility was observed in the sad case of the murder victim, Kitty Genovese. Diffusion of responsibility also occurs in work groups and is referred to as _____ _____. In this situation, the individual group members are not accountable for the work they do. They feel that working harder would only _____ their colleagues' efforts, that they are being _____, or that the work is uninteresting. In the most extreme case of diffusion of responsibility, members of a group lose all awareness of their individuality and sense of self. This is called _____. Deindividuation can lead to disastrous results, including looting, fights, _____, or committing rape.

3-4.   Individuals often do not conform to group pressure and offer help to those in need, acts of _____. These actions could be due to personal convictions or to external influences. Social psychologists have identified several factors that predict independent actions such as whistle-blowing and altruistic behaviour. These include (1) the individual perceives the need for _____, (2) the individual decides to take _____, (3) the individual decides that the costs of doing _____ outweigh the costs of getting _____, (4) the individual has an _____, and (5) the individual becomes _____.

Review of Key Terms

The following is a list of the Key Terms from the section "Individuals in Groups." Make sure you are familiar with each term before taking the matching test on these terms.

conformity   bystander apathy   altruism

diffusion of responsibility   social loafing

groupthink   deindividuation

Matching Self Test 3

Match the appropriate term with its definition or description.

1. _____   In close-knit groups, the tendency for all members to think alike for the sake of harmony and to suppress dissent.

2. _____   In groups or crowds, the loss of awareness of one's own individuality and the abdication of mindful action.

3. _____   The tendency to take action or adopt attitudes as a result of real or imagined pressures.

4. _____   The willingness to take selfless or dangerous action on behalf of others.

4. Cross-Cultural Relations

Read the section "Cross-Cultural Relations" and then answer the following questions. If you have trouble answering any of the questions, re-study the relevant material before going on to the review of key terms and the matching test.

4-1.   The belief that your own culture or ethnic group is superior to all others is known as
_____. Ethnocentrism depends on the concept of "us." Tajfel demonstrated the
power of the "us" category in an experiment with British schoolboys. In this study, the
researchers created in-group _____. The possibility of harmonious relations
between ethnic groups sometimes looks dim due to ethnocentrism. Some people take a
_____ position on differences between ethnic groups arguing that we should
not pass judgment on the customs of others. Other people take an _____
position, maintaining that when cultures violate certain universal human fights, the correct
response is moral indignation. Often the conflicts between cultures is dependent on
_____, summary impressions of a group of people in which all members of the
group are viewed as sharing a common trait. Although stereotypes can often be useful,
psychologists have identified three ways in which they distort reality—(1) they
_____ differences between groups, (2) they produce _____
_____, and (3) they _____ differences within other groups.

4-2.   When negative stereotypes are taken one step further and there is an unreasonable dislike
or hatred of a group or a cultural practice, _____ has occurred. One reason
prejudice may continue is that prejudiced persons often _____ their fears or
feelings of _____ onto the target group. Prejudice also allows people to reduce
_____ problems to one cause. Prejudice is also considered a _____
for low self-esteem. Prejudices can be acquired from _____, entertainment
shows, _____ reports, the process of _____, and parents. The
sociocultural view on prejudice claims that it brings _____ benefits and
justifies the _____ group's dominance. Although studies on prejudice have
shown a decline in the rate of prejudice, most researchers do not feel that this is truly the
case. One major criticism of the studies is that the measure of prejudice was a self report.
Racism, they feel, should be measured using _____ measures. Researchers
have also found that not all prejudice is the same. Some people are _____
racist, sexist, or anti-gay. Others are more _____. And still others hold
remnants of prejudices from childhood but feel _____ about these feelings.

4-3.   One method of combating prejudice is to change the laws that make _____
acceptable. A second approach, the _____ hypothesis, involves bringing
members of both sides together to let them get acquainted. Another possibility involves
going into desegregated schools and businesses and implementing _____
situations. Sherif designed an experiment using two groups of boy scouts that tested
cooperative situations. Although the groups were prejudiced toward each other, Sherif
created projects on which they had to _____ using a policy of _____
in reaching mutual goals. In order for any of these strategies to be effective, four
conditions must be met, (1) both sides must have equal _____ and equal

_____ standing, (2) both sides must _____, (3) both sides must have the moral, legal, and economic _____ of authorities, and (4) both sides must have opportunities to _____ and _____ together.

Review of Key Terms

The following is a list of the Key Terms from the section "Cross-Cultural Relations." Make sure you are familiar with each term before taking the matching test on these terms.

ethnocentrism   prejudice   contact hypothesis

stereotype   symbolic racism

Matching Self Test 4

Match the appropriate term with its definition or description.

1. _____   Cognitive schema or a summary impression of a group, in which a person believes that all members of the group share a common trait or traits (positive, negative, or neutral).

2. _____   The belief that your own ethnic group, nation, or religion is superior to all others.

3. _____   A negative stereotype and strong, unreasonable dislike or hatred of a group or a cultural practice.

4. _____   An approach holding that the best way to end prejudice is to bring members of both sides together and let them get acquainted.

SAMPLE ANSWERS TO *WHAT'S AHEAD* QUESTIONS FROM TEXTBOOK

After you have completed the "Looking Back" section at the end of the chapter by answering the "What's Ahead" questions that preceded each major section of the chapter, compare your answers to the following sample answers. If your answers are not similar to the sample answers, review the pertinent sections of the chapter. The relevant page(s) for each question is(are) provided in the "Looking Back" section in the text.

How do social rules guide behaviour and what is likely to happen when you violate them?

Social norms are rules about how we are supposed to act. Every culture has norms, passed from one generation to another. Norms are the conventions of everyday life that make interactions with other people predictable and orderly. They are enforced by threats of punishment if we violate them. Thus, if you violate a norm, you will punished by law or informally by other people in that you will be made to feel guilty or inadequate.

Do you have to be mean or disturbed to inflict pain on someone just because an authority figure tells you to?

No, you do not have to be mean or disturbed to commit such an act of destructive obedience. The obedience research by Stanley Milgram demonstrated that about two-thirds of the participants obeyed orders to inflict high levels of shock to another person. More than 1,000 participants at several American universities eventually went through the Milgram study. Most of them, men and women equally, inflicted what they thought were dangerous amounts of shock to another person. Researchers in at least eight other countries have also found high percentages of such obedience. Milgram concluded that this obedience was more a function of the situation than of the particular personalities of the participants.

How can ordinary college students be transformed into sadistic prison guards?

Philip Zimbardo, who designed the prison study, would argue that all you need do is put the college students into the role of prison guards, and some of the students would become sadistic prison guards. About a third of the guards in the prison study became tyrannical and abusive. Zimbardo believes that the results of the prison study demonstrate that roles transform people.

How can people be "entrapped" into violating their moral principles?

Entrapment is a process in which individuals increase their commitment to a course of action in order to justify their investment in it. The first steps of entrapment pose no difficult choices with respect to your moral principles, but one step leads to another. Before you realize it, you have become committed to a course of action that poses moral problems, and it is hard to free yourself. For example, in Milgram's study, once participants had given a 15-volt shock, they had committed themselves to the experiment. Unless they resisted authority soon afterwards, they were likely to go on to administer what they believed were dangerously strong shocks. At that point, it was difficult to explain a sudden decision to quit.

In what ways do people balance their ethnic identity and membership in the larger culture?

Four outcomes are possible, depending on whether ethnic identity is strong or weak and whether identification with the larger culture is strong or weak. People who are bicultural have strong ties both to their ethnicity and to the larger culture. Those who choose assimilation have weak feelings of ethnicity but a strong sense of acculturation. Ethnic separatists have a strong sense of ethnic identity but weak feelings of acculturation. And some people feel marginal, connected to neither their ethnicity nor the dominant culture.

What's one of the most common mistakes people make when explaining the behaviour of others?

One of the most common mistakes they make is to overestimate personality factors and underestimate the influence of the situation. This tendency is called the fundamental attribution error. People are especially likely to overlook situational attributions when they are distracted or preoccupied. It is also especially prevalent in Western nations, where middle-class people tend to believe that individuals are responsible for their own actions.

What is the "Big Lie"—and why does it work so well?

Repeat something often enough, even the basest lie, and eventually the public will believe it. The Nazis called this phenomenon the "Big Lie." Its formal name is the validity effect. It works so well because it employs a well-established relationship—we tend to feel more positive toward things we are repeatedly exposed to.

What's the difference between ordinary techniques of persuasion and the coercive techniques used by cults?

In coercive techniques, the manipulator uses harsh tactics, not just hoping that people will change their minds, but attempting to force them to. These tactics are sometimes referred to as brainwashing. Most psychologists, however, prefer the phrase coercive persuasion. The processes that distinguish coercive persuasion from the usual techniques of persuasion include the following. The person is put under physical or emotional distress. The person's problems are defined simplistically, and simple answers are offered repeatedly. The leader offers unconditional love, acceptance, and attention. A new identity based on the group is created. The person is subjected to entrapment. And lastly, the person's access to information is severely controlled.

Why do people in groups often go along with the majority even when the majority is dead wrong?

Some do so because they identify with group members and want to be like them in dress, attitudes, or behaviour. Some want to be liked and know that disagreeing with a group can make them unpopular. Some believe the group has knowledge or abilities that are superior to their own. And some go along to keep their jobs, win promotions, or win votes.

How can "groupthink" lead to bad—even catastrophic—decisions?

Because the group believes that it can do no wrong. It has an illusion of invulnerability. There is no self-censorship. Dissenters decide to keep quiet in order not to rock the boat, offend their friends, or risk being ridiculed. There is direct pressure on dissenters to conform, either by the leader or other group members. By discouraging dissent, leaders and group members create an illusion of unanimity. In brief, without any dissent or doubt, such conformity can lead to bad decisions.

Why is it common for a group of people to hear someone shout for help without one of them calling the police?

The people fail to take action because they believe that someone else will do so. This is a process called diffusion of responsibility—in which responsibility for helping is spread among many people, and individuals fail to take action because they believe that someone else will do so.

What enables some people to dissent, take moral action, or blow the whistle on wrongdoers?

These actions are in part a matter of personal convictions and conscience. There are also many external influences leading to such actions. The individual perceives the need for intervention or help. The individual must decide to take responsibility and that the costs of doing nothing outweigh the costs of getting involved. Having an ally also helps. Lastly, a person may become entrapped. Once having taken the initial step of getting involved, most people will increase their commitment to taking action. Thus, certain social conditions make altruism more likely to occur.

How do stereotypes benefit us—and how to they distort reality?

Stereotypes benefit us by helping us to process new information and retrieve memories. They allow us to organize experience, make sense of differences among individuals and groups, and predict how people will behave. In brief, they allow us to make efficient decisions. Stereotypes, however, also distort reality in three ways. First, they exaggerate differences between groups, making the stereotyped group seem odd, unfamiliar, or dangerous. Second, they produce selective perception; people tend to see only what fits the stereotype and to reject any perceptions that do not fit. Third, they underestimate differences within other groups. Stereotypes create the impression that all members of other groups are the same.

Why does prejudice increase in times of social and economic unrest?

Because one of the most important reasons for prejudice is that it brings economic benefits and justifies the majority group's dominance. Thus, in times of social and economic unrest, prejudice increases in order to maintain the majority group's dominance.

Why do well-intentioned people sometimes get caught up in a "cycle of mistrust" with members of other ethnic or cultural groups?

Some well-intentioned majority group members, although highly motivated to work well with minorities, may be self-conscious and anxious about doing "the wrong thing." Their anxiety makes them behave awkwardly, for instance by blurting out dumb remarks and avoiding eye contact with minority-group members. The minority members, based on their own history of discrimination, may interpret the majority-group members' behaviour as evidence of hostility and respond with withdrawal, aloofness, or anger. The majority members, not understanding that their own anxieties have been interpreted as evidence of prejudice, regard the minority member's behaviour as unreasonable or mysterious, so they reciprocate the hostility or withdraw. This behaviour then confirms the minority members' suspicions about the majority's true feelings and prejudices.

171

***Why isn't mere contact between cultural groups enough to resolve cultural conflict? What
would work?***

Because mere contact does not seem to work. Ethnic groups still form cliques and gangs, fighting
other groups and defending their own ways. Because the origins of tensions between groups in
today's world are so complex, any of the following strategies making discrimination illegal and
increasing contact and cooperation between antagonistic groups would have its greatest impact if
the following four conditions were met. First, both sides must have equal status and equal
economic standing. Second, both sides must cooperate, working together for a common goal.
Third, both sides must have the moral, legal, and economic support of authorities. Fourth, both
sides must have opportunities to work and socialize together, formally and informally. Because
these four conditions are so rarely met, cultural conflicts persist worldwide.

MULTIPLE-CHOICE PROGRESS TEST

*Choose the single best answer for each of the following questions. When you have finished this
progress test, check your answers with those at the end of the chapter. You should review the
indicated pages in the text for the questions you do not answer correctly.*

1. In Milgram's original study on obedience, every single subject administered some shock to
    the learner, and about _____ of all participants obeyed to the fullest extent.
    a. one-fourth
    b. one-half
    c. two-thirds
    d. three-fourths

2. Which of the following statements about the findings of Milgram's obedience studies is
    FALSE?
    a. When the experimenter left the room, people were more likely to disobey.
    b. When two experimenters issued conflicting demands to continue the experiment or to
        stop at once, no one kept inflicting shock.
    c. When the subject worked with peers who refused to go further, they were more likely
        to disobey.
    d. None of the above

3. Which of the following statements about Zimbardo's prison study is FALSE?
    a. The college student volunteers chose which role they wanted, prisoner or guard.
    b. About a third of the guards became tyrannical, and the study was stopped after only six
        days.
    c. According to Zimbardo, this study illustrated the power of roles to transform people.
    d. None of the above

4. In the Milgram obedience studies, some people became so fixated on the "learning task" that they shut out any moral concerns about the learner's demands that he be let out. This illustrates _____.
   a. legitimization of the authority
   b. routinization
   c. the rules of good manners
   d. entrapment

5. Which of the following is a process in which individuals increase their commitment to a course of action in order to justify their investment in it?
   a. validity effect
   b. groupthink
   c. deindividuation
   d. entrapment

6. A strong ethnic identity paired with strong acculturation leads to a _____ pattern of behaviour.
   a. bicultural
   b. assimilated
   c. separatist
   d. marginal

7. Reading about Milgram's obedience findings and thinking that the subjects were sadistic is a good example of the _____.
   a. just-world hypothesis
   b. validity effect
   c. fundamental attribution error
   d. diffusion of responsibility

8. The tendency, in explaining one's own behaviour to take credit for one's good actions and rationalize one's mistakes is the answer to which of the following questions?
   a. What is the fundamental attribution error?
   b. What is the just-world hypothesis?
   c. What is the self-serving bias?
   d. What is the validity effect?

9. Which of the following leads to a dispositional attribution called "blaming the victim"?
   a. just-world hypothesis
   b. entrapment
   c. acculturation
   d. cohort effect

10. The formal name for the effectiveness of familiarity is _____.
    a. the validity effect
    b. the cohort effect
    c. entrapment
    d. acculturation

11. Which of the following is NOT a characteristic of coercive persuasion?
    a. The person is put under physical and emotional distress.
    b. The leader offers unconditional love, acceptance, and attention.
    c. The person's access to information is not controlled.
    d. None of the above

12. Which of the following statements about the experimental findings on conformity is FALSE?
    a. In America, conformity has increased since Asch's work in the 1950s.
    b. People in individualistic cultures are less likely to conform than are people in group-oriented cultures.
    c. Regardless of culture, conformity increases as the number of people giving the wrong answer increases.
    d. None of the above

13. Which of the following is not a symptom of groupthink?
    a. an illusion of invulnerability
    b. lack of self-censorship
    c. no pressure on dissenters to conform
    d. an illusion of unanimity

14. Kitty Genovese was a victim of a process called
    a. deindividuation
    b. ethnocentrism
    c. cognitive dissonance
    d. diffusion of responsibility

15. Social loafing tends to decline when (a) workers feel exploited and (b) workers know their group's
    a. performance will be evaluated
    b. against that of another group.
    c. workers feel that working harder would only duplicate their colleagues' efforts.
    d. the work itself is uninteresting.

16. Deindividuation is likely to occur:
     a. in a large city rather than a small town.
     b. when signs of individuality are covered by masks or uniforms.
     c. in a mob rather than an intimate group.
     d. all of the above

17. Which of the following social and situational factors has a higher probability of leading a person to independent action?
     a. The individual does not perceive the need for intervention.
     b. The individual decides not to take responsibility.
     c. The individual decides that the cost of getting involved does not outweigh the cost of doing nothing.
     d. The individual has an ally.

18. The belief that your own culture or ethnic group is superior to all others is called:
     a. self-serving bias.
     b. ethnocentrism.
     c. social identity.
     d. acculturation.

19. Stereotypes distort reality by:
     a. exaggerating differences between groups.
     b. producing selective perception.
     c. underestimating differences within other groups.
     d. all of the above

20. In his classic Robbers Cave study, Sherif created hostility between the Eagles and Rattlers and then found that he was able to reduce that hostility by:
     a. putting the two groups to work on separate group projects.
     b. putting the two groups in competition for prizes.
     c. putting the two groups in predicaments in which they had to cooperate.
     d. both (a) and (b)

ANSWERS

GUIDED STUDY

1. Roles and Rules

1.1.
social	obedience	conflicting
cultural	electric shocks	man
external	punishment	peers
internal	two-thirds	unethical
norms	experimenter	emotional
role	learner	

1.2.
Zimbardo	third	six
nice	tyrannical	artificial
fair	two	

1.3.   responsibility   entrapment

Matching Self-Test 1

1. social role   2. entrapment   3. social norms

2. Identity Attributions, and Attitudes

2.1.
social	bicultural	marginal
ethnic	assimilation	
acculturation	separatists	

2.2.
attribution	dispositional	bad
situational	Western	just-world
dispositional	self-serving	blaming
fundamental	good	

2.3.	attitude	fear	repeatedly
	cohort	moderate	unconditional
	cognitive	avoid	group
	friendly	coercive	entrapment
	validity	brainwashing	controlled
	admired	distress	
	attractive	simple	

Matching Self-Test 2

1. ethnic identity	4. self-serving bias	7. acculturation
2. attribution theory	5. validity effect	8. fundamental
3. social identity	6. just-world hypothesis	attribution error

---

3. Individuals in Groups

3.1.	conformity	individualistic	ethnicity
	twenty	ambiguous	
	decreased	increases	

3.2.	groupthink	accepted	invulnerability
	agreement	disagree	self-censorship
	wisest	Cuba	dissenters
	liked	Vietnam	unanimity

3.3.	diffusion	duplicate	riots
	social	exploited	
	loafing	deindividuation	

3.4.	altruism	nothing	entrapped
	intervention	involved	
	responsibility	ally	

Matching Self-Test 3

1. groupthink	3. conformity
2. deindividuation	4. altruism

---

4. Cross-Cultural Relations

4.1.

ethnocentrism	absolutist	selective
favoritism	stereotypes	perception
relativist	exaggerate	underestimate

4.2.

prejudice	advertising	unobtrusive
project	news	unapologetically
insecurity	socialization	patronizing
complex	economic	guilty
tonic	majority	

4.3.

discrimination	interdependence	support
contact	status	work
cooperative	economic	socialize
cooperate	cooperate	

Matching Self-Test 4

1. stereotype	3. prejudice
2. ethnocentrism	4. contact hypothesis

ANSWERS TO MULTIPLE CHOICE PROGRESS TEST

Item No.	Answer(s)	Page(s) in Textbook
1.	c. two-thirds	307-308
2.	d. None of the above	308
3.	a. The college student volunteers chose which role they wanted, prisoner or guard.	309-310
4.	b. routinization	311
5.	d. entrapment	311
6.	a. bicultural	313
7.	c. fundamental attribution error	314
8.	c. What is the self-serving bias?	315
9.	a. just-world hypothesis	315
10.	a. the validity effect	317
11.	c. The person's access to information is not controlled.	318
12.	a. In America, conformity has increased since Asch's work in the 1950s.	320-321
13.	c. no pressure on dissenters to conform.	321
14.	d. diffusion of responsibility	322
15.	b. workers know their group's performance will be evaluated against that of another group.	322
16.	d. all of the above	323
17.	c. The individual decides that the cost of getting involved does not outweigh the cost of doing nothing.	324-325
18.	b. ethnocentrism	326
19.	d. all of the above	327
20.	c. putting the two groups in predicaments in which they had to cooperate	333

CHAPTER 10

Psychological Disorders

CHAPTER OVERVIEW

The chapter opens with a description of the criteria for defining mental disorders. These include displaying behaviour that violates cultural standards, maladaptive behaviour, and displaying emotional distress. Means of assessing mental disorders are discussed next. Projective tests such as the Rorschach Inkblot Test and the Thematic Apperception Test as well as more objective means such as the Minnesota Multiphasic Personality Inventory are described. The reliability and validity of these measures are also discussed. The Diagnostic and Statistical Manual of Mental Disorders is described, and possible problems with the use of the manual are outlined.

Anxiety disorders detailed include generalized anxiety disorder, post-traumatic stress disorder, panic disorder, phobia, and obsessive-compulsive disorder. Mood disorders including major depression, dysthymia, and bipolar disorder are discussed. Various theories of depression are presented, including biological, social, attachment, cognitive, and vulnerability-stress explanations. Paranoid, narcissistic, and antisocial personality disorders are also described.

The dissociative disorders of amnesia, fugue, and dissociative identity disorder (multiple personality disorder) are described and critiqued. The biological and the learning models of substance abuse are presented, including criticisms of each model. Lastly, schizophrenic disorders are discussed. Positive and negative symptoms of schizophrenia are described in some detail. In addition, various explanations of schizophrenia are provided.

GUIDED STUDY

1. Defining and Diagnosing Disorder

Read the section "Defining and Diagnosing Disorder" and then answer the following questions. If you have trouble answering any of the questions, re-study the relevant material before going on to the review of key terms and the matching test.

1-1.   The term abnormal behaviour differs from the term _____ illness in several respects. There are three criteria emphasized when determining mental illness. These include (1) violation of _____ standards, (2) _____ behaviour, and (3) _____ distress. Although these criteria are used, the definition of mental disorder is defined broadly as any behaviour or _____ state that causes an individual great _____ or _____; is self-_____ or self-destructive; or is _____ and disrupts either the person's relationships or the larger _____. The term _____ is purely a legal one. One type of test used in the assessment of mental disorder is designed to reveal unconscious motives, feelings, and conflicts, a _____ test. These tests are very _____ in nature and also have low _____ (inconsistent results) and low _____ (they fail to measure what they claim to measure.) One of the most popular projective tests, developed by Hermann Rorschach, is the _____ _____ test. A second popular projective test that involves making up stories about ambiguous pictures is the _____ _____ Test (TAT.) Tests that are more objective in nature are called _____. The most widely used inventory is the Minnesota _____ _____ Inventory (MMPI.)

1-2.   The main diagnostic tool used by clinicians is the Diagnostic and _____ Manual of Mental Disorders (DSM IV.) This contains descriptions of more than _____ disorders. Although a valuable resource, it has several limitations. Firstly, there is a danger of _____, the DSM may encourage the overuse of diagnostic categories. Secondly, there is the problem of diagnostic _____. This was demonstrated in a classic experiment by Rosenhan in which he sent _____ healthy adults to 12 mental hospitals claiming that they were hearing _____. All eight were admitted to the hospitals and diagnosed as suffering from mental disorder. Although they acted normally from that point on, most of the hospital staff viewed their behaviours as _____. Thirdly, there is the problem of confusing serious mental disorders with _____ problems. The last limitation is that the DSM manual gives the illusion of _____ when diagnosis is still very subjective.

Review of Key Terms

The following is a list of the Key Terms from the section "Defining and Diagnosing Disorder." Make sure you are familiar with each term before taking the matching test on these terms.

insanity   Rorschach Inkblot Test   MMPI

mental disorder   TAT   DSM IV

projective test   inventories

Matching Self Test 1

Match the appropriate term with its definition or description.

1. _____   Standardized objective questionnaires requiring written responses; they typically include scales on which people are asked to rate themselves.

2. _____   Psychological tests used to infer a person's motives, conflicts, psychological problems, and unconscious personality dynamics on the basis of the person's interpretations of ambiguous or unstructured stimuli.

3. _____ A projective test that asks respondents to interpret a series of drawings showing ambiguous scenes of people.

4. _____ Any behaviour or emotional state that causes an individual great suffering or worry; is self-defeating or self-destructive; or is maladaptive and disrupts the person's relationships or the larger community.

2. Anxiety Disorders

Read the section "Anxiety Disorders" and then answer the following questions. If you have trouble answering any of the questions, re-study the relevant material before going on to the review of key terms and the matching test.

2-1.   When fear and anxiety are present without any apparent danger, the individual may be suffering from an _____ disorder. When anxiety is continuous and uncontrollable, the individual may be displaying _____ anxiety disorder. Some people have qualities in their own make-up that increase their susceptibility to generalized anxiety disorder, _____ factors. At other times generalized anxiety disorder is set off and maintained by particularly upsetting one-time events or continuing, unsettling situations, _____ factors. People who have lived through particularly harrowing experiences may suffer from _____-_____ stress disorder (PTSD.) When individuals have sudden attacks of intense fear or panic, they may be suffering from _____ disorder.

2-2.   An exaggerated fear of a specific situation, activity, or thing is a _____. One class of phobias deals with situations in which individuals fear they will be observed by others, _____ phobias. One very common social phobia is the fear of being alone in a public place, _____.

2-3.   Recurrent and uncontrollable thoughts, _____, or behaviours, _____, define _____-_____ disorder (OCD.) Compulsions are usually frightening or _____. The most common compulsions are _____ _____, counting, touching, and _____. Recent research has found a physiological basis for OCD. One area of the frontal lobe, the _____ cortex, is responsible for sending messages of danger to the _____ nucleus. It appears that the orbital cortex is not functioning properly in the obsessive-compulsive individual and hence continually sends mistaken fear messages.

Review of Key Terms

The following is a list of the Key Terms from the section "Anxiety Disorders." Make sure you are familiar with each term before taking the matching test on these terms.

generalized anxiety disorder   social phobia

post-traumatic stress disorder (PTSD)   agoraphobia

panic disorder   obsessive-compulsive disorder (OCD)

panic attack   orbital cortex

phobia   caudate nucleus

Matching Self Test 2

Match the appropriate term with its definition or description.

1. _____   An anxiety disorder in which a person who has experienced a traumatic or life-threatening event has symptoms such as psychic numbing, reliving of the trauma, and increased physiological arousal.

2. _____   An exaggerated fear of a specific situation, activity, or object.

3. _____   An anxiety disorder in which a person feels trapped in repetitive, persistent thoughts and repetitive, ritualized behaviours designed to reduce anxiety

4. _____   An anxiety disorder in which a person experiences intense periods of fear and feelings of impending doom, accompanied by physiological symptoms such as rapid breathing and pulse, and dizziness.

5. _____   A continuous state of anxiety marked by feelings of worry and dread, apprehension, difficulties in concentration, and signs of motor tension.

3. Mood Disorders

Read the section "Mood Disorders" and then answer the following questions. If you have trouble answering any of the questions, re-study the relevant material before going on to the review of key terms and the matching test.

3-1.   The common cold of psychiatric disorders is _____. _____ is a chronic form of depression. Those who experience emotional, behavioural, and cognitive changes severe enough to disrupt their usual lives suffer from _____ depression. Some symptoms of major depression include despair and _____, thoughts of death or _____, loss of interest or _____ in usual activities, and loss of _____. The opposite of depression is _____. When individuals experience both depression and mania, they suffer from _____ disorder.

3-2.   Explanations for depression include five possible causes. Firstly, _____ explanations emphasize genetics and brain _____. This view is supported by twin and studies. Secondly, _____ explanations emphasize the _____ of people's lives. For example, this view holds that the reason women are more likely than men to suffer from depression is that they are more likely to lack fulfilling _____ or family _____. Thirdly, _____ explanations emphasize problems with _____ and close _____. This explanation is supported by the fact that depressive episodes are most frequently set off by disruption of a(n) _____ _____. Fourthly, _____ explanations emphasize particular habits of _____ and _____ events. This view holds that depression often results from having a _____ explanatory style. Lastly, _____-_____ explanations draw on all four explanations just described. According to this view, depression results from a(n) _____ between vulnerabilities.

Review of Key Terms

The following is a list of the Key Terms from the section "Mood Disorders." Make sure you are familiar with each term before taking the matching test on these terms.

dysthymia   bipolar disorder

major depression   pessimistic explanatory style

mania   vulnerability-stress model of depression

Matching Self Test 3

Match the appropriate term with its definition or description.

1. _____   An abnormally high state of exhilaration.

2. _____   A mood disorder in which episodes of both depression and mania occur.

3. _____   A mood disorder involving excessive sadness, loss of interest in one's usual activities, thoughts of hopelessness, fatigue, and loss of appetite.

4. _____   A chronic form of depression.

4. Personality Disorders

Read the section "Personality Disorders" and then answer the following questions. If you have trouble answering any of the questions, re-study the relevant material before going on to the review of key terms and the matching test.

4-1.   Rigid maladaptive traits that cause great distress or an inability to get along with others are _____ disorders. _____ personality disorder involves extreme suspiciousness and mistrust of other people, jealousy, secretiveness, and doubt about the loyalty of others. When an individual has an exaggerated sense of self-importance and self-absorption, they are said to have _____ personality disorder.

4-2.   Individuals who can con, cheat and kill without thinking twice about it are referred to as suffering from _____ personality disorder. These individuals used to be called _____ or _____. Antisocial personality disorder is more prevalent in _____ than in _____. It is also believed that antisocial individuals may account for more than _____ of all serious crimes committed in the United States. Antisocial individuals do not respond to _____ that makes most people _____. Their inability to feel emotions such as empathy, guilt, fear of punishment, or anxiety suggests some abnormality in the _____ _____ system. It is also suspected that these individuals have problems in behavioural _____—the ability to control responses to frustration or to inhibit a pleasurable action that may have unpleasant repercussions. Many children who become antisocial have suffered _____ impairments. Other research supports the vulnerability-stress model discussed previously, which holds that _____ damage interacts with _____ deprivation.

Review of Key Terms

The following is a list of the Key Terms from the section "Personality Disorders." Make sure you are familiar with each term before taking the matching test on these terms.

personality disorders   antisocial personality disorder (APD)

paranoid personality disorder   behavioural inhibition

narcissistic personality disorder   vulnerability-stress model of APD

Matching Self Test 4

Match the appropriate term with its definition or description.

1. _____   A disorder characterized by an exaggerated sense of self-importance and self-absorption.

2. _____   A disorder characterized by antisocial behaviour such as lying, stealing, manipulating others, and sometimes violence; lack of social emotions and impulsivity.

3. _____   A disorder characterized by habitually unreasonable and excessive suspiciousness, jealousy, or mistrust.

5. Dissociative Disorders

Read the section "Dissociative Disorders" and then answer the following questions. If you have trouble answering any of the questions, re-study the relevant material before going on to the review of key terms and the matching test.

5-1.   When consciousness, behaviour, and identity are split or altered, one is suffering from a _____ disorder. One type of dissociative disorder, _____, is the inability to remember important personal information, usually pertaining to a traumatic or stressful event. When there is no physical cause for the amnesia, it is said to be _____ or in nature. A second dissociative disorder, _____, involves forgetting your identity and wandering from home. Both amnesia and fugue are _____ and difficult to diagnose.

5-2.   Dissociative identity disorder, previously called _____ _____ disorder (MPD) is used to describe the appearance of two or more distinct identities in one individual. One explanation for this disorder is that it originates in _____ as a means of coping with _____ events. Many people, however, are _____ about MPD. The research supporting MPD has been _____, and many feel that clinicians may actually be _____ the disorder in their clients through the power of _____. An alternative explanation of MPD is provided by the _____ explanation. This view states that MPD is an extreme form of the ability we all have to present different aspects of our personalities to others.

Review of Key Terms

The following is a list of the Key Terms from the section "Dissociative Disorders." Make sure you are familiar with each term before taking the matching test on these terms.

dissociative disorders   dissociative identity disorder   sociocognitive explanation

psychogenic amnesia   multiple personality disorder   fugue state

Matching Self Test 5

Match the appropriate term with its definition or description.

1. _____   A dissociative disorder in which a person flees home and forgets his or her identity.

2. _____   A controversial disorder marked by the appearance within one person of two or more distinct personalities, each with its own name and traits.

3. _____   When no organic causes are present, a dissociative disorder involving partial or complete loss of memory for threatening information or traumatic experiences.

6. Drug Abuse and Addiction

Read the section "Drug Abuse and Addiction" and then answer the following questions. If you have trouble answering any of the questions, re-study the relevant material before going on to the review of key terms and the matching test.

6-1. Substance abuse is defined as "a _____ pattern of substance use leading to clinically significant _____ or distress." The _____ model, put forth by E.M. _____, considers alcoholism a disease. Twin and adoption studies suggest that alcoholism is _____. Alcoholism that begins in adulthood, _____ alcoholism, is not associated with genetic factors. However, alcoholism that begins in adolescence, _____ alcoholism, does seem to be partly heritable.

6-2. Contrary to the biological model, the _____ model holds that addiction to any drug is a central activity of the individual's way of life that depends on _____ and _____. There are several pieces of supporting evidence for this view. Firstly, addiction patterns vary according to cultural _____ and the social _____. When children are taught to drink responsibly and moderately, there is a far lower rate of _____. Secondly, policies of total abstinence tend to _____ rates of addiction rather than _____ them. In the United States, prohibition _____ rates of alcoholism. Thirdly, not all addicts have _____ symptoms when they stop taking a drug. Lastly, addiction does not depend on the drug alone, but also on the _____ for taking it. _____ drinkers drink to reduce negative feelings when they are anxious, depressed, or tense and have _____ drinking problems. _____ drinkers, on the other hand, drink to increase positive feelings when they are tired, bored, or stressed and have _____ drinking problems.

6-3. Proponents of the biological model feel that once an individual is an alcoholic, they are _____ an alcoholic. Proponents of the learning model feel that once an individual no longer _____ to become drunk, they can learn to drink socially and in moderation.

Review of Key Terms

The following is a list of the Key Terms from the section "Drug Abuse and Addiction." Make sure you are familiar with each term before taking the matching test on these terms.

substance abuse disorder	Type I alcoholism	learning model
biological model	Type II alcoholism	

Matching Self Test 6

Match the appropriate term with its definition or description.

1. _____ Alcoholism, which begins in adulthood and is not associated with genetic factors.

2. _____ A maladaptive pattern of substance use, which leads to clinically significant impairment or distress.

3. _____ A model that explains addiction as a central activity of the individual's way of life that depends on learning and culture.

4. _____ Alcoholism, which begins in adolescence and is linked to impulsivity, antisocial behaviour, violent criminality, and does seem to be partly heritable.

7. Schizophrenia

Read the section "Schizophrenia" and then answer the following questions. If you have trouble answering any of the questions, re-study the relevant material before going on to the review of key terms and the matching test.

7-1.   When the personality loses its unity, it is referred to as _____. Schizophrenia is not a _____ or _____ personality. It is a form of _____, a mental condition that involves distorted perceptions of reality and an inability to function in most aspects of life. Symptoms of schizophrenia that involve additions to normal behaviour are active or _____ symptoms. On the other hand, symptoms involving a loss or absence of normal traits are _____ symptoms. The most common positive symptoms include (1) false beliefs, _____, (2) sensory experiences in the absence of sensory stimulation, _____, (3) disorganized, incoherent _____ that consists of a jumble of ideas and symbols linked in a meaningless way called word _____, and (4) disorganized and _____ behaviour. Some schizophrenics completely withdraw into a private world and are immobile for hours in a condition called a _____ stupor. Negative symptoms include loss of _____, poverty of _____, empty replies in _____· and emotional _____. When symptoms of schizophrenia appear suddenly, the prognosis for recovery is _____; but, when symptoms gradually emerge, the outlook is less certain.

7-2.   There are several findings concerning the causes of schizophrenia. Firstly, some individuals with schizophrenia show a decreased _____ weight. Secondly, other individuals with schizophrenia have high levels of activity in brain areas where the neurotransmitter _____ is found. Thirdly, there is a _____ component to schizophrenia. Fourthly, there is evidence that damage to the fetal brain increases the likelihood of schizophrenia. One prenatal cause may be _____. Another prenatal culprit may be the _____ virus. Lastly, some researchers favor the vulnerability-_____ model as an explanation for schizophrenia.

Review of Key Terms

The following is a list of the Key Terms from the section "Schizophrenia." Make sure you are familiar with each term before taking the matching test on these terms.

schizophrenia   negative symptoms   word salad

psychosis   delusions   catatonic stupor

positive symptoms   hallucinations   vulnerability-stress model

Matching Self Test 7

Match the appropriate term with its definition or description.

1. _____ Sensory experiences in the absence of sensory stimulation.

2. _____ Symptoms of schizophrenia that involve the loss or absence of normal traits and abilities

3. _____ A state in which the schizophrenic completely withdraws into a private world, sitting for hours without moving.

4. _____ Symptoms involving an exaggeration or distortion of normal thinking processes and behaviour.

SAMPLE ANSWERS TO *WHAT'S AHEAD* QUESTIONS FROM TEXTBOOK

After you have completed the "Looking Back" section at the end of the chapter by answering the "What's Ahead" questions that preceded each major section of the chapter, compare your answers to the following sample answers. If your answers are not similar to the sample answers, review the pertinent sections of the chapter. The relevant page(s) for each question is(are) provided in the "Looking Back" section in the text.

Why were slaves who dreamed of freedom once considered to have a mental disorder?

Sometimes, a society's notions of mental disorder serve the interests of those in power. This was the case in the early part of the nineteenth century with respect to slaves who dreamed of freedom A physician named Samuel Cartwright argued that many slaves were suffering from drapetomania, an urge to escape from slavery. Thus, doctors could assure slave owners that a mental illness and not the intolerable condition of slavery made slaves seek freedom. Today, of course, psychologists consider drapetomania foolish and cruel.

What's wrong with using tests such as the famous "inkblot" test to diagnose disorders?

Projective tests such as the "inkblot" test have both low reliability and low validity when they are used for assessment or diagnosis. In brief, such tests give inconsistent results and fail to measure what they claim to measure. Thus, they should not be used to diagnose disorders.

Why is the standard guide to psychological and psychiatric diagnosis so controversial?

It is controversial because it has extraordinary impact worldwide, but it has limitations. These limitations include the danger of overdiagnosis, the power of diagnostic labels to influence the perceptions of clinicians and the behaviour of clients, the possible confusion of serious mental disorders with normal problems, and the illusion of objectivity.

What's the difference between ordinary anxiety and an anxiety disorder?

Ordinary anxiety is attached to some dangerous, unfamiliar, or stressful situation. It is adaptive because it energizes and motivates us to cope with the situation. In some individuals, however, anxiety is detached from any apparent danger, or it doesn't turn off when danger is past. These individuals are probably suffering an anxiety disorder.

Why is the most disabling of all phobias known as the "fear of fear"?

The fundamental fear in agoraphobia is of being alone in a public place, where escape might be difficult or where help might be unavailable. Agoraphobia may begin with a series of panic attacks that seem to come out of the blue. The attack is so scary that the agoraphobic-to-be begins to avoid situations that he or she thinks may provoke another panic attack. After a while, any sort of emotional arousal, from whatever source, feels too much like anxiety, and the person will try to avoid it. Because so many of the actions associated with this phobia are designed to help the person avoid a panic attack, it is sometimes known as the "fear of fear."

When is checking the stove before leaving home a sign of caution—and when does it signal a disorder?

It signals a disorder when the behaviour troubles the individual and interferes with the person's life. People who suffer from compulsion disorders feel that they have no control over their behaviour.

How can you tell whether you have major depression or just the blues?

A major depression involves emotional, behavioural, and cognitive changes severe enough to disrupt a person's usual functioning. Emotionally healthy people who are sad or grieving do not see themselves as completely worthless and unlovable, and they know at some level that their sadness or grief will pass. But depressed people have low self-esteem and interpret losses as signs of personal failure and conclude that they will never be happy again.

What are the "poles" in bipolar disorder?

The two "poles" are major depression and mania. Mania is an abnormally high state of exhilaration. The symptoms are exactly the opposite of those in depression. The person is full of energy and feels full of ambitions, plans, and power. The manic person has inflated self-esteem

How do some people think themselves into depression?

Such people may have a pessimistic explanatory style, which leads to depression. They believe that nothing good will ever happen to them, that the future is bleak, and that they cannot do anything to change it. It is also possible that such people may have a "ruminating response style." A person with this response style tends to brood endlessly about their negative feelings.

When does being self-centered become a disorder?

It becomes a narcissistic personality disorder when the person's sense of self-importance and self-absorption becomes extremely exaggerated. Individuals who are narcissistic are preoccupied

190

with fantasies of unlimited success, power, brilliance, or ideal love. They demand constant attention and admiration and feel entitled to special favors, without being willing to reciprocate.

What do a charming but heartless tycoon and a remorseless killer have in common?

They both may have antisocial personality disorder. People with this disorder are without conscience and have no regard for the rights of others. They lack empathy and the ability to feel remorse or sorrow for immoral actions.

Why are some people seemingly incapable of feeling guilt and shame?

The inability of such people to feel emotional arousal suggests some abnormality in the central nervous system. Some researchers believe such people share a common inherited disorder, a genetic disposition toward impulsivity, addiction, or hyperactivity. Other possible causes include being neglected or rejected by parents, having brain damage as a result of birth complications or physical abuse in childhood, and living in a culture or environment that rewards and fosters antisocial traits.

What causes otherwise healthy people to forget who they are?

Such people may be experiencing a dissociative fugue state in which a person forgets his or her identity and also gives up customary habits and wanders far from home. The fugue state may last anywhere from a few days to many years. This fugue state would be a reaction to some traumatic or extremely stressful personal situation. Skeptics point out that it is difficult to determine when people in fugue states have a true disorder and when they are faking.

Why are so many clinicians and researchers skeptical about multiple personality disorder?

Those who are skeptical about multiple personality disorder (MPD) have shown that most of the research used to support the diagnosis is seriously flawed. Skeptics also worry that some clinicians may actually be creating the disorder in their clients through the power of suggestion. In brief, there is little empirical evidence to support MPD. This does not mean that no legitimate cases exist, but great caution is warranted because of the epidemic of cases reported in the last two decades and because so many of those cases have turned out to be a result of psychiatric malpractice.

Why can two people drink the same amount of wine and have two different physical reactions to it?

They can have different reactions because some individuals and ethnic groups have a low tolerance for alcohol. In addition, women generally will get drunker than men on the same amount of alcohol because women are smaller, on average, and their bodies metabolize alcohol differently. Similarly, many Asians have a genetically determined adverse reaction to even small amounts of alcohol.

Why is alcoholism more prevalent in Ireland than in Italy?

This difference is probably due to different cultural practices and social environments in the two countries. Alcoholism is much more likely to occur in societies that forbid children to drink but condone drunkenness in adults (as in Ireland) than in societies that teach children how to drink responsibly and moderately but condemn adult drunkenness (as in Italy).

Why don't policies of total abstinence from alcohol always work?

According to the learning model of addiction, because people are denied the opportunity to learn to drink moderately, they drink excessively when given the chance to drink.

If you take morphine to control chronic pain, does that mean you'll become addicted to it?

No, addiction does not depend on the drug alone, but also on the reasons for taking it. Addicts use drugs to escape from the real world, but people living with chronic pain use some of the same drugs, including morphine, in order to function in the real world and do not become addicted.

What's the difference between schizophrenia and a "split personality"?

People with schizophrenia do not have a "split" or "multiple" personality. Schizophrenia is a fragmented condition in which words are split form meaning, actions from motives, and perceptions from reality. It is an example of a psychosis, a mental condition that involves distorted perceptions of reality and an inability to function in most aspects of life. "Split" or "multiple" personality is a dissociative disorder and not a psychosis.

Why do most researchers consider schizophrenia a brain disorder?

They consider it a brain disorder because there is so much evidence relating schizophrenia to brain abnormalities. For example, some individuals with schizophrenia show decreased brain weight, a decrease in the volume of the temporal lobe or limbic regions, reduced numbers of neurons in the prefrontal cortex, or enlargement of the ventricles. These may all be signs of brain damage. In addition, many people with schizophrenia have high levels of activity in brain areas where the neurotransmitter dopamine is found.

Could schizophrenia begin in the womb?

Evidence is mounting that damage to the fetal brain increases the likelihood of schizophrenia. Another culprit may be an infectious virus during prenatal development. The virus could attack specific areas of the brain, yet remain latent for many years before causing symptoms to appear. Thus, schizophrenia could begin in the womb.

MULTIPLE-CHOICE PROGRESS TEST

Choose the single best answer for each of the following questions. When you have finished this progress test, check your answers with those at the end of the chapter. You should review the indicated pages in the text for the questions you do not answer correctly.

1. Which of the following is a criterion (are criteria) used by mental health professionals when defining mental disorder?
    a. violation of cultural standards
    b. maladaptive behaviour
    c. emotional distress
    d. all of the above

2. Which of the following tests has the highest reliability and validity?
    a. Rorschach Inkblot Test

b. TAT

c. MMPI

d. All of the above have equal reliability and validity.

3. Which of the following is a criticism (are criticisms) of the DSM-IV?
   a. the danger of overdiagnosis
   b. the power of diagnostic labels
   c. the illusion of objectivity
   d. all of the above

4. A _____ is an anxiety disorder in which a person experiences an exaggerated fear of a specific situation, activity, or object.
   a. generalized-anxiety disorder
   b. post-traumatic stress disorder
   c. panic disorder
   d. phobia

5. The most disabling phobia is _____, which accounts for more than half of the phobia cases for which people seek treatment.
   a. claustrophobia
   b. acrophobia
   c. agoraphobia
   d. triskaidekaphobia

6. PET scans find that several parts of the brain (e.g., the orbital cortex) are hyperactive in people with _____.
   a. OCD
   b. post-traumatic stress disorder
   c. panic disorder
   d. agoraphobia

7. When people experience episodes of both depression and mania, they are said to have _____ disorder.
   a. obsessive-compulsive
   b. bipolar
   c. antisocial personality
   d. dissociative identity

8. Which of the following statements about depression is FALSE?
   a. Drugs that decrease the levels of serotonin and norepinephrine sometimes alleviate symptoms of depression.
   b. Depressive episodes are most frequently set off by the disruption of a primary relationship.
   c. The more children they have, the more likely mothers are to become depressed.
   d. None of the above

9.   A _____ personality disorder is characterized by an exaggerated sense of self-importance and self-absorption.
    a. paranoid
    b. narcissistic
    c. antisocial
    d. dissociative

10.   Which of the following statements about antisocial personality disorder is FALSE?
    a. Antisocial personality disorder is more common in males than females.
    b. Individuals with antisocial personality disorder do not respond to punishments that would make most people anxious.
    c. Individuals with antisocial personality disorder lack empathy and have no regard for the rights of others.
    d. None of the above

11.   _____ is a(n) _____ disorder in which a person flees home and forgets his or her identity.
    a. Amnesia; anxiety
    b. Amnesia; dissociative
    c. Fugue; anxiety
    d. Fugue; dissociative

12.   The more commonly used term for dissociative identity disorder is _____ disorder.
    a. obsessive-compulsive
    b. manic-depressive
    c. multiple personality
    d. antisocial personality

13.   Which of the following statements is FALSE?
    a. Many Asians have a genetically determined adverse reaction to even small amounts of alcohol.
    b. Women will generally get drunker than men on the same amount of alcohol.
    c. Type I alcoholism seems partly heritable, but Type II alcoholism is not associated with genetic factors.
    d. None of the above

14.   Which of the following statements is FALSE?
    a. Addiction patterns vary according to cultural practices and the social environment.
    b. Policies of total abstinence tend to decrease rates of addiction rather than increase them.
    c. Not all addicts have withdrawal symptoms when they stop taking a drug.
    d. Addiction does not depend on the drug alone, but also on the reasons for taking it.

15. Problems with drugs are likely to occur when:
    a. a person has a genetic or physiological vulnerability to a drug.
    b. a person believes he or she has no control over the drug.
    c. laws or customs encourage or teach people to take a drug in binges, and moderate use is neither encouraged or taught.
    d. all of the above

16. _____ is a psychosis in which words are split from meaning, actions from motives, and perceptions from reality.
    a. Dissociative identity disorder
    b. Schizophrenia
    c. Fugue state
    d. Paranoid personality disorder

17. Positive symptoms of schizophrenia involve an _____ of normal thinking processes; negative symptoms involve the _____ of normal traits and abilities.
    a. exaggeration; exaggeration
    b. exaggeration; absence
    c. absence; exaggeration
    d. absence; absence

18. The false belief of an individual with schizophrenia that he is Jesus or some other famous person is a _____.
    a. delusion
    b. hallucination
    c. compulsion
    d. obsession

19. Which of the following is a negative symptom of schizophrenia?
    a. disorganized speech
    b. emotional flatness
    c. bizarre delusion
    d. hallucination

20. Which of the following statements about schizophrenia is FALSE?
    a. A particular kind of dopamine receptor is far more common in the brains of schizophrenics than in those of other people.
    b. Nearly 90% of all persons with schizophrenia have a schizophrenic parent.
    c. There is a significant association between exposure to an influenza virus during the second trimester of prenatal development and the onset of adult schizophrenia.
    d. None of the above

ANSWERS

GUIDED STUDY

1. Defining and Diagnosing Disorder

1.1.

mental	defeating	validity
cultural	maladaptive	Rorschach Inkblot
maladaptive	community	Thematic Apperception
emotional	insanity	inventories
emotional	projective	Multiphasic Personality
suffering	ambiguous	
worry	reliability	

1.2.

Statistical	labels	disordered
300	eight	normal
overdiagnosis	voices	objectivity

Matching Self-Test 1

1. inventories
2. projective tests
3. TAT
4. mental disorder

2. Anxiety Disorders

2.1.

anxiety	predisposing	post-traumatic
generalized	precipitating	panic

2.2.

phobia	social	agoraphobia

2.3.

obsessions	repugnant	caudate
compulsions	hand washing	
obsessive-	checking	
compulsive	orbital	

Matching Self-Test 2

1. post-traumatic stress disorder
2. phobia
3. obsessive-compulsive disorder
4. panic disorder
5. generalized anxiety disorder

3. Mood Disorders

3.1.	depression	hopelessness	energy
	Dysthymia	suicide	mania
	major	pleasure	bipolar

3.2.	biological	relations	cognitive
	chemistry	attachment	thinking
	adoption	affiliation	interpreting
	social	relationships	pessimistic
	circumstances	primary	vulnerability-stress
	jobs	relationship	interaction

Matching Self-Test 3

| 1. mania | 3. major depression |
| 2. bipolar disorder | 4. dysthymia |

---

4. Personality Disorders

| 4.1. | personality | Paranoid | narcissistic |

4.2.	antisocial	half	neurological
	psychopaths	punishment	brain
	sociopaths	anxious	social
	males	central nervous	
	females	inhibition	

Matching Self-Test 4

| 1. narcissistic personality disorder | 2. antisocial personality disorder | 3. paranoid personality disorder |

---

5. Dissociative Disorders

| 5.1. | dissociative | dissociative | fugue |
| | amnesia | psychogenic | controversial |

5.2.	multiple personality	flawed	
	childhood	creating	
	traumatic	suggestion	
	skeptical	sociocognitive	

Matching Self-Test 5

1. fugue   2. dissociative identity disorder   3. psychogenic amnesia

---

6. Drug Abuse and Addiction

6.1.   maladaptive   Jellinek   Type II
        impairment   inherited
        biological   Type I

6.2.   learning   alcoholism   reasons
        learning   increase   Coping
        culture   decrease   more
        practices   increased   Enhancement
        environment   withdrawal   fewer

6.3.   always   needs

Matching Self-Test 6

1. Type I alcoholism   3. learning model
2. substance abuse disorder   4. Type II alcoholism

---

7. Schizophrenia

7.1.   schizophrenia   delusions   motivation
        split   hallucinations   speech
        multiple   speech   conversation
        psychosis   salad   flatness
        positive   inappropriate   good
        negative   catatonic

7.2.   brain   genetic   influenza
        dopamine   malnutrition   stress

Matching Self-Test 7

1. hallucinations   3. catatonic stupor
2. negative symptoms   4. positive symptoms

ANSWERS TO MULTIPLE CHOICE PROGRESS TEST

Item No.	Answer(s)	Page(s) in Textbook
1.	d. all of the above	342-343
2.	c. MMPI	343-345
3.	d. all of the above	346-348
4.	d. phobia	349
5.	c. agoraphobia	350
6.	a. OCD	351
7.	b. bipolar	353
8.	a. Drugs that decrease the level of serotonin and norepinephrine sometimes alleviate symptoms of depression.	353
9.	b. narcissistic	357
10.	d. None of the above	357-358
11.	d. Fugue; dissociative	360
12.	c. multiple personality	361
13.	c. Type I alcoholism seems partly heritable, but Type II alcoholism is not associated with genetic factors.	363
14.	b. Policies of total abstinence tend to decrease rates of addiction rather than increase them.	364-366
15.	d. all of the above	367
16.	b. Schizophrenia	368
17.	b. exaggeration; absence	368-369
18.	a. delusion	368
19.	b. emotional flatness	369
20.	b. Nearly 90% of all persons with schizophrenia have a schizophrenic parent.	370-372

CHAPTER 11

Approaches to Treatment and Therapy

CHAPTER OVERVIEW

The chapter opens with a discussion of biological treatments. This includes various drug therapies employing antipsychotic drugs, antidepressant drugs, tranquilizers, and lithium carbonate. Limitations of drug treatments, such as the placebo effect, relapse rates, dosage problems, and long-term risks are also presented. Other biological treatments discussed include psychosurgery, such as prefrontal lobotomies, and electroconvulsive therapy.

The four major schools of psychotherapy are presented next. Psychodynamic therapies, such as Freud's psychoanalysis are discussed first. Key aspects of psychoanalysis such as transference and free association are detailed. Behavioural and cognitive therapies, including systematic desensitization, aversive conditioning, flooding, skills training, and rational emotive therapy are then described. A discussion of the client-centered humanist therapies and the nature of existential therapies follows. Lastly, the differences between family therapies and psychotherapies are discussed.

Various alternatives to psychotherapy, including community psychology programs and rehabilitation programs are described. The clubhouse model of community psychology and a critical view of self-help programs are presented. In terms of evaluating psychotherapy, the scientist-practitioner gap is discussed, as are results from controlled clinical trials on the effectiveness of psychotherapies. The various components of successful psychotherapy are presented, including a discussion of the therapeutic alliance. Lastly, harmful aspects of psychotherapy are noted.

GUIDED STUDY

1. Biological Treatments

Read the section "Biological Treatments" and then answer the following questions. If you have trouble answering any of the questions, re-study the relevant material before going on to the review of key terms and the matching test.

1-1   The most popular biological treatment for psychological disorders is _____.
_____ drugs, or neuroleptics, are used in the treatment of _____ and other psychoses. These drugs block or reduce the sensitivity of brain receptors that respond to the neurotransmitter _____. _____ drugs are used in the

treatment of depression, anxiety, phobias, and obsessive-compulsive disorder. _____ inhibitors elevate the level of norepinephrine and _____. _____ antidepressants boost norepinephrine and serotonin by preventing re-uptake of these substances. Drugs such as Prozac work on a similar principle, but only on the neurotransmitter, _____, and hence are called selective serotonin inhibitors (SSRIs). Drugs such as Valium and Xanax are _____ that increase the activity of the neurotransmitter gamma-aminobutyric acid (_____). These drugs are most commonly used for depressed mood, _____, or anxiety. A salt, _____ carbonate, is used to treat _____ disorder. Although drug treatments are very popular and appear effective, there are several limitations. Firstly, the _____ effect may be operating. That is, some people will respond positively to new drugs just because of the _____ surrounding them. Most people are surprised to discover that one meta-analysis found that antidepressants showed no advantage beyond the _____ effect. Another found no difference in effectiveness of medication versus psychotherapy. Secondly, there are high _____ and _____ rates for drug treatments. Thirdly, there is often a problem in determining the correct _____. Part of the problem stems from the fact that drugs may be _____ differently in men versus women, the old versus the young, and different ethnic groups. Lastly, the long-term are not all known. Some antipsychotic drugs are known to cause _____ dyskinesia and neuroleptic _____ syndrome. Antidepressants can produce many unpleasant _____ reactions.

1-2.   One early type of psychosurgery, _____, was used in the 17th century and involved drilling holes in a patient's skull. In the early 190Os, another form of psychosurgery was developed by Moniz and entailed destroying nerve fibers running from the prefrontal lobes to other brain areas, hence the name _____. Due to the advent of several drug therapies during the 1950s, psychosurgery is rarely used today. Another therapy popular during the 1950s, _____ therapy 0ECT), is becoming popular once again as a treatment for _____. There is controversy, however, surrounding its use.

Review of Key Terms

The following is a list of the Key Terms from the section "Biological Treatments." Make sure you are familiar with each term before taking the matching test on these terms.

antipsychotic drugs	SSRIs	psychosurgery
neuroleptics	tranquilizers	t prefrontal lobotomy
antidepressant drugs	lithium carbonate	electroconvulsive therapy (ECT)
MAO inhibitors	placebo effect	
tricyclics	herapeutic window	

Matching Self Test 1

Match the appropriate term with its definition or description.

1. _____ Drugs commonly but often inappropriately prescribed for patients who complain of unhappiness, anxiety, or worry.

2. _____ Major tranquilizers used primarily in the treatment of schizophrenia and other psychotic disorders.

3. _____ A procedure used in cases of prolonged and severe major depression, in which a brief brain seizure is induced to alter brain chemistry.

4. _____ Antidepressants that boost serotonin levels by preventing the reuptake of serotonin.

5. _____ Antidepressants that elevate the level of norepinephrine and serotonin in the brain by blocking or inhibiting an enzyme that deactivates these neurotransmitters.

2. Kinds of Psychotherapy

Read the section "Kinds of Psychotherapy" and then answer the following questions. If you have trouble answering any of the questions, re-study the relevant material before going on to the review of key terms and the matching test.

2-1. Psychodynamic therapies are based on Freud's method of _____ in which patients gain _____ through talking. In many psychodynamic therapies, the patient engages in _____ _____, saying whatever comes to mind. Patients who displace emotional elements of their life onto the therapist are said to be engaging in _____. Most traditional psychodynamic therapies do not aim to solve an individual's immediate _____. Instead, the goal is _____ not change.

2-2. Behavioural and cognitive therapies focus on helping individuals to change their _____ and _____. Behavioural techniques include behavioural _____ and contracts where the person sets behavioural goals and attempts to meet them step-by-step. A second behavioural technique, _____ _____, is based on counterconditioning. This is typically used to treat fears. When trying to break a bad habit, therapists might use _____ conditioning in which a punishment is substituted for the reinforcement experienced by engaging in the habitual behaviour. Another behavioural treatment, _____, involves taking clients right into feared situations to demonstrate that the situation is not going to kill them. Lastly, behavioural therapists might engage in _____ training.

Cognitive techniques attempts to help people identify the beliefs and expectations that might be unnecessarily prolonging their problems. These beliefs include _____, the belief that the problem is internal rather than external. Another belief, _____, stems from the fact that many individuals think that their problems are permanent. Lastly, many people believe that they have no _____ over their lives. Cognitive therapists aid clients in substituting negative thoughts with positive thoughts. Two of the best known cognitive therapies were developed by Ellis, _____ _____ therapy, and Beck.

2-3. _____ therapies are based on the assumption that people seek self-actualization and self-fulfillment. Carl Rogers developed a nondirective or _____-centered therapy that utilized _____ _____ regard in an attempt to build the client's self-esteem and sense of love. _____ therapy helps clients explore the meaning of _____. Existential therapists encourage patients to take _____ for their life predicament.

2-4. When the family is seen as a kaleidoscope and treated together, _____ therapy is being used. Some family therapists create a family tree of psychologically significant events across many generations, a _____. Even when the entire family is not treated, many therapists treat individuals in a family _____ approach. Clients learn that if they change, even for the better, their families may protest.

2-5. Most therapists do not use just one approach, but draw on methods and ideas from various approaches. Some _____ prefer to use _____ therapy, where people are put together in an attempt to find solutions. Others use the _____ method to aid clients in forming new stories about themselves.

Review of Key Terms

The following is a list of the Key Terms from the section "Kinds of Psychotherapy." Make sure you are familiar with each term before taking the matching test on these terms.

psychoanalysis	behavioural goals	unconditional positive regard
psychodynamic therapies	aversive conditioning	existential therapy
insight	counterconditioning	family therapy
free association	flooding (exposure)	family systems approach
transference	skills training	genogram
dynamic focus	cognitive therapies	group therapy
behaviour therapies	rational emotive therapy	narrative method
behaviour records	humanist therapies	
behavioural goals	client-centered therapy	

Matching Self Test 2

Match the appropriate term with its definition or description.

1. _____ A step-by-step process of desensitizing a client to a feared object or experience.

2. _____ A treatment that takes the client right into a feared situation, with the therapist going along to show that the situation is not going to kill either of them.

3. _____ In psychodynamic therapies, a critical step in which the client transfers unconscious emotions or reactions, such as emotional feelings about his or her parents, onto the therapist.

4. _____ A therapy that aims to help clients identify the beliefs and expectations that might be unnecessarily prolonging their unhappiness, conflicts, and other problems.

5. _____ A cognitive approach in which the therapist uses rational arguments to directly challenge a client's unrealistic beliefs or expectations.

6. _____ A nondirective therapy developed by Carl Rogers.

7. _____ A family tree of psychologically significant events across as many generations as possible.

8. _____ In psychoanalysis, a method of uncovering unconscious conflicts by saying freely whatever comes to mind.

3. Alternatives to Psychotherapy

Read the section "Alternatives to Psychotherapy" and then answer the following questions. If you have trouble answering any of the questions, re-study the relevant material before going on to the review of key terms and the matching test.

3-1. Programs aimed at helping people who are seriously mentally ill or who have disabilities and need more than psychotherapy are _____ and _____ programs. _____ psychologists set up programs to help people who are mentally ill, in their own communities rather than in hospitals. One successful model used by community psychologists is the _____ model through which psychologists may offer rehabilitation counselling, job and training, and a support _____. Rehabilitation psychologists on the other hand, are concerned with the _____ and treatment of people who are _____ disabled. Their treatment may include behaviour therapy, _____ counselling, job training, and _____ intervention.

3-2. About 40 percent of Americans participate in _____-_____ groups that provide emotional support. Groups are available for alcoholics, abusive parents, gay fathers, divorced people, rape victims, widows, widowers, and people suffering from various psychological disorders to name a few. Although these groups offer _____, they do not offer _____ for specific problems.

Review of Key Terms

The following is a list of the Key Terms from the section "Alternatives to Psychotherapy." Make sure you are familiar with each term before taking the matching test on these terms.

community psychologists   clubhouse model   rehabilitation psychologists

self-help groups

Matching Self Test 3

Match the appropriate term with its definition or description.

1. _____   Psychologists concerned with the assessment and treatment of people who are physically disabled, either temporarily or permanently.

2. _____   Psychologists who set up programs to help people who are mentally ill, in their own communities rather than in hospitals.

4. Evaluating Psychotherapy and its Alternatives

Read the section "Evaluating Psychotherapy and its Alternatives" and then answer the following questions. If you have trouble answering any of the questions, re-study the relevant material before going on to the review of key terms and the matching test.

4-1. Scientists and therapists disagree on the relevance of research attempting to evaluate psychotherapy. This is referred to as the _____-_____ gap. Clinical researchers have used _____ clinical trials in an attempt to assess the effectiveness of various kinds of therapy. The overall conclusions of these studies are (1) psychotherapy is better than doing _____, (2) people who have _____ serious problems and are _____ to improve do the best in psychotherapy, (3) for the common emotional problems of life, _____-_____ treatment is usually sufficient, and (4) in some cases, psychotherapy is _____ because of the therapist's incompetence, _____, unethical behaviour, or lack or knowledge.

4-2. Therapy is the most helpful when clients have a strong sense of _____ and are _____ enough to want to work on their problems. Qualities in the therapist are also important. These include empathy, _____, warmth, and _____. The bond between the therapist and the client, the _____ alliance, is also important. It is also important that therapists distinguish normal cultural patterns from individual _____ problems. For example, many Latinos respond to catastrophic stress with an _____ _____, which an uninformed clinician might label as a sign of _____. Latinos also experience _____, loss of soul, as a response to grief or fright. A therapist unfamiliar with this might conclude that the sufferer was delusional or _____.

4-3.   In a recent evaluation of specific therapies, the APA concluded that for many problems and emotional disorders, _____ and _____ therapies are the method of choice. These therapies are particularly effective for anxiety disorders, _____, health problems, and childhood and adolescent _____ problems.

4-4.   Therapy is most likely to be harmful when (1) the client experiences coercion to accept the therapist's advice, _____ intimacies, or other unethical behaviour, (2) there is bias on the part of a therapist who does not understand the client because of the client's gender, _____, religion, or _____ orientation, and (3) there are therapist-induced _____ resulting from inadvertent suggestions or influence.

Review of Key Terms

The following is a list of the Key Terms from the section "Evaluating Psychotherapy and its Alternatives." Make sure you are familiar with each term before taking the matching test on these terms.

scientist-practitioner gap   controlled clinical trials   therapeutic alliance

Matching Self Test 4

Match the appropriate term with its definition or description.

1. _____   Research studies in which people with a given problem or disorder are randomly assigned to one or more treatment groups or to a control group.

2. _____   The breach between scientists and therapists on the issue of the relevance and importance of research findings.

3. _____   The bond of confidence and mutual understanding established between therapist and client, which allows them to work together to solve the client's problems.

SAMPLE ANSWERS TO *WHAT'S AHEAD* QUESTIONS FROM TEXTBOOK

After you have completed the "Looking Back" section at the end of the chapter by answering the "What's Ahead" questions that preceded each major section of the chapter, compare your answers to the following sample answers. If your answers are not similar to the sample answers, review the pertinent sections of the chapter. The relevant page(s) for each question is(are) provided in the "Looking Back" section in the text.

What kinds of drugs are used to treat psychological disorders?

The main classes of drugs employed to treat disorders are anti-psychotic drugs used in the treatment of schizophrenia and other psychoses, anti-depressant drugs used primarily in the treatment of depression, anxiety, phobias, and obsessive-compulsive disorder, tranquilizers for milder cases of depressed mood, panic, or anxiety, and lithium carbonate for bipolar disorder.

Are antidepressants always the best treatment for depression?

Drugs alone may or may not "cure" an emotional disorder. The effectiveness of pills (drugs) for treating emotional disorders depends upon the individual, the problem, and whether the medication is combined with psychotherapy. Without question, drugs have rescued some people from emotional despair, suicide, or years in a mental hospital. We must remember, however, that the brain affects behaviour and behaviour can also affect the brain. Thus, drug therapy with accompanying psychotherapy is the best way to proceed for treating emotional disorders. In fact, certain psychotherapies work as well as drugs do, or even better, for most people who have depression.

Why is "shock therapy" hailed by some clinicians but condemned by others as "a crime against humanity"?

Supporters of electroconvulsive therapy (ECT) argue that it is foolish to deny suffering, depressed patients a way out of their misery, especially if their misery is making them suicidal. They cite research showing that when ECT is used properly, it is safe and effective and causes no long-term cognitive impairment, memory loss, or detectable brain damage. Critics reply that ECT is too often used improperly and that it can indeed damage the brain. Thus, critics condemn it as a crime against humanity.

Why are psychodynamic therapies called "depth" therapies?

These therapies are considered by their proponents to be "depth" therapies because the goal is to delve for unconscious processes rather than concentrate on "superficial" symptoms and conscious beliefs.

How can therapies based on learning principles help you change your bad habits?

Behavioural therapies are based on the principles of classical and operant conditioning. Aversive conditioning is one behavioural therapy that can be used to help you change your bad habits. It substitutes punishment for the reinforcement that has perpetuated a bad habit.

How do cognitive therapists help people get rid of self-defeating thoughts?

A cognitive therapist helps a person substitute positive thoughts for self-defeating ones and encourages the person to seek out situations that confirm the new ways of thinking

Why do humanist therapists focus on the "here and now" instead of the "why and how"?

Humanist therapies generally do not delve into past conflicts, but aim instead to help people feel better about themselves and free themselves from self-imposed limits. To humanists, the most important thing is how a person subjectively perceives his or her own situation, and the important thing to work for is the will to bring about change. This is why they explore what is going on "here and now" and not "why and how."

Why do family therapists prefer to treat families rather than individuals?

Because they maintain that a person's problem developed in his or her family context and that it is sustained by this context. Thus, efforts to isolate and treat one member of the family without the others are doomed. Even when it is not possible to treat the whole family, some therapists will treat individuals in a family systems perspective.

What community resources can help people who have serious mental disorders?

Community psychology programs emphasize community support, including outpatient services at local clinics and close contact with family and friends. The nature of the support depends on the nature of the disorder or disability. For example, people with schizophrenia need a comprehensive program such as the clubhouse model programs.

What can a self-help group offer a person that relatives, friends, and psychotherapies can't?

Self-help groups offer understanding, empathy, and solutions to shared problems. Such groups can be reassuring and supportive in ways that family, friends, and psychotherapists are not because they share the problem.

What is the "scientist-practitioner gap"—and why has it been widening?

The "scientist-practitioner gap" refers to the gap between scientists and therapists in their assessment of the value of empirical research to the practice of therapy. Scientists are concerned that when therapists fail to keep up with empirical findings in the field (e.g., on the most beneficial methods for particular problems), their clients pay the price. Many psychotherapists, however, think that trying to evaluate psychotherapy using the standard methods of empirical research is an exercise in futility. They think that psychotherapy is an art. Thus, clinical experience is more valuable to therapists than research is. The gap has widened because both the scientists and therapists have become more entrenched in their views. Economic pressures and the rise of managed-care health programs, however, should reduce the gap by requiring psychotherapists to produce clear, research-based guidelines for which therapies are most effective, which therapies are best for which disorder, and which therapies are ineffective or potentially harmful.

What does research tell us about the effectiveness of psychotherapy?

The overall results include the following. Psychotherapy is better than doing nothing at all. People who have less serious problems and are motivated to improve do the best in psychotherapy. For the common emotional problems of life, short-term treatment is usually sufficient. In some cases, psychotherapy is harmful because of the therapist's incompetence, biases, unethical behaviour, or lack of knowledge.

What sorts of people make the best therapists and the best clients?

The most successful therapists make their clients feel respected, accepted, and understood. They are actively invested in the interaction with the client, instead of detached in the manner of Freud.

Clients who are likely to do well in therapy have a strong sense of self and are also distressed enough to want to work on their problems. They tend to have support from their families and a personal style of dealing actively with problems instead of avoiding them. In addition, agreeable, positive individuals are more likely to benefit from therapy.

What form of psychotherapy is most likely to help you if you are anxious or depressed?
Behaviour and cognitive therapies are best. Exposure techniques are more effective than any other treatment for reducing severe phobias, and systematic desensitization is most effective with simple phobias. Cognitive-behavioural therapy is recommended for panic disorder, generalized anxiety disorder, and obsessive-compulsive disorder. Cognitive therapy has been most successful in the treatment of mood disorders, especially depression.

Under what conditions can psychotherapy be harmful?
Some clients can be harmed by becoming excessively dependent upon the therapist for all decisions, and some therapists actually foster this dependency for financial or psychological motives. Clients can also be harmed by coercion to accept the therapist's advice, sexual intimacies, or other unethical behaviour; bias on the part of the therapist who does not understand the client because of the client's gender, culture, religion, or sexual orientation; and therapist-induced disorders resulting from inadvertent suggestions or influence.

MULTIPLE-CHOICE PROGRESS TEST

Choose the single best answer for each of the following questions. When you have finished this progress test, check your answers with those at the end of the chapter. You should review the indicated pages in the text for the questions you do not answer correctly.

1. _____ block or reduce the sensitivity of brain receptors that respond to dopamine.
   a. Antipsychotic drugs
   b. Tricyclic antidepressants
   c. MAO inhibitors
   d. Tranquilizers

2. Which of the following drugs is prescribed for depression?
   a. antipsychotic drugs
   b. MAO inhibitors
   c. tranquilizers
   d. none of the above

3. _____ increase the activity of GABA.
   a. Anti-psychotic drugs
   b. Tricyclic antidepressants
   c. MAO inhibitors
   d. Tranquilizers

4. Jack's mood varies from severe depression to manic states. Which of the following drugs should he take for his disorder?
   a. Prozac
   b. Valium
   c. Clozapine
   d. Lithium carbonate

5. Which of the following statements about drug therapy is FALSE?
   a. Prozac is no more effective than the older generation of antidepressants.
   b. Recent meta-analyses have found antidepressant drugs to be far more effective than psychotherapy.
   c. Asian patients require significantly lower doses of antipsychotic drugs than American patients.
   d. None of the above

6. Tardive dyskinesia is a side effect of _____.
   a. antipsychotic drugs
   b. tricyclic antidepressants
   c. MAO inhibitors
   d. tranquilizers

7. Electroconvulsive therapy is used for the treatment of _____.
   a. depression
   b. schizophrenia
   c. obsessive-compulsive disorder
   d. antisocial personality disorder

8. Which of the following types of psychotherapists would be most likely to use free association and transference?
   a. rational emotive therapist
   b. behavioural therapist
   c. psychodynamic therapist
   d. client-centered therapist

9. Systematic desensitization and flooding are _____ therapies.
   a. psychodynamic
   b. cognitive
   c. behavioural
   d. humanist

10. Which of the following habits of thinking does depression usually involve?
    a. internality
    b. stability
    c. lack of control
    d. all of the above

11. In _____ therapy, the therapist uses rational arguments to directly challenge a client's unrealistic beliefs or expectations.
    a. client-centered
    b. rational emotive
    c. existential
    d. aversive conditioning

12. _____ therapies start from the assumption that people seek self-actualization and self-fulfillment.
    a. Humanist
    b. Cognitive
    c. Behavioural
    d. Psychodynamic

13. _____ therapy helps clients explore the meaning of existence and face the great questions of life such as free will with courage.
    a. Rational emotive
    b. Existential
    c. Psychodynamic
    d. Family

14. A genogram would be used by a(n) _____ therapist.
    a. existential
    b. psychodynamic
    c. humanistic
    d. family

15. _____ psychologists are concerned with the assessment and treatment of people who are physically disabled either temporarily or permanently.
    a. Community
    b. Rational emotive
    c. Family
    d. Rehabilitation

16. Which of the following statements about psychotherapy is FALSE?
    a. Psychotherapy is better than doing nothing at all.
    b. People who have less serious problems and are motivated to improve do the best in psychotherapy.
    c. For the common emotional problems of life, short-term treatment is usually sufficient.
    d. None of the above

17. The breach between scientists and therapists on the issue of the relevance and importance of research findings on the effectiveness of psychotherapy has led to the _____.
    a. therapeutic alliance

b. scientist-practitioner gap
c. clubhouse model
d. narrative method

18. The bond of confidence and mutual understanding established between therapist and client is called the _____.
a. therapeutic window
b. therapeutic alliance
c. clubhouse model
d. family systems approach

19. Which of the following pairings of problem and the most successful therapy for that problem is INCORRECT?.
a. childhood behaviour problems and humanist therapy
b. severe phobias and exposure techniques
c. depression and cognitive therapy
d. panic disorder and cognitive-behavioural therapy

20. Therapy clients can be harmed by:
a. coercion to accept the therapist's advice.
b. therapist-induced disorders resulting from inadvertent suggestions.
c. bias on the part of the therapist who does not understand the client's culture.
d. all of the above

ANSWERS

GUIDED STUDY

1. Biological Treatments

1.1.
medication	reuptake	relapse
Antipsychotic	tranquilizers	dropout
schizophrenia	GABA	dosage
dopamine	panic	metabolized
Antidepressant	lithium	risks
MAO	bipolar	tardive
serotonin	placebo	malignant
Tricyclic	enthusiasm	physical
serotonin	placebo	

212

1.2. trepanning   electroconvulsive
      prefrontal lobotomy   depression

Matching Self-Test 1

1. tranquilizers   4. MAO inhibitors
2. antipsychotic drugs   5. SSRIs
3. electroconvulsive therapy

---

2. Kinds of Psychotherapy

2.1. psychoanalysis   free association   problems
      insight   transference   understanding

2.2. behaviour   skills
      attitudes   internality
      records   stability
      systematic desensitization   control
      aversive   rational emotive
      flooding

2.3. Humanist   Existential
      client   existence
      unconditional positive   responsibility

2.4. family   genogram   systems

2.5. group   narrative

Matching Self-Test 2

1. systematic desensitization   4. cognitive therapy   7. genogram
2. flooding (exposure)   5. rational emotive therapy 8. free association
3. transference   6. client-centered therapy

---

3. Alternatives to Psychotherapy

3.1.

community	skills	group
rehabilitation	network	community
Community	assessment	
clubhouse	physically	

3.2.

self-help	support	psychotherapy

Matching Self-Test 3

1. rehabilitation psychologists   2. community psychologists

---

4. Evaluating Psychotherapy and its Alternatives

4.1.

scientist-practitioner	motivated
controlled	short-term
nothing	harmful
less	biases

4.2.

self	therapeutic	susto
distressed	psychological	psychotic
expressiveness	ataque nervioso	
genuineness	pathology	

4.3.

behaviour	depression
cognitive	behaviour

4.4.

sexual	sexual
culture	disorders

Matching Self-Test 4

1. controlled clinical trials   2. scientist-practitioner gap   3. therapeutic alliance

---

ANSWERS TO MULTIPLE CHOICE PROGRESS TEST

Item No.	Answer(s)	Page(s) in Textbook
1.	a. Antipsychotic drugs	380
2.	b. MAO inhibitors	380
3.	d. Tranquilizers	381
4.	d. Lithium carbonate	381
5.	b. Recent meta-analyses have found antidepressant drugs to be far more effective than psychotherapy.	382
6.	a. antipsychotic drugs	383
7.	a. depression	384
8.	c. psychodynamic therapist	386
9.	c. behavioural	387-388
10.	d. all of the above	389
11.	b. rational emotive	389
12.	a. Humanist	390
13.	b. Existential	391
14.	d. family	392
15.	d. Rehabilitation	395
16.	d. None of the above	397-399
17.	b. scientist-practitioner gap	397-39818.
18.	b. therapeutic alliance	399
19.	a. childhood behaviour problems and humanist therapy	400-401
20.	d. all of the above	402

CHAPTER 12

Emotion, Stress, and Health

CHAPTER OVERVIEW

The chapter opens with a discussion of the nature of emotion. This includes a description of the relationship between facial expression and emotion, the structures in the brain responsible for the components of emotion, hormones that help to produce emotion, and the two-factor theory of emotion. The effect of culture on emotion is next addressed through a discussion of the varieties of emotion in different cultures and the various ways to communicate emotion.

The effects of stress on the body and the mind are assessed. This discussion includes coverage of Selye's work on environmental stressors, the relationship between stress and illness, and how optimism and pessimism affect health. In addition, the effects of the emotions of hostility and depression on health are discussed. Lastly, ways to cope with various emotions and stress are discussed. These include cooling off, solving the problem, rethinking the problem, and looking outward.

GUIDED STUDY

1. The Nature of Emotion

Read the section "The Nature of Emotion" and then answer the following questions. If you have trouble answering any of the questions, re-study the relevant material before going on to the review of key terms and the matching test.

1-1   The authors of the text equate the full experience of _____ with a tree. The _____ capacity for emotion is the trunk; _____ and _____ make up the branches, and _____ is the gardener that shapes the tree and prunes it. The most obvious place to look for emotion is on the _____. Paul Ekman has identified _____ basic facial expressions: anger, _____. fear, _____, disgust, _____, and contempt. Ekman has found that the ability to recognize emotions based on facial expressions carries across _____. He calls his theory _____-_____ to emphasize that two factors are involved in facial expression, (1) a universal _____ in the facial muscles associated with certain emotions, and (2) _____-_____ variations in the expression of emotion. People are more likely to recognize _____ faces than they are to recognize expressions of _____ or anger. Emotions are not always revealed through facial expressions;

216

we sometimes use facial expressions to _____ about our feelings. Ekman found a way to determine whether one's facial expression is a valid indicator of one's true emotion. He has developed a coding system that analyzes and identifies each of the _____ of the face. Another factor in interpreting emotion is the _____ in which an observer sees the emotion expressed. Facial expressions can also help people to communicate with _____. According to the facial hypothesis, the facial muscles send messages to the _____ concerning the basic emotion being expressed.

Some researchers have attempted to identify the structures in the _____ responsible for emotion. By studying those with _____ (people who can recognize facial expressions but are unable to identify faces), researchers have determined that these abilities are handled in different areas of the _____ hemisphere. Researchers have also determined that the two hemispheres play differing roles in the experience of emotions. Areas in the _____ hemisphere appear to be specialized for positive emotions, whereas areas in the _____ appear to be specialized for negative emotions. Another brain structure that plays a key role in emotion is located in the limbic system, the _____. The amygdala is responsible for making the initial decision to either _____ or _____ from a person or situation.

Still other researchers focus on how _____ are involved in emotion. Two hormones that activate the sympathetic nervous system and are involved in emotion are _____ and _____.

1-2.   Schachter and Singer proposed the _____-_____ theory of emotion in which they argued that _____ changes are necessary to experience an _____, but are not enough. In addition to physiological arousal, one's _____ interpretation is also important. Many researchers have studied how emotions are influenced by beliefs, _____ of the situation, expectations, and _____. Cognitive research on emotion helps explain why people sometimes feel an emotion that is inappropriate to the situation.

Review of Key Terms

The following is a list of the Key Terms from the section "The Nature of Emotion." Make sure you are familiar with each term before taking the matching test on these terms.

emotion	amygdala	two-factor theory of emotion
neurocultural theory	epinephrine	attributions
facial-feedback hypothesis	norepinephrine	

Matching Self Test 1

Match the appropriate term with its definition or description.

1. _____ The theory that emotions depend on both physiological arousal and a cognitive interpretation of that arousal.

2. _____ The theory emphasizing that two factors are involved in facial expression, the neurophysiology of facial muscles and culture-specific variations in the expression of emotion.

3. _____ The hypothesis stating that the facial muscles send messages to the brain about the basic emotion being expressed.

4. _____ A small structure in the brain's limbic system that plays a key role in emotion.

2. Emotion and Culture

Read the section "Emotion in Cultural Context" and then answer the following questions. If you have trouble answering any of the questions, re-study the relevant material before going on to the review of key terms and the matching test.

2-1. Emotions that are the most recognized the world over and that are biologically based are considered by some researchers to be _____ emotions, whereas they consider emotions that vary by culture to be _____ emotions. Others believe that this distinction is not necessary and that it masks the influence of _____ on every aspect of emotional experience. If some emotions do prove to be biological in nature, _____ determine much of what people feel emotional _____.

2-2. Emotions are also displayed differently depending on a culture's _____ _____ for emotion. Display roles also influence _____ language. When acting out an emotion that we do not really feel, we are engaging in emotion _____. Differing display rules can help explain perceived gender and cultural differences in emotion.

Review of Key Terms

The following is a list of the Key Terms from the section "Emotion in Cultural Context." Make sure you are familiar with each term before taking the matching test on these terms.

primary emotions   display rules   emotion work

secondary emotions   body language

Matching Self Test 2

Match the appropriate term with its definition or description.

1. _____ Expression of an emotion, often because of a role requirement, that a person does not really feel.

2. _____ Emotions that are either "blends" of primary emotions or specific to certain cultures.

3. _____ Social and cultural rules that regulate when, how, and where a person may express (or suppress) emotions.

4. _____ Emotions that are considered to be universal and biologically based.

3. The Nature of Stress

Read the section "The Nature of Stress" and then answer the following questions. If you have trouble answering any of the questions, re-study the relevant material before going on to the review of key terms and the matching test.

3-1.   According to Hans Selye, environmental stressors can force an organism to mobilize its physiological resources in the _____ or _____ response. Selye concluded that stress consists of physiological responses that occur in three phases, (1) the _____ phase, (2) the _____ phase, and (3) the _____ phase. Selye also felt that positive stress, which he called _____, can be beneficial. One of the bodily systems that stress affects is the _____ system. The white blood cells of the immune system are designed to (1) recognize _____ substances (antigens) and (2) destroy or deactivate those substances. It has been found that prolonged stress can _____ some or many of the white cells. Stressors most likely to affect the immune, cardiovascular, and endocrine systems are (1) _____ and loss, (2) noise, _____, and hassles, and (3) poverty and _____. As not all individuals respond to stress in the same way, Seyle's model has been revised by health psychologists who now take into account the psychological qualities of the individual and how the individual copes. In this more complicated view, psychological stress is caused by an interaction of the _____ and the _____.

3-2.   The responses made by individuals to negative life events fall into two categories. Those who think "If something can go wrong for me it will" are classified as _____, and those who think "I'll somehow come through okay" are classified as _____. The pessimistic style is associated with lower _____-_____, less achievement, more _____, and slower emotional recovery from trauma. The optimistic style is better for your _____. Optimists are more likely than pessimists to be active _____ solvers and to seek that can help them.

One type of pessimism that is not associated with negative health outcomes is called _____ pessimism. This view is adopted by many _____, who seem to expect the worst, but work hard to avoid it. Optimism is also related to having a sense of control, referred to as an _____ locus of control. A sense of control affects the immune and _____ systems. The type of control related to health is _____-_____, the belief that you are basically in charge of your own life and well-being. Control in a Western culture is referred to as _____ control, in which people try to influence existing reality by changing other people, events, or circumstances. In an Eastern culture, _____ control, in which people try to accommodate to reality by changing their own aspirations or desires, is more prevalent.

Review of Key Terms

The following is a list of the Key Terms from the section "The Nature of Stress." Make sure you are familiar with each term before taking the matching test on these terms.

stressors e	ustress	locus of control
alarm phase	psychological stress	primary control
resistance phase	pessimistic explanatory style	secondary control
exhaustion phase	optimistic explanatory style	

Matching Self Test 3

Match the appropriate term with its definition or description.

1. _____   An effort to modify reality by changing other people, the situation, or events.

2. _____   The result of a relationship between the person and the environment, in which the person believes the situation is overwhelming and threatens his or her ability to cope.

3. _____   A general expectation about whether the results of your actions are under your own control or beyond your control.

4. _____   An effort to accept reality by changing your own attitudes, goals, or emotions.

4. Stress and Emotion

Read the section "Stress in Emotional Context" and then answer the following questions. If you have trouble answering any of the questions, re-study the relevant material before going on to the review of key terms and the matching test.

4-1.   Emotion and illness were first linked through research on _____ personalities. Type A individuals are determined to _____, have a sense of time _____, are _____, and are _____. Type B people are calmer and less _____. Being a Type A personality alone does not place one at greater risk of heart disease; being Type A and having _____/_____ _____ does seem to place one at greater risk. In addition to hostility, _____ also seems to play a role in the risk of illness, specifically heart disease.

4-2.   Individuals who have the personality trait of _____ _____ constantly try to deny feelings of anxiety, anger, or fear and pretend that everything is fine. These "repressors" are at greater risk of becoming ill versus those who can acknowledge their fears. One explanation for this is that prolonged inhibition of thoughts and emotions requires _____ effort that is stressful to the body. In a study in which college students were asked to either suppress or divulge information concerning traumatic past experiences, those who divulged the information were healthier.

Review of Key Terms

The following is a list of the Key Terms from the section "Stress in Emotional Context." Make sure you are familiar with each term before taking the matching test on these terms.

Type A personalities   cynical/antagonistic hostility   emotional inhibition

Type B personalities   depression   repressors

Matching Self Test 4

Match the appropriate term with its definition or description.

1. _____   People who try to suppress their feelings all of the time.

2. _____   People who are determined to achieve, have a sense of time urgency, are irritable, and are impatient at anyone who gets in their way.

3. _____   The type of hostility displayed by people who are mistrustful of others and quick to have mean, furious arguments.

5. Emotions, Stress, and Health: How to Cope

Read the section "Emotions, Stress, and Health: How to Cope" and then answer the following questions. If you have trouble answering any of the questions, re-study the relevant material before going on to the review of key terms and the matching test.

5-1.   One of the most effective ways to cope with stress is to use _____ techniques. Relaxation training has beneficial effects on the body, lowering stress _____ and enhancing _____ function. Another way to reduce stress is to _____. People who are physically fit have fewer _____ problems and also show less _____ arousal to stressors. Other methods of cooling off can include _____ or listening to _____ music.

5-2.   One type of coping, _____-_____ coping, concentrates on the emotions the problem has caused. _____-_____ coping, on the other hand, focuses on identifying the problem and learning as much about it as possible. Problem-focused coping tends to increase your sense of _____-_____.

5-3.   Another way of coping with stress is to rethink the problem. One method of rethinking the problem is _____ or reassessing its meaning. Another method of coping involves _____ _____, comparing yourself to others who are less fortunate. Lastly, _____ helps those in stressful situations to see the absurd or whimsical aspects of a bad situation.

5-4.   One last coping strategy is _____, to reach out to others. This social support is not only _____ helpful, but _____ beneficial. Two studies supported the fact that those who had few friends and relations were more likely to _____ than those who had many. Social support may be related to better health because it produces beneficial effects on the _____, endocrine, and _____ systems.

Review of Key Terms

The following is a list of the Key Terms from the section "Emotions, Stress, and Health: How to Cope." Make sure you are familiar with each term before taking the matching test on these terms.

relaxation training   problem-focused coping   social comparison

emotion-focused coping   reappraisal

Matching Self Test 5

Match the appropriate term with its definition or description.

1. _____   Choosing to reassess the meaning of a stressor.

2. _____   Coping that concentrates on the emotions the problem caused.

3. _____   Learning to alternately tense and relax the muscles, to lie or sit quietly, or to meditate by clearing your mind and banishing worries of the day.

4. _____   In a difficult situation, comparing yourself to others who you feel are less fortunate.

SAMPLE ANSWERS TO *WHAT'S AHEAD* QUESTIONS FROM TEXTBOOK

After you have completed the "Looking Back" section at the end of the chapter by answering the "What's Ahead" questions that preceded each major section of the chapter, compare your answers to the following sample answers. If your answers are not similar to the sample answers, review the pertinent sections of the chapter. The relevant page(s) for each question is(are) provided in the "Looking Back" section in the text.

Which facial expressions of emotion do people the world over recognize?

Paul Ekman and his colleagues have gathered abundant evidence for the universality of seven basic facial expressions of emotion: anger, happiness, fear, surprise, disgust, sadness, and contempt.

Which side of your brain is most active when you're filled with joy—or despair?

Regions of the left hemisphere appear to be specialized for positive emotions such as joy, whereas regions of the right hemisphere are specialized for negative emotions such as despair.

Which two hormones can make you "too excited to eat"?

The two hormones are epinephrine and norepinephrine, which activate the sympathetic division of the autonomic nervous system. Digestion slows down so that blood flow can be diverted from the stomach and intestines to the muscles and surface of the skin. This is why you may not want to eat when you are excited.

In a competition, who is likely to be happier, the third-place winner or the second-place winner?

In a study of athletes' reactions to placing second and third in the 1992 Olympics and the 1994 Empire State games, the third-place finishers were happier than the second-place winners. Apparently, the athletes were comparing their performance to "what might have been." The second-place finishers, comparing themselves to the first-place finishers, were unhappy that they didn't win. The third-place finishers, comparing themselves to those who did worse than they, were happy that they finished in the top three positions.

Why can't an infant feel shame or guilt?

Infants cannot feel shame or guilt because these emotions require a sense of self and the ability to perceive that you have behaved badly or let down another person, and infants are not cognitively mature enough to have a sense of self or such perceptions of the situation.

Are the "basic" emotions basic everywhere?

Many psychologists believe that the emotions corresponding to the seven universal emotional expressions—fear, anger, sadness, joy, surprise, disgust, and contempt—are also universal and biologically based. These psychologists believe that these seven emotions are the universal primary emotions and that secondary emotions are cultural variations of them. Other psychologists, however, think that the effort to distinguish primary and secondary emotions masks the profound influence of culture on every aspect of emotional experience, starting with which feelings a culture considers "basic." The compromise between these views assumes that even if some basic emotions do prove to be hard-wired biologically, cultures clearly determine much of what people feel emotional about.

Do Germans, Japanese, and North Americans always mean the same thing when they smile at others?

No, the smile has many meanings and uses that are not universal and that depend on a culture's display rules. North Americans tend to smile more frequently than Germans do; this does not mean that North Americans are friendlier than Germans, but that they differ in their notions of when a smile is appropriate. The Japanese smile even more than North Americans, to disguise embarrassment, anger, or other negative emotions whose public display is considered rude and incorrect.

Why do people feel obliged to show sadness at funerals even when they're not feeling sad?

Because they are following the appropriate display rule. Display rules tell us not only what to do when we are feeling an emotion, but also how and when to show an emotion we do not feel. People are expected to demonstrate sadness at funerals, whether they feel this emotion or not. Acting out an emotion we do not feel is referred to as emotion work.

Are women really more emotional than men?

There is little evidence that one sex feels emotions more often than the other. Differing display rules for communicating emotion help explain why many people in Western cultures think women are more emotional than men are. Women in North America tend to be involved in the flight-attendant side of emotion work, persuading others that they are friendly, happy, and warm, conveying deference, and making sure that others are happy. Men tend to be involved in the bill-collection side, persuading others that they are stern, aggressive, and unemotional. These North American gender differences, however, are by no means universal. In addition, even within a culture such as North America, the influence of a particular situation often overrides gender rules.

Why are you more likely to get a cold when you're stressed out?

Of the many bodily systems affected by stress, one of the most intensively studied has been the immune system, which enables the body to fight disease and infection. The white blood cells are important in this fight. Prolonged stress can suppress some or many of these white blood cells. Thus, you are more likely to get a cold when you are stressed out.

Which stressors pose the greatest hazard to your health?

Bereavement and loss; noise, crowding, and hassles; and poverty and powerlessness are all stressors that are especially likely to affect the immune, cardiovascular, and endocrine systems, and thus increase the risk of illness or poor health.

Why do optimists tend to live longer than pessimists?

The pessimistic explanatory style is associated with lower self-esteem, less achievement, more illness, and slower emotional recovery from trauma. It's not what happens to you, but how you think about what happens to you that makes the difference to your state of mind and your physical well-being Optimists are more likely than pessimists to be active problem solvers and to seek information that can help them. They probably also take better care of themselves when they have minor ailments and when they have life-threatening illnesses. Pessimists, in contrast, often do self-destructive things. Taken together, all of these differences lead to a greater life expectancy for optimists.

When is a sense of control good for you, and when is it not?

The kind of control that is related to better health is self-efficacy—the belief that you are basically in charge of your own life and well-being and that if you become sick you can take steps to get better. Health and well-being are not affected by other, more unrealistic kinds of control, such as self-blame or the belief that all disease can be prevented by doing the right thing.

Why are people who are chronically angry and mistrustful their own worst enemy?

Because this type of chronic hostility is far more likely to lead to heart disease. Men who are chronically angry and resentful and who have a hostile attitude are five times as likely as nonhostile men to get heart disease, even when other risk factors, such as smoking, are controlled for.

Which disease is depression most clearly linked to?

Clinical depression is linked to heart attack. There is a common belief that depression is associated with other diseases as well, notably cancer and AIDS, but here the evidence is conflicting.

How can revealing your unresolved feelings about a past trauma help your health?

People who repress such feelings ("repressors") are at greater risk of becoming ill. Once they contract a serious disease, they may even die sooner. There are two ideas as to why emotional inhibition increases the risk of having health problems. First, prolonged inhibition of thoughts and emotions requires physical effort that is stressful to the body. Second, the inability to confide traumatic events may place continuing stress on the immune system. Thus, in either case, revealing such events will help your health.

When you're feeling overwhelmed, what are some ways to calm yourself?

One of the best ways to calm yourself is to use conscious relaxation techniques. Another way is exercise. Other ways include getting a soothing massage, listening to calm music, and taking a refreshing walk. Such activities give the physiological symptoms of stress and intense negative emotions a chance to subside.

Why is it important to move beyond the emotions caused by a problem and deal with the problem itself?

Because problem-focused coping tends to increase your sense of self-efficacy. It encourages you to think critically by considering alternatives and resisting emotional reasoning. You will be a better problem solver, avoid negative emotions such as anger and anxiety, and even reduce physiological arousal.

How can you learn to rethink your problems?

Some of the most effective "rethinking" strategies are: reappraisal, social comparison, and humor. You may not be able to eliminate a stressor, but you can choose to reassess its meaning. Problems can be turned into challenges, losses into unexpected gains. Successful copers also often compare themselves to others who are (they feel) less fortunate. In addition, people who can see the absurd or whimsical aspects of a bad situation are less prone to depression, anger, tension, and fatigue.

When do friends reduce your stress, and when do they just make matters worse?

Friends can help you cope by offering concern and affection. They can help you evaluate problems and plan a course of action. They can offer resources and services. Most of all, they are sources of attachment and connection, which everyone needs throughout life. Of course, sometimes they are not helpful. They may be themselves the source of hassles, unhappiness, stress, and anger. They may behave awkwardly, not knowing what to do or say. They may abandon you or say something stupid and hurtful. Sometimes they offer the wrong kind of support because they have never been in the same situation. And sometimes they can make it difficult for you to change bad health habits, such as drinking or smoking.

MULTIPLE-CHOICE PROGRESS TEST

Choose the single best answer for each of the following questions. When you have finished this progress test, check your answers with those at the end of the chapter. You should review the indicated pages in the text for the questions you do not answer correctly.

1. Which of the following statements is FALSE?
   a. Anger and happiness are universal basic facial expressions of emotion.
   b. Authentic smiles last longer than false smiles.
   c. There are culture-specific variations in the expression of emotion.
   d. None of the above

2. According to the _____, a smile tells us we are happy, and a frown that we are angry or perplexed.
   a. neuro-cultural theory
   b. two-factor theory
   c. facial feedback hypothesis
   d. culture-specific hypothesis

3. Regions of the _____ hemisphere are specialized for positive emotions; regions of the _____ hemisphere are specialized for negative emotions.
   a. right; right
   b. right; left
   c. left; right
   d. left; left

4. The _____, a small structure in the brain's limbic system, plays a key role in emotion.
   a. amygdala
   b. cerebellum
   c. hypothalamus
   d. thalamus

5. Which of the following is NOT a response of the sympathetic division of the autonomic nervous system to arousal?
   a. pupils dilate
   b. heart beats faster
   c. digestion speeds up
   d. breathing speeds up

6.	The _____ theory of emotion assumes that emotions depend on both physiological arousal and a cognitive interpretation of that arousal.
	a.	neuro-cultural
	b.	two-factor
	c.	facial-feedback
	d.	culture-specific

7.	Based on the research on attributions and grades, which of the following students is most likely to feel angry or hostile?
	a.	students who believe they did well because of their own efforts
	b.	students who believe they did well because of a lucky fluke or chance
	c.	students who believe their failures were their own fault
	d.	students who blame others for their failures

8.	Which of the following is FALSE?
	a.	Secondary emotions are the cultural variations of primary emotions.
	b.	Most people express or suppress their emotions without being aware of the display rules they are following.
	c.	There is little evidence that one sex feels emotion more often than the other in Western cultures.
	d.	None of the above

9.	Which of the following is the correct order of the three phases in Selye's theory of stress?
	a.	alarm, resistance, exhaustion
	b.	alarm, exhaustion, resistance
	c.	exhaustion, alarm, resistance
	d.	exhaustion, resistance, alarm

10.	Which of the following is an example (are examples) of eustress?
	a.	competing in an athletic event
	b.	falling in love
	c.	working hard on a project you enjoy
	d.	all of the above

11.	Which of the following statements about the effects of stress is FALSE?
	a.	Short-term stressors are hazardous primarily for anxious people who are quick to react.
	b.	Noise and crowding are most harmful to your health when they are not controllable.
	c.	In the workplace, executives and managers suffer most from job stress.
	d.	None of the above

12.	Which of the following is NOT associated with a pessimistic explanatory style?
	a.	low self-esteem
	b.	more illness
	c.	more achievement

227

d. slower emotional recovery from traumas

13. People who are optimistic and have positive illusions:
    a. do not deny their problems.
    b. are more likely than pessimists to be active problem solvers.
    c. take better care of themselves when they have ailments and illnesses.
    d. all of the above

14. An internal locus of control helps to:
    a. reduce pain.
    b. improve adjustment to surgery and illness.
    c. speed up recovery from some diseases.
    d. all of the above

15. Health and well-being are affected by:
    a. self-efficacy.
    b. self blame.
    c. the belief that all disease can be prevented by doing the right thing.
    d. all of the above

16. _____ cultures emphasize _____ control in which people try to influence existing reality by changing other people, other events, or circumstances.
    a. Western; primary
    b. Western; secondary
    c. Eastern; primary
    d. Eastern; secondary

17. Which of the following is the characteristic of Type A people that is dangerous to them?
    a. determination
    b. hostility
    c. impatience
    d. intensity

18. Which of the following styles of coping is associated with the greatest longevity in women diagnosed with breast cancer?
    a. positive/confronting
    b. denial/avoidance
    c. fatalistic/helpless
    d. positive/avoidance

19. A low level of physical fitness is associated with:
    a. decreased life expectancy.
    b. fewer health problems.
    c. less physiological arousal to stress.
    d. fewer visits to the doctor.

20. Of the following rethinking strategies, which is (are) effective for dealing with stress?
    a. reassessing the meaning of the stressor
    b. comparing yourself to others who are less fortunate
    c. seeing the humorous aspects of the stressful situation
    d. all of the above

ANSWERS

GUIDED STUDY

1. The Nature of Emotion

1.1.
emotion	neuro-cultural	brain
biological	neurophysiology	prosopagnosia
thoughts	culture-specific	right
explanations	happy	left
culture	sadness	right
face	lie	amygdala
seven	muscles	approach
happiness	context	withdraw
surprise	themselves	hormones
sadness	feedback	epinephrine
cultures	brain	norepinephrine

1.2.
two-factor	emotion	perceptions
bodily	cognitive	attributions

Matching Self-Test 1

1. two-factor theory
2. neuro-cultural theory
3. facial feedback hypothesis
4. amygdala

---

2. Emotion in Cultural Context

2.1.
primary	culture	about
secondary	cultures	

2.2.
display rules	body	work

Matching Self-Test 2

1. emotion work
2. secondary emotions
3. display rules
4. primary emotions

---

3. The Nature of Stress

3.1.
fight	eustress	crowding
flight	immune	powerlessness
alarm	foreign	psychological
resistance	suppress	person
exhaustion	bereavement	environment

3.2.
pessimists	problem	neuroendocrine
optimists	information	self-efficacy
self-esteem	defensive	primary
illness	Asians	secondary
health	internal	

Matching Self-Test 3

1. primary control
2. psychological stress
3. locus of control
4. secondary control

---

4. Stress in Emotional Context

4.1.
Type A	irritable	cynical/antagonistic
achieve	impatient	hostility
urgency	intense	depression

4.2.   emotional inhibition   physical

Matching Self-Test 4

1. repressors
2. Type A personalities
3. cynical/antagonistic hostility

---

5. Emotions, Stress, and Health: How to Cope

5.1.
relaxation	exercise	massage
hormones	health	calm
immune	physiological	

5.2.	emotion-focused	Problem-focused	self-efficacy
5.3.	reappraisal	social comparison	humor
5.4.	looking outward psychologically	medically die	cardiovascular immune

Matching Self-Test 5

1. reappraisal
2. emotion-focused coping

3. relaxation training
4. social comparison

ANSWERS TO MULTIPLE CHOICE PROGRESS TEST

Item No.	Answer(s)	Page(s) in Textbook
1.	b. Authentic smiles last longer than false smiles.	412
2.	c. facial feedback hypothesis	412
3.	c. left; right	413-414
4.	a. amygdala	414
5.	c. digestion speeds up	414
6.	b. two-factor	415
7.	d. students who blame others for their failures	416
8.	d. None of the above	408-410
9.	a. alarm, resistance, exhaustion	422
10.	d. all of the above	422
11.	c. In the workplace, executives and managers suffer most from job stress.	424
12.	c. more achievement	425
13.	d. all of the above	426
14.	d. all of the above	426
15.	a. self-efficacy	426-427
16.	a. Western; primary	427
17.	b. hostility	428-429
18.	a. positive/confronting	430
19.	a. decreased life expectancy	431
20.	d. all of the above	433-434

CHAPTER 13

The Major Motives of Life: Love, Sex, Food, and Work

CHAPTER OVERVIEW

The chapter covers a variety of motives in our lives. Firstly, the motive to love is discussed. This includes a description of various theories of love and types of love. Also included is a discussion of how gender and culture affect love. The second motive discussed is the motive for sex. This discussion encompasses the biological aspects of sex, including how hormones affect sexual behaviour and an evolutionary view of sexual behaviour. The psychological viewpoint on sexual behaviour holds that the sexiest sex organ is actually the brain. Cultural variations in sexuality and different sexual orientations are also discussed.

The third motive presented is the motive to eat. Topics covered include the genetics of weight, cultural influences on weight and eating, and dilemmas involved in dieting. The last motive discussed is the motive to work. The questions of how motivation affects work and how work affects motivation are discussed. Self-efficacy, need for achievement, and need for power are examined. The chapter ends with a discussion of conflicting motives as might occur in approach-avoidance situations.

GUIDED STUDY

1. The Social Animal: Motives for Love

Read the section "The Social Animal: Motives for Love" and then answer the following questions. If you have trouble answering any of the questions, re-study the relevant material before going on to the review of key terms and the matching test.

1-1 _____ is defined as an inferred process within a person or animal that causes that organism to move toward a goal or away from an unpleasant situation. Early research on motivation focused on _____-reduction. One of the deepest and most universal human motives is the need for _____. The most intense attachment is _____. One distinction made between different types of love is that between _____ love and companionate love. According to John Alan Lee's theory of love, there are six different styles of love—game-playing love, _____; romantic, passionate love, _____; affectionate, friendly love, _____; possessive, dependent love, _____, logical, pragmatic love, _____; and unselfish love, _____. According to Shaver and Hazan, adults, just like babies, can have attachments that are _____, or

_____-ambivalent. Steinberg thinks that there are three ingredients of love—_____, intimacy, and _____. Differing varieties of love occur because of the ways people combine these three elements. For example, intimacy alone leads to _____, whereas intimacy plus commitment leads to _____ love. Intimacy plus passion leads to _____ love, and passion alone is referred to by Steinberg as _____. Passion plus commitment is _____ love, and commitment alone is _____ love. The ideal form of love, _____ love, combines all three elements.

1-2.   Although both sexes become equally attached and suffer equally when a love relationship ends, women and men do differ in terms of how they _____ love. Many women define intimacy as shared _____ of feelings, whereas many men define intimacy as being together _____.

Review of Key Terms

The following is a list of the Key Terms from the section "The Social Animal: Motives for Love."
Make sure you are familiar with each term before taking the matching test on these terms.

motivation	social motives	six styles of love
drive reduction theory	passionate love	attachment theory of love
need for affiliation	companionate love	triangle theory of love

Matching Self Test 1

Match the appropriate term with its definition or description.

1. _____ A theory of love specifying three ingredients—intimacy, commitment, and passion.

2. _____ An early theory of motivation that emphasized biological needs resulting from states of physical deprivation.

3. _____ One of the deepest and most universal of human motives.

4. _____ A theory of love specifying that adults can have secure, avoidant, or anxious-ambivalent attachments.

2. The Erotic Animal: Motives for Sex

Read the section "The Erotic Animal: Motives for Sex" and then answer the following questions.
If you have trouble answering any of the questions, re-study the relevant material before going on to the review of key terms and the matching test.

2-1.   Psychologists do not agree on whether human sexuality is a _____ drive. One

biological factor that promotes sexual desire is the hormone _____.
Testosterone contributes to sexual _____, but sexual activity also produces
_____ levels of testosterone. One of the first researchers of sexual behaviour
to promote the idea that males and females were alike in their basic anatomy and
physiology was _____. This research was supported and elaborated upon by
_____ and Johnson in the 1960s. Masters and Johnson did, however, disagree
with Kinsey's assertion that women have a _____ sexual capacity than men.
One limitation of the work by Masters and Johnson was that they did not look at sexual
differences between those of different _____, experiences, or
_____.

_____ psychologists have promoted a biological approach to sexuality.
According to this view, it is evolutionarily _____ for males to compete with
other males for access to young and fertile females and to try to win and
_____ as many females as possible. Females, on the other hand, need to shop
for the best _____ deal. Critics maintain that the evolutionary view is an
_____-_____-_____ explanation of a stereotype. In
addition, critics also argue that among human beings, sexual behaviour is extremely
_____ and changeable.

2-2. Researchers have repeatedly found that the sexiest sex organ is the _____. For
most individuals, the primary reasons for sex are to express _____ and
intimacy, to feel _____, and to feel _____ pleasure. There are
also several negative reasons for having sex, including exacting _____ on a
previous partner, to get _____, to _____ another person, or to
fulfill a perceived _____. Research on college students has found that many
men and women say they have had sex when they did not want to, due to
_____ pressures. Men and women differ, however, in the reasons they give for
having unwanted sex, and they differ dramatically in their perceptions of sexual
_____. In one study, _____ percent of the women claimed that
men had forced them to do something sexually that they did not want to do but only
_____ percent of the men said they had ever forced a woman into a sexual act.
The most extreme example of sexual coercion is _____. Malmuth found that
sexually aggressive males are characterized by a cluster of traits they call
_____ masculinity. This entails being _____, defensive, hostile
toward women, and wishing to _____ women.

2-3. There are many cultural variations in sexuality. These include what parts of the
_____ and what style of _____ are erotic, what sexual acts and
_____ are erotic or repulsive, and whether sex is seen as something
_____ and beautiful, or as something ugly and _____. The rules
and requirements about sex are transmitted via sexual _____. Sexual scripts
teach men and women how to behave during _____ and sex. The origins of
sexual scripts and gender differences according to many psychologists have to do with a
culture's _____ and _____ arrangements.

2-4. The words _____ and _____ were not even invented until the mid-nineteenth century. Today, many researchers feel that sexual orientation is primarily determined by _____ and other biological factors. Although most psychological theories of homosexuality, such as that of _____ mothers or _____ fathers, have never been supported, some researchers are still skeptical of biological explanations for two reasons. Firstly, sexual identity and behaviour take so many different forms that no _____ cause is likely to ever be found. Secondly, the biological research has too many serious _____ to lead to any firm conclusions. The most reasonable conclusion at present is that sexual identity and behaviour involve an interaction of _____, _____, and experiences and that the route to sexual identity for one person may not be the same for another.

Review of Key Terms

The following is a list of the Key Terms from the section "The Erotic Animal: Motives for Sex." Make sure you are familiar with each term before taking the matching test on these terms.

evolutionary psychology   gender roles   homosexual

hostile masculinity   sexual script   heterosexual

Matching Self Test 2

Match the appropriate term with its definition or description.

1. _____ A script that teaches men and women how to behave during dating and sex.

2. _____ The branch of psychology putting forth that sex differences in courtship and mating practices evolve in response to a species' survival needs.

3. _____ A cluster of traits displayed by sexually aggressive males.

3. The Hungry Animal: Motives to Eat

Read the section "The Hungry Animal: Motives to Eat" and then answer the following questions. If you have trouble answering any of the questions, re-study the relevant material before going on to the review of key terms and the matching test.

3-1. It was originally believed that being overweight was a sign of _____ _____. A major theory of weight assumes that there is a biological mechanism that keeps a person's body weight at a genetically influenced _____ _____. This is the weight a person stays at when neither trying to gain or lose weight. In addition, this theory holds that we each have a genetically programmed rate at which we burn calories, _____ _____ rate, and a fixed number of

_____ cells, which can change in size but not in _____. Genetic research on obesity has isolated a gene called "_____" which causes fat cells to secrete a hormonelike protein, _____, which travels through the blood to an area in the hypothalamus that regulates appetite. Leptin levels signal how large or small the body's fat cells are, and the brain adjusts appetite accordingly. Thus, some obese people may gain weight rapidly because they have a variant form of "obese" and have _____ levels of leptin. Others who are obese may have a gene that prevents cells in the brain from responding normally to leptin's signals.

3-2.   Culture influences what people eat, _____ they eat, and with _____ they eat. Culture also influences our perceptions of what the _____ body should look like. The cultural ideal for body size in the United States has been getting _____ in recent decades. Silverstein proposed that this is because men and women associate the curvy, big-breasted female body with femininity, _____, and motherhood. Hence, this body type is more fashionable in eras that celebrate women's role as mothers. People also associate femininity and nurturance with _____. Thus, at times when women want to enter traditionally male roles in terms of education or work, they try to look thin and _____. Sometimes the obsession for thinness goes too far, and _____ disorders may result. The two most common eating disorders are _____ and _____ _____. These eating disorders are _____ times more common in _____ than in _____.

3-3.   Researchers are divided on whether obese individuals should try to fight their _____ _____ or whether they should try to fight society's _____. Some feel that dieting is _____, and others feel that weight loss can help reduce _____ risks.

Review of Key Terms

The following is a list of the Key Terms from the section "The Hungry Animal.' Motives to Eat."
Make sure you are familiar with each term before taking the matching test on these terms.

basal metabolism rate	"obese"	bulimia
set point	leptin	anorexia nervosa

Matching Self Test 3

Match the appropriate term with its definition or description.

1. _____ A hormonelike protein that travels through the blood to an area in the hypothalamus that regulates appetite.

2. _____ The rate at which the body bums calories for energy.

236

3. _____ The genetically influenced weight range for an individual, thought to be maintained by a biological mechanism that regulates food intake, fat reserves, and metabolism.

4. _____ An eating disorder in which the sufferer stops eating almost completely because of a delusional belief that she or he is too fat.

4. The Competent Animal: Motives to Work

Read the section "The Competent Animal: Motives to Work" and then answer the following questions. If you have trouble answering any of the questions, re-study the relevant material before going on to the review of key terms and the matching test.

4-1. _____/_____ psychologists have studied work motivation. When we have expectations concerning how well we will do at something and then behave in such a way as to make the prediction come true, we are employing the _____-_____ prophecy. The motivation to work is also influenced by having _____. Goals are most likely to improve performance when (1) the goal is _____, (2) the goal has a _____, and (3) the goal is but achievable. Approaching a problem with helplessness or mastery is unrelated to _____. Success is predicted by the way in which people _____ about the goals they set for themselves and how _____ they feel about reaching them. According to Dweck, those who are motivated by _____ goals frequently decide failures are their fault and stop trying to improve. On the other hand, those motivated by _____ and _____ goals are more interested in increasing their _____ and _____. They tend to regard failure as a source of useful _____ that will help them to improve. When a goal has been reached, people feel _____. This in turn is related to self-_____ according to _____. Bandura further states that self-efficacy is acquired from four sources: (1) having experiences in mastering new _____ and overcoming _____, (2) having successful and competent _____ _____, (3) getting _____ and _____ from others, and (4) learning how to read and manage your own _____ state. McClelland argued that people have a need for _____, which he measured with the _____. The TAT has also been used to measure the need for _____. David Winter has found that when _____ motivation rises in leaders, _____ is likely. When it falls, war is less likely. On the other hand, when the _____ motive rises, wars are averted.

4-2. Working _____ greatly affect the motivation to work. One study found that the degree of _____ and _____ a job provides are very important aspects of a job. The strongest motivator at work is _____ pay, bonuses that are given upon completion of a goal. Achievement tends to be low in those who work in _____-_____ jobs. Work motivation and satisfaction depend on the right fit between the qualities of the _____ and _____ of the work.

Review of Key Terms

The following is a list of the Key Terms from the section "The Competent Animal: Motives to Work." Make sure you are familiar with each term before taking the matching test on these terms.

self-fulfilling prophecy   learning goals   Thematic Apperception Test (TAT)

value   self-efficacy   need for power incentive pay

performance goals   need for achievement

Matching Self Test 4

Match the appropriate term with its definition or description.

1. _____ A learned motive to dominate or influence others.

2. _____ A person's belief that he or she is capable of producing desired results, such as mastering new skills and reaching goals.

3. _____ An expectation that comes true because of the tendency of the person holding it to act in ways that confirm it.

4. _____ A learned motive to meet personal standards of success and excellence in a chosen area.

5. When Motives Conflict

Read the section "When Motives Conflict" and then answer the following questions. If you have trouble answering any of the questions, re-study the relevant material before going on to the review of key terms and the matching test.

5-1.   Researchers have identified four kinds of motivational conflicts. _____-_____ conflicts occur when you are equally attracted to two or more possible activities or goals. _____-_____ conflicts occur when you have to choose between the lesser of two evils. _____-_____ conflicts occur when a single activity or goal has both positive and negative aspects. Lastly, _____ approach-avoidance conflicts occur in situations that offer several possible choices, each containing _____ and _____. Another viewpoint on the competing motives in our lives was put forth by _____. He referred to our motives as a hierarchy of _____. According to Maslow, the bottom of the hierarchy contains _____ needs, whereas the top of the hierarchy represents self-_____ and self-_____. Although this theory is very popular, it has not been supported by _____.

Review of Key Terms

The following is a list of the Key Terms from the section "When Motives Conflict." Make sure you are familiar with each term before taking the matching test on these terms.

approach-approach conflict avoidance-avoidance conflict Abraham Maslow

approach-avoidance conflict multiple approach-avoidance conflicts hierarchy of needs

Matching Self Test 5

Match the appropriate term with its definition or description.

1. _____ Conflicts that require that you choose between the lesser of two evils.

2. _____ Situations that offer several possible choices, each containing advantages and disadvantages

3. _____ Maslow's theory in which he envisioned people's motivational strivings on a pyramid.

SAMPLE ANSWERS TO *WHAT'S AHEAD* QUESTIONS FROM TEXTBOOK

After you have completed the "Looking Back" section at the end of the chapter by answering the "What's Ahead" questions that preceded each major section of the chapter, compare your answers to the following sample answers. If your answers are not similar to the sample answers, review the pertinent sections of the chapter. The relevant page(s) for each question is(are) provided in the "Looking Back" section in the text.

What kind of lover defines love as jealousy and possessiveness, and what kind defines it as just the opposite calm compatibility?

Mania lovers are possessive and suffer from jealousy. Pragmatic lovers are just the opposite and choose partners based on a shopping list of compatible traits.

Do men and women differ in the ability to love?

Neither sex loves more than the other in terms of "love at first sight," manic love, erotic love, selfless love, or companionate love over the long haul. Both sexes become equally attached and both suffer when a love relationship ends. Women and men, however, do differ, on average, in how they express love.

What part of the anatomy do psychologists think is the "sexiest sex organ"?

Researchers have shown repeatedly that the sexiest sex organ is actually the brain, where perceptions begin. People's values, expectations, fantasies, and beliefs profoundly affect sexual desire and responsiveness.

How do the sexual rules for heterosexual couples foster misunderstandings?

In the U.S. and Canada, the sexual scripts for heterosexual couples create conflicting motives for sexuality and misreadings of one another's behaviour. For example, what is a sexual signal? Men and women often answer this question differently. A woman's intent might be to look attractive, but a man may interpret her dress and demeanor as indicating sexual interest.

Can psychological theories about "smothering mothering" or "absent fathers" explain why some men become gay?

No. Homosexuality is unrelated to "smothering mothers," "absent fathers," psychopathology, or parental practices and role models.

Why can some thin people eat anything they want without gaining weight, whereas some heavy people can diet without losing weight?

One theory that integrates such findings holds that a biological mechanism keeps a person's body weight at a genetically influenced set point—the weight the person stays at when not consciously trying to gain or lose. Everyone has a genetically programmed basal metabolism rate and a fixed number of fat cells. The fat cells can change in size but not in number. A complex interaction of metabolism, fat cells, and hormones keeps people at the weight their bodies are designed to be. Thus, when a heavy person diets, the body's metabolism slows down to conserve energy and fat reserves. When a thin person overeats, metabolism speeds up, burning energy.

What disorders can occur when the psychological need to be thin collides with the body's need to store some fat?

The two most common ones are bulimia, in which the sufferer binges and then purges by vomiting or using laxatives, and anorexia nervosa, in which the sufferer stops eating almost completely because of a delusional belief that she or he is too fat.

Why is "doing your best" an ineffective goal to set for yourself?

Because a goal is more likely to be met if the goal is specific. You need to be specific in defining your goals.

When you're learning a new skill, should you concentrate on mastering it or performing it well in front of others?

You should concentrate on mastering it. Then failure and criticism will not discourage you because you will realize that learning takes time. This is not true when you concentrate on performance. Then you tend to stop trying to improve when you do poorly. In addition, if you concentrate on mastering the skill, you will feel greater intrinsic pleasure in the task.

What kind of power motivation distinguishes poor leaders from highly effective ones?

Effective leaders have a higher motivation to use power to improve society rather than to further their own ambitions.

What kind of conflict do you have when you want to study for a big exam but you also want to go out partying?

You have an approach-approach conflict in which you are equally attracted to two activities.

Do you have to satisfy basic needs for security and belonging before you can become "self-actualized"?

This idea has not been supported by research. People have simultaneous needs for comfort and safety and for attachments, self-esteem, and competence. Individuals who have met their lower needs do not inevitably seek higher ones, nor is it the case that people behave badly only when their lower needs are frustrated. Higher needs may even take precedence over lower ones.

MULTIPLE-CHOICE PROGRESS TEST

Choose the single best answer for each of the following questions. When you have finished this progress test, check your answers with those at the end of the chapter. You should review the indicated pages in the text for the questions you do not answer correctly.

1. Passionate love is _____ emotionally intense and _____ sexualized than companionate love.
    a. less; less
    b. less; more
    c. more; less
    d. more; more

2. According to John Alan Lee's styles of love classifications, romantic, passionate love is called _____.
    a. Iudus
    b. eros
    c. pragma
    d. agape

3. Those who score high on *storge* on the Love Attitudes Scale:
    a. believe in instant chemistry (love at first sight).
    b. like to play the game of love with several partners at once.
    c. choose partners on the basis of a shopping list of compatible traits.
    d. yearn desperately for love but suffer from jealousy and worry when they find it.

4. According to the attachment theory of love, _____ lovers are not jealous or worried about being abandoned.
    a. securely attached
    b. anxious
    c. ambivalent
    d. avoidant

5. According to the triangle theory of love, companionate love is:
    a. intimacy alone.
    b. intimacy plus passion.

    c. intimacy plus commitment.

    d. commitment alone.

6.   In studies of dating and married couples, which of the following combinations RARELY turn(s) up?

    a. ludic-ludic

    b. manic-manic

    c. avoidant-avoidant

    d. all of the above

7.   Which of the following statements about gender and love is FALSE?

    a. Men are more ludic and avoidant than women, and women are more romantic and anxious than men.

    b. Neither sex loves more than the other in terms of manic or erotic love.

    c. Both sexes become equally attached and both suffer when a love relationship ends.

    d. None of the above

8.   Which of the following statements about sex is(are) FALSE?

    a. Psychologists agree that sex is a primary drive.

    b. Testosterone promotes sexual desire in men but not women.

    c. Women have a lesser capacity for sexual response than men.

    d. All of the above

9.   Which of the following findings would NOT support the evolutionary view of sexuality?

    a. Men are more interested than women in the youth and beauty of their sexual partners.

    b. Men are quicker than women to have sex with partners that they do not know well.

    c. Men are more inclined than women toward polygamy and promiscuity.

    d. Men emphasize the financial resources or prospects of a potential mate more than women.

10.   Which of the following statements about cultural variations and sexuality is (are) TRUE?

    a. Cultures differ in what parts of the body are erotic.

    b. Cultures differ in the sexual acts that are considered erotic.

    c. Cultures differ in whether sex is seen as something joyful and beautiful or as something ugly and dirty.

    d. All of the above

11.   Which of the following statements about sexual orientation is FALSE?

    a. The words *homosexual* and *heterosexual* were not invented until the mid-19th century.

    b. Women with a history of prenatal exposure to high levels of androgen are more likely to become bisexual or lesbian.

    c. Homosexuality is unrelated to smothering mothers and absent fathers.

    d. The vast majority of homosexual men and women have a close gay relative.

12. According to the set point theory of weight,
    a. everyone has a fixed number of fat cells, which can change in size but not number.
    b. when a heavy person diets, the body's metabolism slows down to conserve energy.
    c. when a thin person overeats, metabolism speeds up, burning energy.
    d. all of the above

13. Compared to the role it plays in mice, leptin's role in human obesity:
    a. is simpler.
    b. is more complicated.
    c. is about the same.
    d. is minor.

14. With respect to the relationship of culture and weight, which of the following is FALSE?
    a. People tend to eat with those of their own social status or higher.
    b. The cultural ideal for body size in the U.S. has been getting decidedly thinner, especially for women.
    c. College women who develop eating disorders are more likely to say that their fathers think their mothers are unintelligent.
    d. None of the above

15. In _____, the sufferer binges and then purges by vomiting or using laxatives. This disorder and other eating disorders are more common in _____.
    a. bulimia; men
    b. bulimia; women
    c. anorexia nervosa; men
    d. anorexia nervosa; women

16. A goal is most likely to improve performance when:
    a. you define the goal as "doing your best."
    b. you give yourself an indefinite amount of time.
    c. the goal is challenging but achievable.
    d. all of the above

17. People who are motivated by concerned with increasing their competence and skills and discouraged by criticism and failure.
    a. learning and mastery goals; are
    b. learning and master goals; are not
    c. performance goals; are
    d. performance goals; are not

18. According to Bandura, self-efficacy is acquired from:
    a. having experiences in mastering new skills and overcoming obstacles.
    b. having successful and competent role models.

c. learning how to read and manage your own physiological states.
d. all of the above

19. Novice parachute jumpers must choose between the fear of jumping and the fear of losing face if they do not jump. This is an example of an _____ conflict.
   a. approach-approach
   b. avoidance-avoidance
   c. approach-avoidance
   d. avoidance-approach

20. Which of the following statements about Maslow's hierarchy of needs pyramid is TRUE?
   a. Basic survival needs are at the top level of the pyramid.
   b. Social needs for belonging and affection are below security needs in the pyramid.
   c. This theory has not been supported by research.
   d. None of the above

ANSWERS

GUIDED STUDY

1. The Social Animal: Motives for Love

1.1.
Motivation	mania	liking
drive	pragma	companionate
affiliation	agape	romantic
love	secure	infatuation
passionate	avoidant	fatuous
Iudos	anxious	empty
eros	passion	consummate
storge	commitment	

1.2.
express	revelations	comfortably

Matching Self-Test 1

1. triangle theory of love
2. drive-reduction theory
3. need for affiliation
4. attachment theory of love

---

2. The Erotic Animal: Motives for Sex

2.1.		
primary	Masters	adaptive
testosterone	lesser	inseminate
arousal	ages	genetic
higher	cultures	after-the-fact
Kinsey	Evolutionary	varied

2.2.		
brain	dominate	rape
love	obligation	hostile
desirable	psychological	insecure
erotic	coercion	dominate
revenge	22.8	
money	2.8	

2.3.		
body	joyful	dating
clothing	dirty	economic
positions	scripts	social

2.4.		
homosexual	smothering	limitations
heterosexual	absent	biology
genetic	single	culture

Matching Self-Test 2

1. sexual script   2. evolutionary psychology   3. hostile masculinity

---

3. The Hungry Animal: Motives to Eat

3.1.	
emotional disturbance	number
set point	"obese"
basal metabolism	leptin
fat	low

3.2.	where	incompetence	ten
	whom	muscular	women
	ideal	eating	men
	thinner	bulimia	
	nurturance	anorexia nervosa	

| 3.3 | set point | prejudices | unhealthy health |

Matching Self-Test 3

1. leptin
2. basal metabolism rate

3. set point
4. anorexia nervosa

---

4. The Competent Animal: Motives to Work

4.1.	Industrial/organizational	competent
	self-fulfilling	efficacy
	goals	Bandura
	specific	skills
	time limit	obstacles
	challenging	role models
	ability	feedback
	think	encouragement
	competent	physiological
	performance	achievement
	learning	TAT
	mastery	affiliation
	competence	power
	skills	war
	information	affiliation

4.2.	conditions	incentive	conditions
	flexibility	dead-end	
	autonomy	individual	

Matching Self-Test 4

1. need for power
2. self-efficacy

3. self-fulfilling prophecy
4. need for achievement

---

5. When Motives Conflict

5.1.
Approach-avoidance	Maslow
Avoidance-avoidance	needs
Approach-avoidance	basic
multiple	actualization
advantages	transcendence
disadvantages	research

Matching Self-Test 5

1. avoidance-avoidance conflicts   3. hierarchy of needs
2. multiple approach-avoidance conflicts

ANSWERS TO MULTIPLE CHOICE PROGRESS TEST

Item No.	Answer(s)	Page(s) in Textbook
1.	d. more; more	442
2.	b. eros	443
3.	b. like to play the game of love with several partners at once.	443
4.	a. securely attached	443
5.	c. intimacy plus commitment	444
6.	d. all of the above	444
7.	a. Men are more ludic and avoidant than women, and women are more romantic and anxious than men.	446
8.	d. All of the above	447-449
9.	d. Men emphasize the financial resources or prospects of a potential mate more than women	449
10.	d. All of the above	452-453
11.	d. The vast majority of homosexual men and women have a close gay relative.	454-456
12.	d. all of the above	457
13.	b. more complicated	458
14.	d. None of the above	459
15.	b. bulimia; women	460
16.	c. the goal is challenging but achievable.	463
17.	b. learning and mastery goals; are not	463
18.	d. all of the above	464
19.	b. avoidance-avoidance	469
20.	c. This theory has not been supported by research.	470

APPENDIX

Statistical Methods

Appendix Overview

The appendix covers three topics from statistics. Firstly, methods of organizing data are examined. These include constructing frequency distributions and graphing data. Secondly, various descriptive statistics and frequency distributions are considered. Measures of central tendency, measures of variability, percentile ranks, standard scores, and normal and skewed frequency distributions are discussed. Lastly, inferential statistics are introduced at a cursory level. A discussion of the null hypothesis versus the alternative hypothesis is presented along with a brief introduction to hypothesis testing.

GUIDED STUDY

1. Organizing Data

Read the section "Organizing Data" and then answer the following questions. If you have trouble answering any of the questions, re-study the relevant material before going on to the review of key terms and the matching test.

1-1.   Per the example in the appendix, the _____ data were the scores obtained on the mood disturbance scale. These data were used in constructing a _____ distribution that showed how often each possible score actually occurred. When data sets are very large, it is easier to construct a _____ frequency distribution in which adjacent scores are broken into equal sized _____ or _____.

1-2.   The most common statistical picture is a _____ that depicts numerical relationships. A graph constructed from a frequency distribution shows the score values along the _____-axis and the frequencies along the _____axis. When rectangles or bars are drawn above each score, we are representing the data in a _____ or bar graph. Another way to represent data is in a frequency _____ or _____ graph, in which the frequency of each score is indicated by a point placed directly over the score on the horizontal axis at the appropriate frequency on the vertical axis. The points are then connected by a line.

Review of Key Terms

The following is a list of the Key Terms from the section "Organizing Data." Make sure you are familiar with each term before taking the matching test on these terms.

frequency distribution   graph

histogram (bar graph)   frequency polygon (line graph)

Matching Self Test 1

Match the appropriate term with its definition or description.

1. _____ A graph in which rectangular bars are drawn above each score indicating the number of times it occurred.

2. _____ A graph in which each score is indicated by a point placed directly over the score on the horizontal axis, at the appropriate height on the vertical axis.

3. _____ A distribution that indicates how often each possible score actually occurred.

2. Describing Data

Read the section "Describing Data" and then answer the following questions. If you have trouble answering any of the questions, re-study the relevant material before going on to the review of key terms and the matching test.

2.1. Procedures for summarizing and describing data are known as _____ statistics. One descriptive statistic is a measure of _____ central _____ that characterizes a set of data in terms of a single number. The most popular measure of central tendency is the _____, which is computed by adding all of the scores in the set and dividing by the total number of scores. Although the mean is a popular measure of central tendency, it can very easily be thrown off "centre" by one or more extremely, _____ scores or one or more extremely _____ scores. In such cases, it is more appropriate to use the _____, or the midpoint in a set of scores that are ordered from highest to lowest. The last measure of central tendency is the _____, the most frequently occurring score.

2-2. In addition to a measure of central tendency, it is also beneficial to have a measure of _____ that indicates whether the scores are clustered closely around the mean or widely scattered. The simplest measure of variability is the _____, which is found by subtracting the lowest score from the highest score. A more accurate measure of variability is the _____ _____. This gives us an idea of how much, on average, scores in a distribution differ from the mean. A large standard deviation indicates that the scores are _____ scattered, while a small standard deviation indicates that the scores are clustered _____ near the mean.

2-3. Frequently researchers do not want to work with raw scores. Hence, they might transform raw scores into _____ scores, scores that give the percentage of people who scored at or below a given raw score. Another type of transformed score is a z-score or

_____ score. This tells us how many standard deviation units a given raw score is above or below the mean. For example, if your exam score is 43 in a distribution with a mean of 50 and a standard deviation of 7, then the corresponding z-score would be _____.

2-4.   In addition to knowing the variability of our scores, it is also beneficial to know the pattern of their distribution. When the pattern forms a bell-shaped curve, it is called a _____ curve. The normal curve has several properties. These include (1) one half of the curve is _____ to the other, (2) the _____, median, and _____ all have the same value, and (3) _____ scores are clustered near the mean and _____ scores are in the "tails." More specifically, _____ percent of the scores will fall between plus and minus 1 standard deviation from the mean, _____ percent of the scores will fall between plus and minus 2 standard deviations from the mean; and _____ percent of the scores will fall between plus and minus 3 standard deviations from the mean. Not all distributions are normal, some are lopsided or _____. When the tail of the distribution is toward the right, the distribution is skewed right, or _____ skewed. When the tail of the distribution to toward the left, the distribution is skewed left, or _____ skewed. In a skewed curve, the mean, median, and mode fall at different points.

Review of Key Terms

The following is a list of the Key Terms from the section "Describing Data." Make sure you are familiar with each term before taking the matching test on these terms.

descriptive statistics	standard deviation	left (negatively) skewed distribution
measure of central tendency	percentile score	mode
mean	normal curve	range
median	right (positively) skewed distribution	z-score

Matching Self Test 2

Match the appropriate term with its definition or description.

1. _____   The midpoint in a set of scores or observations.

2. _____   A statistical measure of how much, on average, scores in a distribution differ from the mean.

3. _____   The most frequently occurring score in a distribution.

4. _____ A statistic that tells you how far a given raw score is above or below the mean, using the standard deviation as the unit of measurement.

5. _____ A symmetrical, bell-shaped curve.

3. Drawing Inferences

Read the section "Drawing Inferences" and then answer the following questions. If you have trouble answering any of the questions, re-study the relevant material before going on to the review of key terms and the matching test.

3-1.   When researchers attempt to make inferences about the entire population based on a particular sample, they are using _____ statistics. The hypothesis stating that experimental manipulations will have no effect on the subjects' behaviour is the _____ hypothesis. The experimental or research hypothesis, stating that the experimental manipulation will have an effect, is called the _____ hypothesis.

3-2.   The theoretical distribution called the _____ distribution of the difference between means is based on potential population data and is used in testing the null hypothesis. The theoretical sampling distribution represents what we would expect by chance if we did our study many times, testing the entire population. We figure out how far the mean difference between the groups in one study is from the _____ of the sampling distribution. If it is very different, out in one of the _____ of the sampling distribution, then it is statistically significant. When a result is said to be statistically significant, it means that if only _____ were operating, the result would be highly improbable (5% or less). Thus, we are fairly safe in concluding that more than chance was operating, namely that the _____ variable was operating. We can reject the null hypothesis. Statistically significant results are not always psychologically important. Thus, it is useful to know its _____ size, how much of the total variability in scores was accounted for by the independent variable

Review of Key Terms

The following is a list of the Key Terms from the section "Drawing Inferences. " Make sure you are familiar with each term before taking the matching test on these terms.

null hypothesis	effect size	statistically significant
sampling distribution	alternative hypothesis	

Matching Self Test 3

Match the appropriate term with its definition or description.

1. _____ The hypothesis that states that on the average, the experimental group will behave differently than the control group.

2. _____ When a finding is improbable based on chance, hence we feel safe in concluding that the independent variable led to this effect

3. _____ The hypothesis stating that the experimental manipulations had no effect.

MULTIPLE-CHOICE PROGRESS TEST

Choose the single best answer for each of the following questions. When you have finished this progress test, check your answers with those at the end of the chapter. You should review the indicated pages in the text for the questions you do not answer correctly.

1. A graph in which rectangular bars are drawn above each score, indicating the frequency of the score by the bar's height, is called a _____.
    a. frequency distribution
    b. histogram
    c. frequency polygon
        line graph

2. The measure of central tendency that is the arithmetic average is called the
    a. mode
    b. median
    c. mean
    d. range

3. The midpoint in a set of scores is called the _____, and the most frequent score is called the
    a. median; mode
    b. mode; median
    c. median; mean
    d. mean; median

4. Consider the following set of scores: 4, 5, 4, 4, 3, 6, 5, 2, 4, 3, 5, 4, 4, 3, and 4. Which of the following statements is TRUE?
    a. The mean and the median both = 4.
    b. The mean is greater than the median.
    c. The mean is less than the median.
    d. The range = 5.

5. Which of the following statements is (are) TRUE?
   a. A large standard deviation signifies that the mean is not very typical of the population.
   b. A small standard deviation signifies that the mean is representative of the population.
   c. The drawback of percentile scores is that they do not tell us how far apart people are in terms of raw scores.
   d. All of the above

6. Assume the mean for a psychology test is 70 and the standard deviation is 8. Bill scored 62 on the test. Thus, Bill's z-score is:
   a. -1
   b. +1
   c. -2
   d +2

7. About _____ of the scores in a normal distribution fall between + 2 and - 2 standard deviations from the mean.
   a. 34%
   b. 5O%
   c. 68%
   d. 95%

8. The percentile score for a score that is 1 standard deviation above the mean in a normal distribution is roughly _____.
   a. 34%
   b. 68%
   c. 84%
   d. 95%

9. Which of the following statements is (are) TRUE?
   a. In a normal distribution, the mean = the median = the mode.
   b. In a left-skewed distribution, the mean is greater than the median.
   c. In a right-skewed distribution, the mean is less than the median.
   d. All of the above

10. Which of the following statements is FALSE?
    a. The alternative hypothesis in an experiment can be stated precisely and tested directly.
    b. A result is considered to be statistically significant if the likelihood of its occurring by chance is 5% or less.
    c. To see whether a statistically significant result has practical importance, its effect size should be checked.
    d. None of the above

Answers

GUIDED STUDY

1. Organizing Data

1.1. raw   grouped   intervals
      frequency   classes

1-2. graph   y   polygon
      x   histogram   line

Matching Self-Test 1

1. histogram (bar graph)
2. frequency polygon (line graph)
3. frequency distribution

---

2. Describing Data

2.1. descriptive   high   mode
      tendency   low
      mean   median

2.2. variability   standard deviation   closely
      range   widely

2.3. percentile   standard   -1

2.4. normal   most   99.74
      equal   few   skewed
      mean   68.26   positively
      mode   95.44   negatively

Matching Self-Test 2

1. median   3. mode   5. normal curve
2. standard deviation   4. z-score or standard score
